COLERIDGE AND MILL

To my father
who taught me to love scholarship

Coleridge and Mill

A Study of Influence

CHRISTOPHER TURK

Lecturer in English, University of Wales
Visiting Fellow, Yale University
Visiting Fellow, ISSCO, University of Geneva
Paul Mellon Fellow, Yale Center for British Art

Avebury

Aldershot · Brookfield USA · Hong Kong · Singapore · Sydney

Published by

Avebury

B
1607
.T87
1988

Gower Publishing Company Limited,
Gower House, Croft Road, Aldershot,
Hants. GU11 3HR, England

Gower Publishing Company,
Old Post Road, Brookfield, Vermont 05036
USA

British Library Cataloguing in Publication Data
Turk, Christopher, 1942-
    Coleridge and Mill : a study of influence.
    1. English philosophy. Mill, John Stuart,
    1806-1873. Influence of Coleridge, Samuel
    Taylor, 1772-1834
    I. Title
    192

LIBRARY OF CONGRESS
Library of Congress Cataloging-in-Publication Data

Turk, Christopher.
    Coleridge and Mill : a study of influence / Christopher Turk.
        p.   cm. -- (Avebury series in philosophy)
    Bibliography: p.
    Includes index.
    ISBN 0-566-05668-2 : $35.00
    1. Mill, John Stuart, 1806-1873. 2. Coleridge, Samuel Taylor,
1772-1834--Influence--Mill. I. Title. II. Series.
B1607.T87 1988
192--dc19   88-10537
                                                                CIP

ISBN 0-566-05668-2

Printed and bound in Great Britain by
Athenaeum Press Limited, Newcastle-upon-Tyne

Contents

Preface

I have always had a fascination for argument. Partly, I suppose, this is because nothing stimulates thinking as much as contest. But it is also because, having been brought up in liberal educational institutions, I have never been able to understand the purblind advocates of one side only. Perhaps, with these interests, it is not surprising that I found Coleridge and Mill absorbing. They are the greatest of the early nineteenth century liberals, whose breadth of insight enabled them to see wider issues than the party-hacks of the day. Not surprising, they were aware of each other, though Coleridge was an old man, his head ringing with metaphysics, when John Mill, then a young hopeful, first met him.

The history of this awareness made, for me at least, an instructive study. It embraces most of the ideas which we now label Victorian liberalism, and it gives us glimpses into the intellectual life and attitudes of the period. This book is not a survey of the ideas of the 1830s and 1840s in Victorian England, but the reader will have touched on most of the concerns of the day by the time he is through. He will also, I suspect, meet ideas and attitudes which will add to his stock of useful truths, and which can be applied elsewhere. This ideal itself is one curiously typical of the period. "A man may find Truth mixed up even with the mud that is flung upon him" one of the characters in this history declares, and I suppose even now this is the aim of liberal, humanitarian education. The account of the relationships between the careers and ideas of Coleridge and Mill is a journey into the routes of humane idealism. We still live with the fruits.

The work on which this book is based began in the late 1960s, when the claim that Mill learnt a significant amount from Coleridge was rather new. It has now become an accepted proposition in the history of ideas. Accounts elsewhere put the interaction into a wider context, but this study goes back to the documents, papers, letters and journals of the time to substantiate the claim. What it perhaps lacks in breadth I hope it makes up for in detail. There is probably not much in the writings of the group who form the core of this study which has been missed. This is a large claim for any scholar to make, but many stones were turned to find the facts given here. The inevitable result is a dense maze of footnotes and references; anyone wanting to re-trace the details of Mill's reading of Coleridge will find ample clues here.

This book is aimed at two groups. Firstly, the scholar of the period, perhaps working on either of the two figures, or merely wanting more period thought about how they were transmitted. The scholar will find a lot of quotation, reference and detail. Secondly, the book is for the student of the history of ideas int the early nineteenth century. He or she will find most of the major currents of ideas mentioned, and many pointers to sources elsewhere, in which the various threats which make up this study can be followed. This book is a collection of contemporary detail rather than a summary of the latest critical research, and should be understood in that light, though I hope it is not thereby made unreadable.

Llanvair Discoed
November 1987

Acknowledgements

My thanks are due to David Daiches and Michael Moran at the University of Sussex who read and commented on the work in its early stages. I also had help from Graham Hough, and many other people too numerous to mention. Special thanks are due to John Beer, who first expressed the hope that the work would appear in print. Secondly, the University of Wales, Cardiff who gave me a year's sabbatical from my permanent post there. Thirdly, to a great university of the New World, which is the oldest of the three by nearly two centuries, Yale, where I spent the sabbatical.

I cannot effectively thank all the people on the way who have assisted my work in ways large and small. A numerous body of librarians, secretaries and colleagues have helped push the work along. But I should mention Debbie Manning, who did much of the final typing, and Catherine Aldred who helped with proof reading, and many, many other things. Thanks, too, to my father who made the index.

1 The seminal mind

It vexes and grieves me to the heart, that when he is gone, as go he will, nobody will believe what a mind goes with him, – how infinitely and ten-thousand-thousand-fold the mightiest of his generation. — Robert Southey[1]

But being thought to have influence is the surest way of obtaining it really. — J.S.Mill[2]

The nineteenth century fascination with influence is a curious phenomenon. The source of an idea, and how original it was, seemed to many minor thinkers almost more important than the significance of the idea itself. Honesty about literary property, and modesty of an effusive kind, when his mind was darkened with the shadow of a greater figure, were the hallmarks of the nineteenth century minor intellectual. Perhaps one cause was the cooling of Romanticism. Individual creativity, original brilliance and innovation on a revolutionary scale were the legacy of the recent past, and perhaps the careful husbandry of ideas was a compensation. Whatever the reason, "influence" was an important issue in the intellectual climate of the 1830's. To be thought to have influence was major praise; to be influenced by one greater than oneself required detailed acknolwedgement.

The Coleridgeans were no exception to this rule. Coleridge's admirers in the nineteenth century (and modern ones too) seem to

---

[1]Letter from Robert Southey, 23 June, 1803, in J.W.Robberds, *A Memoir of the Life and Writing of the Late William Taylor of Norwich*, 2 vols. (London, John Murray, 1843), I, 462.

[2]*The Letters of John Stuart Mill*, ed. H.S.R.Elliot, 2 vols. (London, Longmans Green and Co., 1910), I, 225.

claim almost everything for him. He is the most seminal of all the English minds of the nineteenth century, if his disciples are to be believed. But the painstaking literary historian can find little evidence of this influence.[3] Coleridge's importance and relevance in modern terms needs little arguing – he has come to take a central place in our literature – but it is still important to the literary historian to be able to specify with some certainty Coleridge's real influence on the other thinkers of the nineteenth century.

This study is intended as a contribution towards this task. It will look at the paradox of Coleridge's reputation by examining in detail one beneficiary of this influence. John Stuart Mill was of the opposite "school" to Coleridge, yet he wrote in 1840 the most widely read of all assessments of Coleridge, in which he claimed Coleridge was a "seminal mind," one of "the teachers of the teachers."[4] For this reason, and because Mill is a highly representative figure in the nineteenth century, the facts of Coleridge's influence will be explored in terms of his influence on Mill. To do this the dimensions of the myth of Coleridge's influence will first be established, before looking at Mill himself, his education and ideas, to see what contact he had with Coleridge, and how this contact influenced him.

In summary form, my conclusion is that despite his criticisms of intuitionism, Mill seems to have learned a great deal from Coleridge, especially from Coleridge's eclecticism, and his idea of the "clerisy," as well as from his political methodology, his religious thought, and his aesthetics. This evidence provides a new, and more detailed, background to the lavish generalisations heaped on Coleridge's importance. It is, however, Coleridge's reputation itself which forms the substance of the first chapter. Luckily, the Victorian's concern for literary property is scattered in many letters and journals of the period. These became the books of account for intellectual debt, the bills of sale and invoices payable of the intellectual life of the time. They record a rich transaction of ideas, which helps us to judge Coleridge

---

[3]See H.D.Trail, *Coleridge*, English Men of Letters (London, Macmillan and Co., 1884), p.196.

[4]*Mill on Bentham and Coleridge*, with an introduction by F.R.Leavis (London, Chatto and Windus, 1962), pp.39-40.

through their eyes, and thereby to flesh out the modern claims for his importance.

"So Coleridge passed, leaving a handful of golden poems, an emptiness in the heart of a few friends, and a will-o'-the-wisp light for bemused thinkers."[5] With these words, E.K.Chambers ends his modern biography of Coleridge, adding to the old belief that Coleridge's only achievement was a wasted life, a few sparks of genius in the thick gloom of obscurity or, as Carlyle put it, "a mass of richest spices putrefied into a dunghill."[6] This same view was put more recently by F.R.Leavis, who writes, "[it is] a commonplace that what he actually accomplished with his gifts . . . appears, when we come to stock-taking, disappointingly incommensurate." He comes to a "depressing conclusion: Coleridge's prestige is very understandable, but his currency as an academic classic is something of a scandal."[7] In contrast to Leavis's view, most commentators on the nineteenth century insist on Coleridge's importance as a seminal thinker. But when one looks closely there is very little concrete evidence offered by the supporters of either of these opposed views to enable us to arbitrate between them. The question of just how far Coleridge is to be credited with being a "seminal" force in the nineteenth century in a major sense remains open.

The intensity of nineteenth century admiration of Coleridge as a guiding influence argues that his was a remarkable achievement. Many disciples who were themselves important and influential thinkers are explicitly indebted to him. But the reception of his work by the public at large, and by the reviewers of the nineteenth century, argues equally strongly against this conclusion.   From this conflict arises the "scandal," and the unsubstantiated myth.

---

[5]E.K.Chambers, *Samuel Taylor Coleridge, A Biographical Study* (Oxford, Clarendon, 1938), p.331.

[6]Letter to John Carlyle, in James Anthony Froude, *Thomas Carlyle, A History of the First Forty Years of Life, 1795-1835*, 2 vols. (London, Longmans, Green, and Co., 1891), I, 303-304.

[7]F.R.Leavis, "Coleridge in Criticism," *Scrutiny*, IX (1940-41), 57, 69.

I

Coleridge's modern fame is limitless. Since I.A.Richards' mechanistic psychology met Coleridge's idealist aesthetics in a curiously harmonious embrace,[8] his reputation and importance have not ceased growing. His spices have not putrefied, but purified with the passage of time; the fitful will-o'-the-wisp light has become a steady beacon. His philosophy, once an absurdity, has become a subject of serious study,[9] his aesthetics have undergone a wholesale renaissance,[10] his politics have been exhumed and justified,[11] his once gladly forgotten life has become a subject of much biography,[12] his cormorant reading and hidden glints of imagery have attracted scholarly and recondite detection,[13] and even his trunks full of jottings and fragments form the material of a vast and faithful editorial task – though so much still remains unpublished that one suspects the germ of Coleridge's procrastination even now lurks contageously among his manuscripts.   Altogether a vast amount of detailed scholarship has been devoted to him; and it has become commonplace to write about Coleridge in the panegyric mood – in several languages.

Coleridge, like Shakespeare, is so gilded with scholarship that no

[8] See I.A.Richards, *Coleridge on Imagination* (London, Routledge and Kegan Paul, 1934).

[9] *e.g.* J.H.Muirhead, *Coleridge as Philosopher* (London, Allen and Unwin, 1954); H.Marcoux, "The philosophy of Coleridge," *Revue de l'Université d'Ottawa*, XVIII (1948), 38-52, 150-169, 235-249.

[10] *e.g.* R.H.Fogle, *The Idea of Coleridge's Criticism*, Perspectives in Criticism, 9 (Berkeley and Los Angeles, California University Press, 1962); J.V.Baker, *The Sacred River, Coleridge's Theory of the Imagination* (Lousiana State University Press, 1957); J. R. de J. Jackson, *Method and Imagination in Coleridge's Criticism* (London, Routledge and Kegan Paul, 1969).

[11] *e.g.* John Colmer, *Coleridge, Critic of Society* (Oxford, Clarendon, 1959); Carl R.Woodring, *Politics in the Poetry of Coleridge* (Madison, University of Wisconsin Press, 1961).

[12] *e.g.* E.K.Chambers, *op.cit.*; Maurice Carpenter, *The Indifferent Horseman, The Divine Comedy of Samuel Taylor Coleridge* (London, Elek Books, 1954).

[13] *E.g.* John Livingstone Lowes, *The Road to Xanadu, a Study in the Ways of the Imagination* (London, Constable and Co., 1933), and Patricia M.Adair, *The Waking Dream, A Study of Coleridge's Poetry* (London, Edward Arnold, 1967).

attacks can damage his reputation. *Biographia Literaria*,[14] for example, has been claimed as "almost the Bible of modern criticism,"[15] Although Coleridge left only samples of what he might have achieved, these samples class him as the "most germinative mind" of the nineteenth century.[16] He is claimed to have been an important influence on fields as divergent as surrealism[17] and theology.[18] He is accredited as "a very great religious philosopher," and "the first voice of Christian Socialism."[19] He was, it is said, vital in changing theology from Necessitarianism to Idealism, and in combatting the "meliorist ethical basis" of the nineteenth century with his spirituality.[20] As an historian and political theorist he is called an important and continuing opponent of the errors of the German Post-Kantian Idealists.[21] But it is religious thought that is supposed to have received its clearest impulse from Coleridge. His guidance preserved it through the evolutionary controversy,[22] and coloured all subsequent theology.[23]

---

[14]S.T.Coleridge, *Biographia Literaria, or Biographical Sketches of my Literary Life and Opinions*, 2 vols. (London, Rest Fenner, 1817).

[15]S.E.Hyman, *The Armed Vision* (New York, Alfred A. Knopf, 1952), p.11.

[16]J.C.Shairp, *Studies in Poetry and Philosophy* (Edinburgh, Edmonston and Douglas, 1868), pp.122,186.

[17]Irving Babbit, "Coleridge and the Moderns," *The Bookman*, LXX (October 1929), 122.

[18]A.W.Benn, *The History of English Rationalism in the Nineteenth Century*, 2vols. (London, Longmans, Green, and Co., 1906), I, 281-282.

[19]J.C.Shairp, *op.cit.*, p.266; G.C.Binyon, *The Christian Socialist Movement in England* (London, S.P.C.K., 1931), p.31.

[20]S.F.Gingerich, "From Necessity to Transcendentalism in Coleridge," *P.M.L.A.*, XXXV (1920), 59; Howard R.Murphey, "The Ethical Revolt against Christian Orthodoxy in Early Victorian England," *American Historical Review*, LX (1955), 800-801.

[21]R.Preyer, *Bentham, Coleridge, and the Science of History*, Leipziger Beiträge zur Englischen Philologie, 41 Heft (Bochum-Langendreer, Verlag Poppinghaus, 1958), p.26.

[22]Graham Hough, *The Last Romantics* (London, Gerald Duckworth and Co., 1949), p.135.

[23]John Tulloch, *The Movement of Religious Thought in Britain During the Nineteenth Century* (London, Longmans, Green and Co., 1885), pp.7-10; see also Mark Pattison, "Tendencies of Religious Thought in England, 1688-1750," in his *Essays*, ed H.Nettleship, 2.vols (Oxford, Clarendon, 1889), II, 51; D.C.Somervell, *English Thought in the Nineteenth Century* (London, Methuen and Co., 1929), p.66.

Coleridge restored the science of criticism.[24] He made it "sympathetic and interpretative," and created a "vital and thought-engendering" body of criticism.[25] In fact Coleridge's importance "stands today higher than ever."[26]

This modern importance needs neither exposition nor explanation – it is self-evident from any library shelf. William Walsh has put his finger closer to the heart of Coleridge's fame than most, when he writes,

> Coleridge was a seminal mind – and I believe the term is peculiarly appropriate to him ... Coleridge established no movements ... founded no institutions, sat on no committees (the picture of Coleridge the committee-man is an alarming one) ... even his literary works are fragmentary and incomplete. And yet ... it is Coleridge who is unconfined by time and Coleridge who is increasingly relevant to us in the twentieth century ... Coleridge's influence worked at a more profound level, at the roots of action, where the quality of practice is determined. Coleridge's influence was seminal in that it operated in depth among motives and purposes, assumptions and values. ... If we ask why Coleridge should have been able to exercise so intimate an influence on the modern mind, the answer must be, I think, that Coleridge himself represented ... the first truly modern consciousness ... Coleridge's works ... so disturbed and unsatisfactory ... are ... analogies of the modern mind. They also compose a kind of *summa* of

[24]Emerson R.Marks, "Means and Ends in Coleridge's Critical Method," *E.L.H.*, XXVI (1959), 399.

[25]T.H.S.Escott, "Coleridge as a Twentieth-Century Force," *London Quarterly Review*, CXXI (1914), 233; Anna Helmholz, *The Indebtedness of Coleridge to A.W. von Schlegel*, Bulletin of the University of Wisconsin, CLXIII (Madison, University of Wisconsin Press, 1907), p.291.

[26]Rene Wellek, "The Romantic Age," *A History of Modern Criticism, 1750-1950*, 4 vols. (London, Jonathan Cape, 1955), II, 151. For further comment on Coleridge's importance see, for instance, Jean Pucelle, *L'Idéalism en Angleterre, de Coleridge à Bradley* (Neuchâtel, La Baconnière, 1955), p.18; John Bayley, *The Romantic Survival, A Study in Poetic Evolution* (London, Constable and Co., 1957), p.10; Alec R.Vidler, *F.D.Maurice and Company* (London, S.C.M.Press, 1966), p.206; Leslie Stephen, "The Importance of German," in *Studies of a Biographer*, 4 vols. (London, Duckworth and Co., 1898-1902), II, 56; Graham Hough, "Coleridge and the Victorians," in *The English Mind, Studies in the English Moralists, Presented to Basil Willey*, ed. Hugh Sykes Davies and George Watson (Cambridge University Press, 1964), pp.175-192.

suggestiveness.[27]

This study is not, however, about Coleridge's modern fame, for this has been amply established, but about his influence on the nineteenth century, and though the same qualities in his work gave him this influence, the results and the reasons are different. Some nineteenth century reaction to Coleridge was ecstatic; it was so jubilant that it drowned the opposition. Hare[28] is as fulsome as any. He writes of,

> those who knew Coleridge . . . and not a few there are – whose hearts glow with gratitude and love toward him, as their teacher and master, the establisher of their faith, and the emancipator of their spiritual life from the bondage of the carnal understanding.[29]

Hare is by no means the only eulogist. Allston, writing in the *Daily Telegraph* (1885) is convinced that,

> it is to the pure white light of that sleepless, all embracing, all penetrating intellect, far more than to any individual faculty in its comprising prism, that the late homage of his countrymen should be offered up.[30]

In America, too, his influence was, according to the Bishop of Albany, a considerable one, "his philosophy, he said, was taught in some of the class-books of their universities, his poetry was instilled in the highest education of the young men of the United States."[31] But this apparently general praise seems to have been more the unlimited generosity of a few disciples than a universal experience. But it is undoubtedly to this small and enthusiastic group of disciples that Coleridge owed the survival and extension of his fame. The Coleridgeans, as they were known, were a group with a common classical background, and a common dissatisfaction with Lockean mechanistic psychology. In Burke, and most fully in Coleridge, they found an alternative. Although several of them were "accomplished

---

[27]William Walsh, *The Use of Imagination; Educational Thought and the Literary Mind* (London, Chatto and Windus, 1959), pp.52-53.

[28]Julius Charles Hare (1795-1855).

[29]J.C.Hare, "Samuel Taylor Coleridge and the English Opium Eater," *British Magazine*, VII (January, 1835), p.25.

[30]Quoted by Lucy E.Watson, *Coleridge at Highgate* (London, Longmans, Green, and Co., 1925), p.70.

[31]Ibid., p.100.

German scholars,"[32] they saw in Coleridge the highest exponent of the new Idealism.

Among the most enthusiastic of these disciples were Julius Hare, F.D.Maurice,[33] John Sterling and Thomas Arnold. There were plenty of minor disciples who spread Coleridge's ideas; such as Heraud,[34] Charles Lloyd in is novel *Edmund Oliver*,[35] and J.H.Green,[36] the surgeon who devoted a lifetime to trying to disentangle Coleridge's Logic. All in various ways spread Coleridge's ideas or testified to his importance.

Hare's love and admiration for Coleridge knew no bounds. He "would almost shamelessly declare his debt to Coleridge."[37] His *Guesses at Truth* is full of Coleridge's ideas, which Hare readily enough acknowledges.

> So frequently have I strengthened my mind with the invigorating waters which stream forth redundantly in Mr. Coleridge's works, that, if I mistake not, many of my thoughts will appear to have been impregnated by his spirit.[38]

Hare spread Coleridge's influence. He "soon became the recognised exponent of Coleridgean ideas in Cambridge,[39] and he was the exponent not only of Coleridge, but of German Romantic Idealism in general. He became a friend of Bunsen, whose book[40] with Coleridge's

---

[32]Preyer, op.cit., p.16.

[33]Frederick Denison Maurice (1805-1872).

[34]John A.Heraud (1799-1887), poet and dramatist.

[35]Charles Lloyd (1775-1839), *Edmund Oliver*, 3 vols. (Bristol, 1798).

[36]Joseph Henry Green (1791-1863).

[37]G.F.McFarland, "J.C.Hare: Coleridge, DeQuincey, and German Literature," *Bulletin of the John Reynolds Library*, XLVII (1964-65), 188; see also "The Early Career of J.C.Hare," *Ibid.*,XLVI (1963-64), 42-83.

[38]Julius Charles and Augustus William Hare, *Guesses at Truth, by Two Brothers*, 2vols. (London, John Taylor, 1827), II, 279-280.

[39]Graham Hough, "Coleridge and the Victorians," *op.cit.*, p.183.

[40]Christian Carl Josias von Bunsen. His work, *Die Verfassung der Kirche der Zukunft* (Hamburg, 1845), translated by the author as *The Constitution of the Church of the Future* (London, Longmans, and Co., 1847), may owe something to Coleridge.

Church and State,[41] was to help to introduce new concepts of the function of Church institutions in society. And he amassed a library of German books, still remarkable in size, which became a lending library for the better undergraduates whom he befriended. Another important disciple was F.D.Maurice. He wrote in the introduction to his *Kingdom of Christ*,

> It seems to me that the doctrine which I have endeavoured to bring out in what I have said respecting the relations between Church and State, is nothing but an expansion of Mr. Coleridge's remarks.[42]

Maurice, his commentators claim, learnt more from Coleridge than from Plato.[43] "Maurice came nearer to treating Coleridge as a master than he did anyone else."[44] His importance as a disciple of Coleridgean ideas lies in his later friendship with Kingsley,[45] and his transmission of Coleridgean ideas to the important Broad Church movement.[46] John Sterling[47] is less important historically yet, through his friendship with Mill, Carlyle, Maurice and many others,[48] he must have helped to transmit Coleridgean ideas. He was the most ardent of Coleridge's disciples. "To Coleridge," he said, "I owe *education*."[49]

Thomas Arnold, too, was a Coleridgean disciple and by reason of his position as an educator must be regarded as one of the most important and influential. Arnold called Coleridge,

> a very great man indeed, whose equal I know not where to find in England. . . . What a great man [he] . . . was, that is, intellectually!

[41]S.T.Coleridge, *On the Constitution of Church and State, with Reference to the Idea of Each, with Aids towards a Right Judgement on the Late Catholic Bill* (London, Hurst, Chance, and Co., 1830).

[42]*The Kingdom of Christ*, II, 357.

[43]Herbert G.Wood, *Frederick Denison Maurice* (Cambridge University Press, 1950), p.33.

[44]A.R.Vidler, *op.cit.*, p.215; see also Frederick Maurice, *The Life of Frederick Denison Maurice*, 2 vols. (London, Macmillan and Co., 1884), I, 164.

[45]Charles Kingsley (1819-1875).

[46]See C.R.Saunders, *Coleridge and the Broad Church Movement* (Durham, N.C., Duke University Press, 1942), p.91.

[47]John Sterling (1806-1844).

[48]E.g. Richard Chenevix Trench (1807-1886); William Johnson Fox (1786-1864).

[49]Quoted by J.C.Hare, "Introduction," to John Sterling, *Essays and Tales*, ed. J.C.Hare, 2 vols. (London, J.W.Parker, 1848), I, xv.

for something I suppose must have been wanting to hinder us from
calling him a great man απλοσ. But where has he left his equal?. . . I
think with all his faults old Sam was more of a great man than any
one who has lived within the four seas in my memory.[50]

Even Arnold's son, Matthew, although more remote in time and
influence, was important in spreading Coleridgean ideas. Many of his
ideas are close to Coleridge's[51] and he has similar attitudes to trade
unions and to the Church.[52]

Many of Coleridge's famous contemporaries were lavish in their
praise after his death, despite the inequalities of Coleridge's
relationship to them in the early years of the century. Hazlitt and De
Quincey were both generous enough when Coleridge died,[53] though De
Quincey's attitude was ambiguous, patently owing much to Coleridge,
yet betraying little of friendship.[54] Lamb, at least, never wavered in his
generosity. For him Coleridge was "the proof and touchstone of all my
cogitations."[55] Even Carlyle, despite the ungenerosity of his direct
comments, seems to owe much to Coleridge's ideas.[56] But if these were
Coleridge's friends writing his obituaries, those who knew Coleridge
only remotely could be as enthusiastic as his friends. Marsh was a
great admirer, approaching Kant only through Coleridge and using
Coleridge's idea of the clerisy himself.[57] He also probably directed
Emerson to Coleridge.[58] Emerson was disappointed by his first

---

[50]Arthur Penrhyn Stanley, *The Life and Correspondence of Thomas Arnold, D.D.*, 7th ed.
(London, B.Fellowes, 1852), pp.347, 368, 394.

[51]Lionel Trilling, *Matthew Arnold* (London, Allen and Unwin, 1939), pp.55-57.

[52]Leon Gottfried, *Matthew Arnold and the Romantics* (London, Routledge and
Kegan Paul, 1963), pp.169-176.

[53]Herschel Baker, *William Hazlitt* (London, Oxford University Press, 1962),
pp.351-352.

[54]Thomas De Quincey, "Samuel Taylor Coleridge," *Tait's Edinburgh Magazine*, I
(1834), 509-520, 588-596, 685-690, II (1835), 3-10. Reprinted in *Recollections of the
Lakes and the Lake Poets*, in *Works* (Edinburgh, Adam and Charles Black, 1862), II,
38-122.

[55]Quoted by L.E.Watson, *op.cit.*, pp.164-165; her reference is to a letter dated
November 21st, 1834, in *Monthly Magazine*, February 8th 1845.

[56]See Charles Frederick Harrold, *Carlyle and German Thought, 1819-1834* (New
Haven, Yale University Press, 1934), pp.50-54.

[57]J.Dewey, "James Marsh and American Philosophy," *J.H.I.*, II (1941), 132, 144.

[58]*Ibid.*, 137.

interview with Coleridge,[59] but there is enough evidence to show his interest in and use of Coleridge.[60] Through Marsh and Emerson the whole American "Transcendental" movement received the impulse of Coleridge's ideas. Other Americans were also impressed by Coleridge. Washington Allston[61] confessed of Coleridge that, "to no other man do I owe so much intellectually as to Coleridge."[62] Allsop regarded him as a "wonderful . . . myriad-minded man."[63] Many other admirers in England, as well as in America, recorded lavish praise. Edward Irving[64] told Coleridge that "you have been more profitable . . . to my spiritual understanding . . . than any or all of the men with whom I have entertained friendship,"[65] though it is doubtful whether he caught the "higher spirit" of Coleridge's ideas.[66]

There were also more major figures who owed a great deal to Coleridge. Thus J.H.Newman, although he was instinctively opposed to Coleridge's tolerant and broad theology and only read Coleridge in his maturity, yet was "surprised how much that I thought mine is to be found there."[67] Perhaps, finally, the most ardent of Coleridge's later disciples was D.G.Rossetti. He wrote, "I worshiped him on the right side of idolatry,"[68] though only as a poet, since he thought that indolence and sloth had overpowered Coleridge's intellectual genius.[69] The diversity of people who praised Coleridge is amazing, and so is their warmth. A euphoria suffused all these grateful

---

[59]L.E.Watson, *op.cit.*, p.152.

[60]John S.Harrison, *The Teachers of Emerson* (New York, Sturgis and Walton Co., 1910), pp.297-298.

[61]Washington Allston (1779-1843).

[62]Watson, *op.cit.*, p.69.

[63]T.Allsop, *Letters, Conversations and Recollections of S.T.Coleridge* (London, Edward Moxon, 1836), I, x.

[64]Edward Irving (1792-1834).

[65]Edward Irving, *For Missionaries after the Apostolical School, A Series of Orations in Four Parts* (London, Hamilton, Adams, and Co., 1825), pp.vii-viii.

[66]John Tulloch, *op.cit.*, p.157.

[67]Wilfred Ward, *The Life of Cardinal Newman*, 2 vols. (London,Longmans, 1912), I, 58 and note.

[68]T.Hall Caine, *Recollections of Rossetti* (London, Elliot Stock, 1882), p.147.

[69]Arthur Christopher Benson, *Rossetti* (London, Macmillan and Co., 1904), p.141; see also pp.172, 222.

acknolwedgements which was food for the myth. For a myth it certainly was that surrounded Coleridge after his death. Poetic reputations often rise and fall but,

> there is nothing more curious than the way in which the long silence of the outer world was broken in 1834 when Coleridge died. . . .Lights will sometimes flicker over a newly filled grave, but this was more like the noisy inebriety of an Irish funeral.[70]

After the relative neglect of the eighteen-twenties, the obituaries marked the beginning of a steady rise in his posthumous reputation, until it reached surprising proportions. His influence was "greatly exaggerated" and "mythically exalted" leaving "distinct traces of a Coleridgean legend which has only slowly died out."[71] It is this legend which is the substance of the modern claims for Coleridge; and Leavis', or Chambers', or Carlyle's remarks are not a misjudgement, but an indication of how thin that substance really is. Aside from the commendable gratitude of some warm friends and like, but inferior, spirits, what evidence is there to establish Coleridge's importance? Few would now doubt that Coleridge was a major figure, but what exact lines of influence can be demonstrated?

II

A reasonable start to the task of tracing Coleridge's importance might be to look at the effect and history of his published work. Yet this only deepens the mystery. His reception in the early nineteenth century presents a strange contrast to the enthusiasm of his disciples. Among the reviews of the time it is noticeable that "the *Quarterly* regularly praised the work of Tory men of letters, except Coleridge, whom no one defended with any consistency."[72] The *Edinburgh Review* was steadily against Coleridge, "their utmost energy must be put forth in resisting the little band of writers that had found a rallying point in the Lake country." *Biographia Literaria* was also

[70]Henry Taylor, *Autobiography, 1800-1875*, 2 vols. (London, Longmans, Green, and Co., 1885), I, 191.

[71]H.D.Traill, *op.cit.*, pp.206-207.

[72]George L.Nesbitt, *Benthamite Reviewing: The First Twelve Years of the Westminster Review, 1824-1836* (New York, Columbia University Press, 1934), p.12.

badly received, "*Blackwoods* pronounced its opinions to be 'wild ravings'."[73] Few writers can have had such a silent reception who were later to have such a noisy following. The only one of Coleridge's mature prose works which was at all well received when it was first published was *Aids to Reflection*.[74] Yet even this, which was Coleridge's most important book in the eyes of the nineteenth century, was poorly received by the reviewers. It was not mentioned by any of the leading ones.[75] But, despite this, the book sold 1,000 copies in two years.[76] New editions were demanded "at regular intervals" for about twenty years.[77] It seems to have become a manual of religious devotion for many, especially in America.

> Mr.Thomas Walker, a former editor of the *Daily News* ... writes: 'In a blessed hour I met with the "Aids to Reflection." and ... I have kept up the habit of re-reading the "Aids" yearly ever since'.[78]

Similarly, "William Howitt, F.S.A., tells us that 'some of Coleridge's works are "Class-books in the American Universities" and his "Aids to Reflection" has perhaps more than any other production formed the minds of the studious young men of the United States'."[79] Again, Marsh calls the publication of *Aids to Reflection* in Vermont in 1829 "an event of considerable intellectual importance."[80]

Confessions of an Inquiring Spirit,[81] published posthumously, provoked something like a similar reaction. The conservative religious press was horrified, and the book was severely castigated in company with the work of some of Coleridge's disciples in an article entitled "On

---

[73]T.Hall Caine, *Life of Samuel Taylor Coleridge* (London, Walter Scott, 1887), pp.113-114, 134.

[74]S.T.Coleridge, *Aids to Reflection, in the Formation of a Manly Character* (London, William Pickering, 1825).

[75]J.D.Boulger, *Coleridge as Religious Thinker* (New Haven, Yale University Press, 1961), p.4.

[76]L.E.Watson, *op.cit.*, p.49.

[77]H.F.Traill, *Recollections of Rossetti*, p.178.

[78]L.E.Watson, *op.cit.*, p.98.

[79]*Ibid.*, p.96.

[80]J.Dewey, *op.cit.*, 131.

[81]S.T.Coleridge, *Confessions of an Inquiring Spirit*, edited from the author's MS by Henry Nelson Coleridge, esq., M.A. (London, William Pickering, 1840).

Tendencies Towards the Subversion of Faith."[82] But liberal theologians were delighted with the book. Dr. Arnold thought it represented the opening of "an era in Theology the most important that had occurred since the Reformation,"[83] though even this approval did not make it a commercial success for the publishers.

The rest of Coleridge's books were even less popular. *Biographia Literaria* was not reprinted until thirty years after its publication;[84] *The Friend* took nearly twenty years between second and third editions;[85] and *Church and State*, which was printed twice in 1830, was only printed twice more in England until after the Second World War, once in 1839, and once in 1852.[86] So Coleridge's works were far from a success when they were first printed. But about the middle of the century interest in them revived. In the early 1840's all his main works were readily available in reprint, boosted by generous selections of *Table Talk* and *Literary Remains*.

Towards the end of the century this interest vanished. The lectures and marginalia were published in the 1880's, and then there was a gap of forty years between the *Anima Poetae* in 1895,[87] and the modern editions of Coleridge's fragments by T.M.Raysor and Kathleen Coburn.[88] There are also fewer commentaries between 1895 and 1925 than at other times.[89]

There are thus two distinct gaps in the uneven flow of the

---

[82]*The English Review*, X (1848), 399-444.

[83]J.C.Shairp, *op.cit.*, p.260.

[84]The second edition is London, William Pickering, 1847.

[85]Second edition, London, Rest Fenner, 1818; third edition, London, William Pickering, 1837.

[86]First and second edition, London, Hurst, Chance, and Co., 1830; third edition, London, Edward Moxon, 1839; fourth edition, London, Edward Moxon, 1852.

[87]S.T.Coleridge, *Anima Poetae*, ed. E.H.Coleridge (London, W.Heinemann, 1895).

[88]*e.g. The Philosophical Lecturers*, ed. Kathleen Coburn (London, Pilot Press, 1949); *The Notebooks of Samuel Taylor Coleridge, 1794-1808*, ed. Kathleen Coburn, 4 vols. (London, Routledge and Kegan Paul, 1957); *Coleridge's Miscellaneous Criticism*, ed. T.M.Raysor (London, Constable and Co., 1936); *Coleridge's Shakespearean Criticism*, ed. T.M.Raysor, 2 vols. (London, Constable and Co., 1930).

[89]See *The New Cambridge Bibliography of English Language and Literature*, ed.G.Watson, 5 Vols. (Cambridge University Press, 1969), III, columns 231-234.

publication of Coleridge's works, that between the first editions and
the Victorian reprints, and that between the cessation of the printing
of his political works and the modern revival of interest in his critical
marginalia. It is a curious history full, not of sound and fury, but of
strange silences and gaps. Despite his achievement of a solid place in
conventional literary history, the vast majority of Coleridge was
unavailable in an edition printed in this century until the late 1960's.

There is no simple reason why Coleridge's prose works were
ignored by the majority of the reading public. To some extent they
were difficult, fragmentary and unrewarding. "He never fully solved
the problem of communicating these intrinsically valuable ideas to
others,"[90] writes one commentator, and certainly his writing is far from
popular in style. Even *The Friend*, intended as a popular periodical,
was "too cumbrous" to achieve any success.[91] It is a sad comment on
his books that he "revealed himself most intimately and completely as
an annotator of hundreds of books written by other men."[92] Coleridge,
the most fertile of minds, left as his best work unwanted scribbles in
other men's books; many of them still unlocated.[93]

Of course, this fragmentation has its advantages. It strengthens
the shock of pleasure when Coleridge suddenly welds the pieces of his
discourse into a lasting insight. Equally, to have exercised an influence
as diverse as that claimed for him, his mind was bound to have been
dispersive. Moreover, it is indeed,

> striking testimony to Coleridge's real speculative power that, in spite
> of these obvious shortcomings in the form of its presentation, his
> philosophical teaching should have made such a deep impression upon
> the readers of his books.[94]

Coleridge's fragmentary and discursive mind, those unbelievable
sentences which keep the reader on the rack for a full page or more,

---

[90] John Colmer, *op.cit.*, p.167.

[91] Gingerich, *op.cit.*, p.35.

[92] John Louis Haney, "Coleridge the Commentator," in *Coleridge: Studies by
Several Hands*, ed. Edmund Blunden and E.L.Griggs (London, Constable and Co.,
1934), p.109.

[93] John Louis Haney, "The Marginalia of STC," *Schelling Anniversary Papers by
his Former Students* (New York, The Century Co., 1923), p.174.

[94] James Seth, *English Philosophers and Schools of Philosophy* (London, J.M.Dent and Sons,
1912), p.319.

the very palpable grammatical darkness from which the flashes of insight shine, indeed most of the characteristics of Coleridge's prose militate against any ready acceptance of his books. To the majority of the reading public, then as now, Coleridge's style was painfully indigestible.

Another error, a cardinal sin in public relations, was the persistent procrastination to which his work was subject. It came out after long delays, which amounted nearly to decades in some instances. Undoubtedly the expectation aroused by his early poems had evaporated, and his name had been half forgotten before he published anything else. Indeed, what should have been the solid core of Coleridge's work was never finished. Had the *Magnum Opus* been printed it might have been little read – but it would have done his reputation much good. As it is, "if we wish to know what he tried in vain to accomplish we must go to his contemporaries in Germany."[95]

Coleridge suffers the reputation of a mind weak and afraid of work, a procrastinator. What he did publish came so late on the expectation, that the interest aroused by his ideas was utterly poisoned by the condemnation of his apparent idleness. In fact, he was far from idle[96] and, when he says that such and such a work is publishable, he may be nearer the truth than he is credited with. His publications are, even when finished, often diffuse. Many of his manuscripts are near enough the standard of his published works to warrant his boasts. We must remember that most of those who accused him of procrastination and dishonesty in his claims were practising journalists, who valued the word actually printed more than the thought. But this was irrelevant to the public. Indeed, the very boasts of what was ready for the press which must have seeped from Highgate by layers through the interested public, merely acted as a catalyst to the poison of delay.

But there was yet another reason why his works were ignored. Matthew Arnold's moral distaste for Coleridge exemplifies it well. "The most obvious successor of Coleridge as a religious thinker is

[95]A.C.Bradley, *English Poetry and German Philosophy in the Age of Wordsworth* (Manchester University Press, 1909), pp.7-8.

[96]A.D.Snyder, *Coleridge on Logic and Learning* (New Haven, Yale University Press, 1929), p.viii.

Matthew Arnold,"[97] and it is indeed possible to draw compelling parallels between Arnold and Coleridge. Coleridge's firm link between morality and style, his clerisy (Arnold's remnant), and his hatred of mechanism, all are echoed in Arnold's writings. Indeed there are passages in Coleridge which ring exactly like Arnold's prose. Coleridge wrote, for instance, in a notebook,

> Surely, surely, we are adapting all to the Vulgar, instead of raising the Vulgar to the best.[98]

Had Coleridge the flow of didactic prose which Arnold had at his command, Arnold's work might have been done earlier. We would thus expect Coleridge to be a major, and unacknowledged influence on Arnold. But Leon Gottfried, although he insists in a detailed study that this is so, is unable to find any important mention of Coleridge in Arnold's work to support it. He finds, instead, a surprising lack of any reference. This leads him to suppose that Arnold absorbed Coleridge as part of the intellectual atmosphere at university. But he also notes that Arnold "never showed signs of anything but contempt"[99] for the weaknesses of Coleridge's life, and could only admire Coleridge "in spite of the disesteem – nay, repugnance – which his character may and must inspire."[100]

This moral reprobation of Coleridge was not unusual, and may account in some measure for the silence and apparent lack of interest which greeted Coleridge's publications even after he had conquered his addiction to opium. There are discreet references to this among his disciples when they talk of his influence. Maurice, for instance, felt that he had not properly acknowledged his debts to Coleridge in the first edition of *The Kingdom of Christ*.

> Twenty years ago you might have attributed such an omission to a cowardly and dishonourable dread of being associated with an unpopular name.[101]

---

[97]Graham Hough, "Coleridge and the Victorians," *op.cit.*, p.190.

[98]*Notebooks*, ed. Coburn, *op.cit.*, II entry 2339.

[99]Gottfried, *op.cit.*, pp.191-193.

[100]Matthew Arnold, *Lectures and Essays in Criticism*, ed. R.H.Super, The Complete Prose Works of Matthew Arnold, Vol. III (Ann Arbor, University of Michigan Press, 1962), p.190.

[101]*Kingdom of Christ*, II, 349.

Maurice sees Coleridge's difficulties in obtaining a favourable reception as partly due to the abstruse character of his speculations, but he also mentions "many other [disadvantages] of an outward kind which I need not hint at in writing to you."[102] Maurice's tact – he is writing to Coleridge's nephew – precludes any specific comment, even should he have wished to make it. But he is clearly conscious of the presence of those difficulties which he is anxious to forget in Coleridge's life, which were sufficient to cause a dread, however cowardly, of being associate with him in the public mind. Dr. Arnold hinted at the same thing when he qualified his praise of "old Sam" with the reflection, "but yet there are marks enough that his mind was a little diseased."[103]

H.N.Coleridge too writes of the "extensive, but now decreasing, prejudice" which has hitherto "deprived [his prose works] of that acceptance with the public which their great preponderating merits deserve."[104] This prejudice is clear enough in the Victorian comments on Coleridge. He was regarded at best as "one of the weakest of good men."[105] And even Hort, in attempting to refurbish Coleridge's image, must first admit that,

> everyone knows that Coleridge was an opium-eater; and with many censors that is enough to condemn, not his character only, but even his writings.[106]

Some writers accused Coleridge of dishonesty at every level. Thus Benn comments on Coleridge's theology,

> love of truth and sincerity have to be flung away as they were flung away by Coleridge, who, as Sterling told Caroline Fox, 'professed doctrines he did not believe in order to avoid the trouble of controversy'.[107]

The contrast between this and the sort of reverence given to even

---

[102]*Ibid.*, 352.

[103]Stanley, *op.cit.*, p.394.

[104]S.T.Coleridge, *Table Talk and Omniana*, ed.T.Ashe (London, G.Bell and Sons, 1923), p.3. This edition is subsequently referred to as *Table Talk*.

[105]A.W.Benn, *op.cit.*, II, 72.

[106]F.J.A.Hort, "Coleridge," *Cambridge Essays* (London, J.W.Parker, 1856), p.297.

[107]A.W.Benn, *op.cit.*, I, 391. The passage he refers to is in *Memories of Old Friends, Being Extracts from the Journals and Letters of Caroline Fox, 1835-18,71*, ed. H.N.Pym, 2 vols. (London, Smith, Elder and Co., 1882), I, 287-288.

Coleridge's most difficult ideas today is a sign of how powerful the
biographical estimate common in the nineteenth century was. In every
way, Coleridge was difficult for the nineteenth century to approve. He
even failed to fit any simple category since he was apparently never
unreservedly friend or foe to any sect.

> Can we wonder that his name so generally awakens a kind of
> suspicious awe, a dim shrinking, as from some power not altogether
> evil, with which, however, it is on the whole safer not to hold
> personal intercourse?" [108]

A fine example of early Victorian prejudice against Coleridge at its
strongest is given by Clement Carlyon, at one stage a close
acquaintance of Coleridge. Carlyon, the Tory, is still incensed at
Coleridge's early Jacobinism.

> It need not be said how much more he would have consulted his own
> future fame, had he pleaded guilty to this foul offence committed in
> his day of political frenzy, instead of attempting to fritter away its
> atrocity by mental fallacies and a sort of psychological special
> pleading, which essayed to set up the pretensions of ill-defined
> motives, and a licentious imagination, in opposition to the plainest
> letter of the law. . . . the gravamen of the charge against Coleridge,
> after all, is not so much that he entertained sentiments which so
> many political visionaries entertained in common with him at the
> breaking out of the French Revolution . . . but that subsequently,
> when he saw his error, and repudiated the tenets and projects of his
> earlier years, he never appears to have made the *Amende
> Honourable*. . . it was a great aggravation of his offence, that he
> should have attempted to palliate [it] by dint of sophistry, and have
> even presumed to affront by such a compound of metaphysical jargon
> and fictitious philosophy, a company of whom no less men than Scott
> and Davy formed part. [109]

It is a remarkable testimony of bigotry, yet this is the measure of
the typical Victorian reaction to Coleridge's undisguisable
shortcomings. It is clear that the disciples felt the weight of a moral
reprobation of Coleridge – whether it was due to his procrastination,
his desertion of his wife, his politics, his opium-taking, or his
plaguarism is unimportant – for it had a strongly adverse effect on the
working of his influence. After his death, when his influence was at

[108]Hort, *op.cit.*, p.292.

[109]Clement Carlyon, *Early Years and Late Reflections*, 4 vols. (London, Whittacker and
Co., 1836-1858), I, 2, 76-77.

last beginning to show signs of bearing fruit, they were anxious to counterbalance this reprobation.

The consciousness of a general feeling against Coleridge – a feeling causing not active disapproval, but a dread of any association with him – throws light on the silence that greeted his publications for so many years. It explains Arnold's silence, and John Stuart Mill's guarded public references to Coleridge and conviction that the essay on Coleridge he was eventually to publish would not be "popular."[110] It would explain the very general lack of support in the documents of the time for the almost universal contention among his disciples, now taken over by the commentators, that Coleridge was seminal to his age. Coleridge, it would appear, became the centre not of controversy and interest, but of dread, and it was only those close to him who knew the real value of his achievement and preserved it. After Coleridge's death, however, the personal antipathy was largely forgotten, and even Arnold was contemplating an essay on Coleridge before he died in 1888.[111]

But even after these explanations the mystery of how "this indolent, desultory man. . . . yet exercised an influence which few other men did over the minds of his countrymen"[112] is still unsolved. But this is the mystery of genius – the trite, here, is true. The silence was a silence, not of intellectual disregard, but of moral disapprobation. Thus the praise of Coleridge's disciples is unusually fulsome, precisely because the spell needed breaking, and it is a feature, even more common to moral misjudgements than to intellectual ones, that righting them requires extravagance. It needed exaggeration, and a certain bravado, to be a disciple of Coleridge in the early nineteenth century.

[110]*The Collected Works of John Stuart Mill*, ed. F.E.L.Priestley, Vols. XII and XIII, "The Earlier Letters, 1812-1848," ed. F.E.Mineka (University of Toronto Press, 1963), XIII, 411.

[111]Gottfried, *op.cit.*, p.169.

[112]John H.Overton, *The English Church in the Nineteenth Century, 1800-1833* (London, Longmans, Green, and Co., 1894), p.209.

III

So much for the myth, what of the reality? What were the channels of Coleridge's influence and how did they affect the nineteenth century? Coleridge himself, while anxious to be of value, felt that his influence would not flow in the usual channels. In 1796 he believed that, although "I am not *fit* for *public* Life; yet the Light shall stream to a far distance from the taper on my cottage window."[113] Nearly ten years later Coleridge's tone has changed, though his hopes remain the same.

> I have lain too many eggs in the hot sands of this wilderness, the world, with ostrich carelessness and ostrich oblivion. The greater part indeed have been trod under foot, and are forgotten; but yet no small number have crept forth into life.[114]

The contrast between the two images, between "streaming" and "creeping" contains a decade of experience. Coleridge himself saw that the influence which he expected to have must pass through the few men who were close to him, and not through his printed works, and at Highgate he applied himself to the task of teaching by word of mouth those who came to listen. It was thus as a talker, not a writer that Coleridge was in the end to achieve fame and influence.

If Coleridge's prose works were felt to be disappointing, and were largely ignored, to the relatively few who heard him talk, his genius was never in doubt. He was frequently compared to Dr. Johnson, and the only regret his hearers express is that he had no assiduous Boswell. To many of these hearers, Coleridge's talk was a source of wonder. H.N.Coleridge writes,

> Throughout a long-drawn summer's day, would this man talk to you . . . marshalling all history, harmonizing all experiment, probing the depths of your consciousness, and revealing visions of glory and of terror to the imagination . . . leading you . . . for ever through a thousand windings, yet with no pause, to some magnificent point in which, as in a focus, all the parti-coloured rays of his discourse should

---

[113]*Collected Letters of Samuel Taylor Coleridge*, ed. E.L.Griggs, 4 vols. (Oxford, Clarendon, 1956-1959), I, 277.

[114]*Biographia Literaria*, ed. J.Shawcross, 2 vols. (Oxford, Clarendon, 1907), I, 32. It was a popular image with Coleridge; he also used it several times in letters, see *Collected Letters* ed. Griggs, II, 1011; III, 126, 131, 133, 145.

converge in light.[115]

Coleridge seems to have owed much of this impressiveness to the manner of his delivery. Collier promised that, "I shall never forget the peculiarly emphatic tone and rich voice."[116] A little girl who was taken to Highgate records a more vivid picture of how,

> that poor, mad poet, Coleridge, who never held his tongue, stood pouring out a deluge of words meaning nothing, with eyes on fire, and his silver hair streaming down to his waist.[117]

It was the potential which Coleridge displayed in his talk which contributed more than anything else to the disappointment most of his contemporaries felt with his actual productions. Coleridge found strange impediments in the way when he tried to write. Whether it was the fruit of habitual procrastination, or the moral weakness which Carlyle found in every line of his being,[118] or some inexplicable constitution of his mind, or perhaps that his ideas were more fitted to the potentially endless stream of discourse than to the precision and sharp limitations of print – whatever it was that made it so difficult for Coleridge to commit his ideas to writing, it never impeded his talk.[119]

Cottle, Coleridge's early publisher and friend, remarked jealously that "he often poured forth as much as half an 8vo volume in a single evening, and that in language sufficiently pure and connected to admit of publication."[120] Hazlitt felt that Coleridge's prose was "utterly abortive," but it was again the standard of the talk by which he was judging it.

> Hardly a gleam is to be found in it of the brilliancy and richness of those stores of thought and language that he pours out incessantly . . . Mr.Coleridge . . . has done little or nothing to justify to the world or to posterity, the high opinion which all who have ever heard

[115]*Table Talk*, p.5.

[116]John Payne Collier (1789-1883), in *Coleridge the Talker, A Series of Contemporary Descriptions and Comments,* ed. Richard W.Armour and Raymond F.Howes (New York, Cornell University Press, 1940), p.167. Subsequently referred to as *Coleridge the Talker.*

[117]*Ibid.,* p.91.

[118]Thomas Carlyle, *The Life of John Sterling,* World's Classics, CXLIV (London, Oxford University Press, 1933), pp.56-57.

[119]See *Table Talk,* p.7; see also *Coleridge the Talker,* p.352.

[120]Joseph Cottle (1770-1853) in *Coleridge the Talker,* p.186.

him converse . . . with one accord entertain of him.[121]

Coleridge himself, however, pleaded for a different estimate of his achievement.

> But are books the only channel through which the stream of intellectual usefulness can flow? . . . is the diffusion of truth to be estimated by publications?. . . Would that the criterion of a scholar's utility were the number and moral value of the truths, which he has been the means of throwing into the general circulation; or the number and value of the minds, whom by his conversation or letters he has excited into activity, and supplied with the germs of their after-growth! A distinguished rank might not indeed, even then, be awarded to my exertions; but I should dare look forward with confidence to an honourable acquittal.[122]

The talk by which he hoped to compensate for the inadequacies of his writings was undoubtedly successful to a large extent in influencing those who came to listen. Even Carlyle's cruelly funny account of Coleridge, "and how he sung and snuffled . . . 'om-m-mject' and 'sum-m-mject', with a kind of solemn shake or quiver, as he rolled along"[123] is prefaced with a characteristic admission of Coleridge's genius. "He distinguished himself," Carlyle writes, "to all that ever heard him as at least the most surprising talker extant in this world."[124] But if all found him surprising, not all found him interesting. "There were, indeed, some whom Coleridge tired, and some whom he sent asleep,"[125] H.N.Coleridge mildly records.

Carlyle, using his command of satire, called Coleridge a pump, whose listeners were expected to sit passively and be filled like buckets.[126] But for once another writer, James Fenimore Cooper, found the best image. "Coleridge," he wrote, "reminded me of a barrel to which every other man's tongue acted as a spigot, for no sooner did the latter move, than it set his own contents in a flow."[127] But whatever his critics thought of his social manners, there were plenty who took his talk seriously enough. It is here, perhaps, in the efforts of

---

[121]*Ibid.*, p.257.
[122]*Biographia Literaria*, ed. Shawcross, I, 149-150.
[123]Carlyle, *op.cit.*, p.57.
[124]*Ibid.*, p.56.
[125]*Table Talk*, p.5; see also *Coleridge the Talker*, p.198.
[126]Carlyle, *op.cit.*, p.58.
[127]James Fenimore Cooper (1789-1851), in *Coleridge the Talker*, p.182.

Coleridge's admiring hearers to explain their experiences, as they listened to him and contemplated afterwards the insights they had gained from him, that the image of the "seminal thinker" was born. Certainly, if Coleridge was seminal, it was at Highgate surrounded by these men that he sowed most liberally and fruitfully. It was undoubtedly true that "the *chair* would sometimes assume the solemn gravity of the *pulpit*"[128] as Coleridge talked, and yet, despite all the criticism, Coleridge was never accused of being dogmatic – an impressive tribute to a man who talked so much, not always to the pleasure of all present.

The records of his talk show that it was scattered with the same brilliant insights and images which are found in his prose works, insights which cohere round the few central distinctions which were the basis of his thinking. But what these records, inevitably, lack is the connectedness of his talk. H.N.Coleridge wrote,

> I can well remember occasions when I have gone away with divers splendid masses of reasoning in my head, the separate beauty and coherency of which I deeply felt; but how they had produced, or how they bore upon, each other, I could not then perceive.[129]

But what he did remember shows that Coleridge talked at length about the same ideas which fill his prose works. He talked of his "system" and of the need to reconcile conflicting half-truths; he expounded the central distinctions between Reason and Understanding, Genius and Talent, and Imagination and Fancy; he criticised the materialistic and prudential philosophy of the Enlightenment; and he illustrated his "favourite maxim – extremes meet."[130] But, towards the end of his life, his scheme for the reform of the Church and for the clerisy occupied his time more and more,

> he spoke upon it with an emotion which I never saw him betray upon any topic of common politics, however decided his opinions might be.[131]

Hartley Coleridge recorded that his father was more radical in his sympathies at the end of his life than was generally known, and was as

---

[128] *Ibid.*, p.202.
[129] *Table Talk*, p.8.
[130] *Ibid.*, pp.9-11.
[131] *Ibid.*, p.11.

much occupied with schemes for reform as with a conservative philosophy.

Coleridge at Highgate, far from drifting deeper and deeper into metaphysics, was on the contrary formulating ever more clearly, and impressing on the minds of those who heard him, his convictions on the way in which the nation could be regenerated, and his idea of the "clerisy" which was to be so influential in years to come. It was this Highgate sage, propagating his ideas like a teacher or a priest, rather than like a literary figure, who was such an influence in the nineteenth century. It was not Coleridge the poet, not Coleridge the visionary radical, but Coleridge the lecturing philosopher whose ideas were so fruitfully sown in so many diverse minds.[132]

IV

This is the outline of the growth of the myth of Coleridge's influence. I have chosen to explore the details of this influence on one figure, John Stuart Mill. Mill is, if not the most obvious, the most useful choice among the important figures who acknowledged Coleridge's influence. That Coleridge's "place as one of the seminal minds of the age should have been defined by the utilitarian John Stuart Mill is evidence enough of his persuasive, all but inescapable influence."[133] Mill's position as a member, if a very broad-minded one, of the opposing school does make him an unusually impartial witness. But Mill was also receiving Coleridge's influence at a time when it was most ignored by the public at large, around 1828-31, and was receiving it largely through the disciples. Mill is therefore ideally placed to contribute useful evidence towards an understanding of Coleridge's influence on the nineteenth century. It is not generally believed that Mill, despite his essay on Coleridge, knew a great deal about his subject, but it is admitted that,

> Mill's attempt to absorb, and by discrimination and discarding to unify, the truths alike of the utilitarian and the idealist positions is, after all, a prologue to a very large part of the subsequent history of

---

[132]See Graham Hough, "Coleridge and the Victorians," *op.cit.*, pp.177-178, 183-184.
[133]Gottfried, *op.cit.*, p.164.

English thinking.[134]

To show the extent of Coleridge's role in Mill's thought could establish then, not only his real influence on Mill but also his place in the intellectual history of the century. But Mill's special attraction for this role is his own, and counteracting, importance in comparison with Coleridge's. Despite Mill's fair-minded essay, his own ideas "told heavily and increasingly against Coleridge's."[135] Mill is, for all his partisan upbringing, as central to the Victorian temper of mind as any one figure can be.

> If one man ever represented an epoch, Mill represented Victorianism. To such an extent, indeed, is this the case that any fair description of Victorianism sounds almost like a projection of Mill's private beliefs and aspirations.[136]

He had an enormous influence on the mind of his age and "possessed . . . an authority in the English Universities . . . comparable to that wielded forty years earlier by Hegel in Germany and in the Middle Ages by Aristotle."[137] Mill thus came to have a "firm hold on the rising thought of Oxford and Cambridge."[138] His *Logic* was the text book of philosophy until, with T.H.Green's appointment to the Oxford chair of Philosophy in 1871, Hegelianism became the dominant ideology.[139] His "authority among the educated youth of England was greater than may appear credible to the present generation. His work *On Liberty* was to the younger body of Liberal statesmen a political

[134]Raymond Williams, *Culture and Society, 1780-1950* (London, Chatto and Windus, 1958), p.49.

[135]D.G.James, "The Thought of Coleridge," in *The Major English Romantic Poets; A Symposium in Reappraisal*, ed.Clarence D.Thorpe, Carlos Baker and Bennet Weaver (Carbondale, Southern Illinois University Press, 1957), p.100.

[136]R.P.Anschutz, "J.S.Mill: Philosopher of Victorianism," in *1840 and After*, ed. Arthur Sewell (Auckland, N.Z., 1939), p.131.

[137]Arthur James Balfour, *Theism and Humanism* (London, Hodder and Stoughton, 1915), p.138.

[138]James M'Cosh, *An Examination of J.S.Mill's Philosophy* (London, Macmillan and Co., 1866), p.1.

[139]Melvin Richter, *The Politics of Conscience; T.H.Green and his Age* (London, Weidenfeld and Nicholson, 1964), p.150.

manual."[140] Mill is the ideal choice not only because of his historical importance, but also because he is as precise, as honest, and as impartial a witness in intellectual matters as can be found.[141] Very few writers had his openness of mind;

> because he believed in the importance of ideas, he was prepared to change his own if others could convince him of their inadequacy, or when a new vision was revealed to him, as it was by Coleridge.[142]

Even more important, Mill's background was hostile to everything Coleridge stood for. His training had refined this hostility to a pure impartiality, but he remained totally remote from the panegyrics and myth-making of the disciples. He was, rather, in initial sympathy with the reprobators of Coleridge's immorality. "Mill never, any more than Carlyle, found it easy to admire Coleridge."[143] That such a man, a sharply discriminating radical, and a paragon of Liberal Victorian virtues, should have anything to say for Coleridge is evidence in itself. Mill read Coleridge, not because he felt he ought to, not carried away by enthusiasm, or blinded by prejudice, but because Coleridge was worth reading. Coleridge's place in Mill's mind was due to his value, not to his reputation.

The account of Mill's experience of Coleridge's ideas is thus the best witness we have of the truth of Coleridge's influence. The evidence is made the easier to collect by the fact that Mill left a most unusually complete and full account of the history of his mind. His education was an experiment, and he fully bore his share of the responsibility in making the result of the experiment freely and openly available in the *Autobiography*.[144] Mill is, finally, the best choice because it is his assessment of Coleridge as a "seminal mind", a "teacher of the teachers" which has proved to be the most

---

[140]A.V.Dicey, *Lecture on the Relation Between Law and Public Opinion in England During the Nineteenth Century* (London, Macmillan and Co., 1914), p.386.

[141]See Vernon F.Storr, *The Development of English Theology in the Nineteenth Century, 1800-1860* (London, Longmans, Green, and Co., 1913), p.319.

[142]Sir Isiah Berlin, *John Stuart Mill and the Ends of Life* (London, Council of Christians and Jews, 1959), p 32.

[143]Shirley R.Letwin, *The Pursuit of Certainty* (Cambridge University Press, 1965), p.305.

[144]J.S.Mill, *Autobiography* (London, Longmans, Green, Reader, and Dyer, 1874).

influential.[145] Almost every account of Coleridge's importance now quotes Mill, and the importance of Mill's essay as testimony of Coleridge's influence is well recognised.[146] Yet it is curious that although there is more evidence for Coleridge's influence on Mill than there is of his influence on, for example, Matthew Arnold or J.H.Newman – subjects which have been attempted[147] – the details of Coleridge's influence on Mill have not been extensively studied.

V

I will conclude this introductory chapter with a summary of the line the subsequent argument is to follow, and a discussion of the general points which are raised by the offer to study the influence of a writer on a philosopher. It seems clear, for instance, that the process of examining Coleridge's role in the development of Mill's ideas must start by establishing the background of Mill's own education. An exposition of his early training will be followed by an account of the varying interpretations of Mill's mental crisis in 1825-6, and an attempt to establish a tenable cause and effect relationship between the crisis and the new opinions which were flooding into his mind at that time. Mill's explicit expressions of debt to Coleridge in the *Autobiography*, and in an earlier letter, lead us to a discussion of the evidence of Mill's reading of Coleridge.

Next it will be necessary to establish the background of ideas before looking at any parallels in thought between the two writers. Mill's career as an epistemological empiricist, intermittently committed to total relativism and a hybrid ontology, is in sharp contrast to Coleridge's erratic progress through associationism and Kantianism to a personal, mystic form of Platonism, deriving as much from

---

[145] J.S.Mill, *Autobiography* (London, Longmans, Green, Reader, and Dyer, 1874).

[146] A.W.Benn, *op.cit.*, I, 285-286; Waler H.Pater, *Appreciations* (London, Macmillan and Co., 1890), p.82.

[147] Gottfried, *op.cit.*, pp.151-199; H.F.Davis, "Was Newman a Disciple of Coleridge?" *Dublin Review*, CCXVII (October, 1945), 165-173; W.R.Castle, "Newman and Coleridge," *Sewanee Review*, XVII (1909), 139-152. Mill has also been compared to Newman, see Leslie Stephen, *An Agnostic's Apology and other Essays* (London, Duckworth and Co., 1937), pp.113-114.

seventeenth century English theology as from continental sources. These differing growths of ideas, as well as the criticisms each makes of the opposing doctrine, will not seem to promise any common beliefs, or influence. But, although Coleridge and Mill are clearly Platonist and Aristotelian, a common relativism, and devotion to the realities of individual experience prevent any similarities being rejected without examination.

Subsequent analysis of their ideas on political methodology, on religion, on aesthetics, on the role of an established church, and on eclecticism will then show that they did, in fact, have considerable areas of belief in common, and that Mill learnt from Coleridge in a fruitful way. Finally, Mill's essays on "Bentham" and "Coleridge" will be discussed, and the rather ambiguous assessment of Coleridge found in them explained in terms of Mill's decreasing interest in Coleridge as his mature political and philosophical concerns increasingly employed his energies. It will be possible to conclude that Coleridge had a real, if minor, role to play in Mill's thought.

It is not necessary, and it is certainly not the intention of this study, to show that Coleridge was in any way an overriding, or even a major, component of Mill's thought. It is only intended to show that he was taking a real place beside the other forces of the age in the thought of a highly representative figure. To establish this is to provide factual support for the contention that Coleridge's achievement, far from being ignored, was able to exercise a valuable influence in the nineteenth century.

More, of course, will emerge from this study than detailed evidence of Coleridge's influence. Inevitably light is cast on Mill, and on the early nineteenth century. Mill's role in the considerable modifications which Utilitarianism underwent as it was transformed from the doctrinaire Benthamism of James Mill to Liberalism, is clarified. Equally, the role of idealism, in a broad sense, in the nineteenth century is discussed. Coleridge's idealism was not the common philosophy of the nineteenth century; his ideals were unconventional, his enthusiastic disciples a minority. Coleridge's mystical Platonism, saturated in German metaphysics, was alien to the main tenor of the English tradition, if not of the sixteenth and seventeenth centuries then of the tradition established in the eighteenth century by Locke and Hume. In the nineteenth century this tradition was, and continued to be, strictly materialistic, empirical and utilitarian in fact, if not fully in admission. Yet this tradition contained new elements of idealism.

Mill's modified utilitarianism is a convenient focus to study this mixture, and Coleridge's idealism is a source of many of the new elements. In literature too, romanticism and Victorianism are totally different in flavour, if the roots of the one in the other are clear enough. In both these areas the forces of Coleridge's idealist outlook combine with Mill's utilitarianism to form strands of the Victorian outlook. In the cross-pollination of these two traditions is seen the birth of the new outlook.

2 A change of opinions

A grief without a pang, void, dark and drear,
A stifled, drowsy, unimpassioned grief,
Which finds no natural outlet, no relief,
In word, or sigh, or tear. – S.T.Coleridge[1]

Coleridge, in whom alone of all writers I have found a true
description of what I felt." – J.S.Mill[2]

Perhaps the only fact about John Stuart Mill which everyone
knows, apart from his authorship of *On Liberty*, is that he underwent
in his early twenties a mental crisis which left him a changed man. No
other event in the history of ideas can have been so thoroughly
interpreted, and mis-interpreted, as this one. Any scholar at all familiar
with the literature of Mill studies must yawn at the prospect of being
taken, once again, on a guided tour of this popular exhibit; the
fragments of Mill's mind distributed by his crisis into discrete and
incompatible ideas.

Yet Mill himself invited the thorough inspection he received. No
writer of comparable importance left such a complete, careful account
of the genesis and development of his ideas.[3] But although he was

[1]S.T.Coleridge, *Complete Poetical Works*, ed. E.H. Coleridge, 2 vols. (Oxford, Clarendon, 1912), I, 364.

[2]J.S.Mill, *Autobiography*, 3rd. ed. (London, Longmans, Green, Reader, and Dyer, 1874), p.140. Subsequently referred to as *Autobiography*.

[3]Catherine M.Cox, *The Early Mental Traits of Three Hundred Geniuses* (London, Harrup & Co., 1926), p.155.

remarkably honest and generous in his description of his intellectual debts and experiences, there are places nevertheless where he is inevitably over-simplifying.[4] It is these places that have attracted comment.

It is not necessary to examine in any depth the complex arguments that now surround the *Autobiography*. But the outline of Mill's education and change of opinions must be recapitulated in order to assess Coleridge's role in them. With this background established, the problems of the chronology, and the causative relationship of the events of the year of the crisis will be dealt with before examining Mill's detailed descriptions of his debt to Coleridge. Next will come a thorough catalogue of Mill's reading of Coleridge's works. The picture of Mill's acquaintance with Coleridge will be completed by recording his personal contacts with Coleridge himself and, more importantly, his vociferous disciples, the Coleridgeans. John Sterling is the most important of these.

In the following chapters this evidence of Mill's knowledge of Coleridge will underlie a discussion of Coleridge's and Mill's philosophical ideas, their methodology, religion, politics, art and eclecticism. From this, parallels will emerge which will provide the material for an estimate of Coleridge's influence on Mill.

I

Jeremy Bentham and his friend, James Mill, designed John Stuart Mill's education from the first as an experiment. Both believed that association and the pleasure-pain principle were the ultimate and complete laws of the formation of the human mind and character; and they saw John's mind as a 'Tabla Rasa' on which they could imprint their philosophy.

Mill was required by his exacting father to be unusually learned at an early age.[5] Then, at the age of sixteen, this precocious and diverse learning was suddenly galvanised into a plan of action, a weapon of attack. He read Bentham for the first time. Although he,

---

[4]See Robert D. Cumming, "Mill's History of his Ideas," *J.H.I.*, XXV (1964), 235-256.
[5]*Autobiography*, p.30.

had always been taught to apply [the Benthamite principle of the greatest happiness], yet in the first pages of Bentham it burst upon me with all the force of novelty ... When I laid down the last volume of the *Traité* I had become a different being ... It gave unity to my conceptions of things. I had now opinions; a creed, a doctrine, a philosophy; in one among the best senses of the word, a religion; the inculcation and diffusion of which could be made the principal outward purpose of a life.[6]

It was a conversion indeed. With this equipment, and this catalytic experience, Mill set out on the first stages of his remarkable career.

By the age of eighteen he was the centre of an active group of young radicals, and although he was nearly the youngest he was regarded as their intellectual leader. When he first emerged into the political world, the Utilitarians thought of him as their prodigy, and the opposing schools as a "made" man.[7] His early writings betray the immaturity of his ideas. He believed that the road to happiness was discovered, and insisted that all that remained to be done was to teach everyone how to follow this road.

The glibness of his positions at this time foretells disaster. The self-assurance was, perhaps, no more than that of any precocious adolescent, but his education, which had in no way discouraged the child from finding his own justifications for the truth, had never seriously suggested inadequacies in the system it taught. When Mill did meet serious opposition to his father's ideas, in the form of the conservatism represented by Macaulay,[8] in the form of the Coleridgeans, and in the form of the demands of his own growing inner needs, the crumbling of his self-assurance was as exaggerated as the assurance itself had been.

Mill had proposed to himself the propagation of Bentham's ideas as a religion, and his "conception of my own happiness was entirely identified with this object."[9] But, called on to face and explain the

---

[6]*Ibid.*, pp.64-67.

[7]*Ibid.*, p.155.

[8]T.B.Macaulay, "Mill's essay on Government," *Edinburgh Review*, XCVII (March, 1829), 159-189; reprinted in *Critical and Miscellaneous Essays*, 5 vols. (Philadelphia, Carey and Hart, 1841-44), V, 328-367.

[9]*Autobiography*, p.132.

complex manifestations of his growing personality, this simplified ideal
of life suddenly seemed to him to be inadequate. He asked himself the
distinct question,

> 'Suppose that all your objects in life were realised . . . would this be
> a great joy and happiness to you?' And an irrepressible self-
> consciousness distinctly answered, 'No!' At this my heart sank within
> me: the whole foundation on which my life was constructed fell
> down.[10]

The 'crisis' which was to transform his opinions as surely as his
first reading of Bentham had hardened them, was upon him. Through
the winter of 1826-7 he was haunted by a nameless depression, for
which, even from the much later perspective of the *Autobiography*, he
was unable to find a satisfactory explanation.

There have been more than enough attempts to supply the
deficiency. The crisis has been subjected to many interpretations, both
interesting and bizarre. Alexander Bain kindly attributed the
depression almost solely to overwork;[11] John Bowring, on the other
hand, was maliciously witty at Mill's expense. Mill, he said, "was most
emphatically a philosopher, but then he read Wordsworth, and that
muddled him, and he was been in a strange confusion ever since,
endeavouring to unite poetry and philosophy."[12] W.T.Courtney, in a
small life of Mill published in 1889, is even more astringent, concluding
his account of the crisis with a flourish of moral homily.

> This is the shipwreck of Rationalism . . . The teaching of the older
> Mill had been throughout the suppression of feeling . . . and the issue
> is seen in John Mill sitting down in despair, with all his schemes of
> life and human regeneration lying in ruins around him.[13]

A similar comment comes from W.Ward.

> The Autobiography will ever remain as a most pathetic human
> record, the story of an unnatural experiment in mental vivisection

---

[10]*Ibid.*, pp.133-134.

[11]Alexander Bain, *John Stuart Mill, a Criticism* (London, Longmans, Green & Co.,
1882), p.38.

[12]Caroline Fox, *Memories of Old Friends, Being Extracts from the Journals and
Letters of Caroline Fox, from 1835 to 1870*, ed.H.N.Pym, 2 vols. (London, Smith,
Elder and Co., 1882), I, p.216. Subsequently referred to as *Fox*.

[13]William Leonard Courtney, *Life of John Stuart Mill* (London, Walter Scott, 1889),
pp.57-58.

exercised on a little child, issuing in a somewhat maimed and
impoverished nature, and of an heroic and partly successful attempt
at recovery.[14]

Even A.O.J.Cockshut, in a sensible account of Mill's poetics, tells
us that the crisis shows that, "the saint of rationalism possessed in the
depths of his mind the fiery conscience of a covenanter."[15]

This is the kind of commentary to which Mill is unfortunately
open, and its exaggerations discourage serious attempts to disentangle
the problems of the crisis. By contrast, Mill's own account seems much
more acceptable. But more recent, and closer, examinations have
disclosed factual conflicts in it which cannot be ignored. The
chronology Mill gives of his states of mind at this time is contradictory.
In one chapter he records that in 1826-7 the debating society was
revived by his enthusiasm, and in the next chapter that the work he
did in 1826-7 was done mechanically, with no sense of purpose. The
last page of the preceding chapter, however, says that the article
written in 1828 was a "labour of love."[16]

There are similar discrepancies in Mill's description of the process
of the crisis. For instance, of 1826 Mill writes, "the whole foundation
on which my life was constructed fell down,"[17] but of 1830 he writes,
"I never allowed . . . the fabric of my old . . . opinions . . . to fall to
pieces."[18] R.D.Cummings comes to the conclusion that Mill's account is
"not historical,"[19] and that he explained the crisis according to two
successive theories of the mind, which left conflicting interpretations.

There is no doubt that Mill's own history of his crisis is
inadequate. Indeed, in a later discussion of it, he makes it clear that
the process was more complex and gradual than his first account would
suggest. "These few selected points," he warns the reader, "give a very
insufficient idea of the quantity of thinking which I carried out

[14]Wilfred Ward, "John Stuart Mill," *Quarterly Review*, CCXIII (1910), 291.

[15]A.O.J.Cockshut, *The Unbelievers, English Agnostic Thought, 1840-1890* (London,
Collins, 1964), p.29.

[16]*Autobiography*, p.131.

[17]*Ibid.*, p.134.

[18]*Ibid.*, p.156.

[19]R.D.Cummings, *op.cit.*, p.243.

respecting a host of subjects during these years of transition."[20]

It is possible to show that Mill's crisis was to a large extent a gradual affair, yet the fact remains that Mill felt he needed the idea of 'crisis' to express his own conception of what had occurred. The problem of the crisis can thus only be solved if due respect is first given to his own explanations of it, before probing its inconsistencies.

II

Mill's own account of his crisis shows that he seized on anything plausible to decipher the state of uncertainty in which he found himself. His range of explanations includes the inadequacies of his education, his neglect of emotional culture, the loss of his life-aims, the consequent evaporation of all motives in his life, and the self-consciousness theories of Carlyle. Two of these explanations established themselves in his subsequent narrations as the most important ones – his criticism of his education, and his consequent neglect of emotional culture. It is notable that the other explanations, loss of life-aims, and self-consciousness theories, which were prominent at first were not developed.

The immediate result of the crisis was a state of depression. There seem to have been two major strands in this depression, which are given equal importance in Mill's account, although he neither distinguished, nor integrated them. One strand was the failure of his life-aims; the other was the sudden sense of a lack of feeling, the belief that he was a stick or a stone. Neither of these things necessarily involves the other. But Mill seems to regard them as congruent experiences, although it can be agued that they are significantly diverse.

His early utilitarian 'life-aims' did not include extensive emotional satisfaction. The sense that he was emotionally deficient seems oddly inapplicable to the feeling that Bentham no longer presented the leading light that he did when Mill first read him. The explanation probably lies in the origins of both beliefs in a new theoretical awareness. Mill became conscious of the inadequacies of Benthamism

---

[20] *Autobiography*, p.168.

through reading Macaulay at the same time as he discovered the importance of the emotions through reading the Romantics. To him they represented the same thing; the new intellectual horizons which made Benthamism seem narrow. But in fact they were different things.

The diversity of the two strands is seen in the results of the crisis. Mill continues his account in the *Autobiography*,

> The experiences of this period had two very marked effects on my opinions and character. In the first place they led me to adopt a theory of life, [which treated] ... not happiness, but some end external to it, as the purpose of life. .... The other important change which my opinions at this time underwent, was that I, for the first time, gave its proper place, among the prime necessities of human well-being, to the internal culture of the individual. .... I now began to find meaning in the things which I had read or heard about the importance of poetry and art as instruments of human culture.[21]

The first change is a change in life-aims, here explained in terms of the self-consciousness theories of Carlyle. The second is a change in theoretical awareness. The two changes might, again, be regarded as, in the abstract, opposed ones. The first is a determination to turn away from the direct pursuit of emotional fulfillment, in the belief that it flees from conscious intention; the second is a determination to give more deliberate and direct attention to the cultivation of emotional satisfaction in art forms.

Mill's initial failure to make anything systematic out of these diverse insights shows how complex the crisis was. The new opinions did not replace his old ones, they merely required to be joined on to them.[22] The mixture is a curious one, and will provide a key to unravel Mill's apparently bland, but in reality complex accounts of his crisis. The dual explanation of the crisis finally crystallized as a distrust of his education, and a belief that he had been starved of emotional culture. These two things can be dealt with separately.

Mill's interest in his education was absorbing. The *Autobiography* was written mainly to give an account of it, and its results. Although his education was undoubtedly remarkable and beneficial in many directions, he felt it to be inadequate to the needs of the whole man.

---

[21] *Ibid.*, pp.141-144.
[22] *Ibid.*, p.143.

The early draft contains references to the "ungainliness, awkwardness" and "thoroughly ineffective and bungling manner"[23] of the education and its product, and "the bitterness of some of his language . . . bear[s] witness to a strong feeling in the matter."[24] Most of these criticisms were later deleted, but those that were left in the published version, although often mild in tone, show considerable dissatisfaction. He makes a great deal of the fact that his education left him mentally dextrous, but practically handicapped, and concludes that "my father . . . demanded of me not only the utmost that I could do, but much that I could by no possibility have done."[25] All the criticism is couched in the general, public terms which characterize the *Autobiography*, but the personal reaction is only thinly disguised. Mill attributes his crisis largely to the inadequacies of his education. "I was," he writes, "left stranded at the commencement of my voyage, with a well-equipped ship and rudder, but no sail."[26]

But Mill was too much involved with the process of his education to see it in perspective. Whatever its inadequacies, it was unlikely to have contributed entirely to the state of depression he found himself in. For, although the education was unusual in its intentions, it was surely by no means unusual in its results. Intended to produce a Utilitarian philosopher instead of a Christian gentleman, it succeeded partially and was partially inadequate. If his education was more thorough in its formative effects than usual, it also encouraged him to question what he learnt, and taught him to think for himself, "almost from the first."[27] As he reached manhood, and his ideas became substantially real to him, he revolted from the traditions of his upbringing in a way akin to the revolt of many gifted children. Samuel Butler comes to mind; Canon Butler and James Mill have some resemblance of personality, despite antagonisms of creed. John Mill was only unusual because this revolt took the form of a questioning of the adequacy of

---

[23]Quoted in Jack Stillinger, ed., *The Early Draft of Mill's Autobiography* (Urbana, University of Illinois Press, 1961), p.18.

[24]*Ibid.*

[25]*Autobiography*, pp.5-6; see also p.33.

[26]*Ibid.*, p.139; see also James Mill, *Analysis of the Phenomena of the Human Mind*, 2 vols. (London, Baldwin and Cradock, 1829), II, 212-213.

[27]*Autobiography*, p.29.

rationalism, instead of the more usual questioning of the value of an established religion. It was fundamentally a healthy process.[28]

Mill had little opportunity to see his education in this light. It was surrounded from the first by a sense of its abnormality. When James Mill talked with his son before sending him off to stay with friends in France, he reminded him of the unusualness of his achievements.[29] Whatever John Mill may have felt about his own share in this precosity, he had no reason to believe himself normal in any way. James Mill did not doubt the efficacy of his scheme; John Mill had not the experience to make his own judgement. He ignored the natural process of growth in himself, as much as his father's pride in his training ignored the possibility of its inadequacy. There thus grew out of the education a family myth, and Mill's attack on it was also therefore an attack on the family gods in a more personal sense than usual, as commentators have been quick to point out.[30]

But Mill's education does not seem to have been as peculiar as both father and son believed,[31] nor was its 'failure' in the crisis as destructive an experience as John Mill's account implies. The list of works Mill was engaged in at the time of the crisis shows that he was probably suffering as much from overwork as anything; the depression was partly at least the result of exhaustion. The essays Mill wrote before and after show no evidence of any real failure of his mental powers. Equally, any radical doubt as to his own abilities might have been quickly forgotten in the sublimation which engulfs all totally painful experiences. But he seems to have remained interested in what had happened to him, and evidently regarded it as a useful experience.

The crisis is clearly a positive, and not a negative event in Mill's life. Rather than any real experience of total doubt, what happened to

---

[28]Shirley R.Letwin, *The Pursuit of Certainty* (Cambridge University Press, 1965), p.211; see H.O.Pappe, *John Stuart Mill and the Harriet Taylor Myth* (Melbourne University Press, 1960), p.1; also cf. Bertrand Russell, *Autobiography, 1972-196 9*, 3 vols. (London, George Allen and Unwin, 1967-1969), I, 146.

[29]*Autobiography*, p.34.

[30]See A.W.Levi, "The Writing of Mill's *Autobiography*," *Ethics*, LXI (1950-51), 284-296.

[31]Anna Jean Mill, *John Stuart Mill's Boyhood Visit to France, 1820-21* (Toronto University Press, 1960), p.xvi.

him was similar to what occurred when he first read Bentham. The concepts which were to transform his mind were already part of it, but when the crisis turned them into "substantial knowledge" they took on all the force of novelty. Becoming suddenly real to him, his thought appeared to be transformed. This experience of finding reality in ideas previously uninteresting is part of the normal process of growth, and Mill's crisis was thus neither unhealthy, nor permanently damaging. It was only the difficulty of seeing the process of his education and the growth of his mind in perspective which lead Mill to interpret his crisis as primarily the result of a special inadequacy in his education.

The second strand of Mill's account of his crisis was the belief that he lacked proper cultivation of the feelings. The crisis presented itself, in part, as "the thought that all feeling was dead within me."[32] James Mill had undervalued and neglected feeling and "from this neglect, both in theory and in practice of the cultivation of feeling, naturally resulted, among other things, an undervaluing of poetry, and of Imagination generally, as an element of human nature."[33] But the truth was that John Mill had not been totally cut off from the sources of culture. Indeed,

> long before I had enlarged in any considerable degree, the basis of my intellectual creed, I had obtained in the natural course of my mental progress, poetic culture of the most valuable kind.[34]

It was not a new discovery of poetry, but a new understanding of its importance which produced the sense of crisis. Before this time Mill had been mainly familiar with Augustan poetry, particularly Pope's poems and translations, but he had no theoretical means of understanding the "keen enjoyment" which even then poetry gave him.[35] During the crisis, however, he discovered Romantic poetry, and the Romantic theories of the mind. Mill was aware of the value of art before the crisis, for he turned, as if by habit, to music and poetry to relieve his depression. But he had been "theoretically indifferent."[36] It was this theoretic indifference which Wordsworth and Coleridge

---

[32] *Autobiography*, p.141.

[33] *Ibid.*, p.112

[34] *Ibid.*, p.113

[35] *Ibid.*, p.10.

[36] *Ibid.*, p.112

conquered.

There seems no reason to regard the unusualness of his education as responsible, by itself, for the resulting 'crisis.' It was contact with what that education omitted that sparked off the turmoil. There is an important difference between these things. No education can be a total preparation for life; all education omits important things. It was not the omissions which mattered, it was the new ideas which filled the gap. Had Mill not met these new ideas, had no acceptable contradictory system to Benthamism been available, it is unlikely that a 'crisis' would have occurred.

The link of causation thus lies between the new ideas and the crisis, and not between the deficiencies of the old ideas and the crisis. But in which direction did this causative link operate? Mill's account says that after the crisis his opinions broadened. The crisis, he suggests, was *causa sui*, the effect was his new contacts with intuitionism. Yet a close look at his own statements suggests that the cause and effect relationship is by no means so simple, or so uni-directional. Mill claimed the crisis directed his attention to the need for emotional culture, yet he had read poetry before the crisis.[37] He had also been in contact with new ideas before the crisis. Most significantly, the crisis was due to a sense of lack of feeling, and Mill turned, first, without any prompting, to art, to music, and to poetry, to find the remedy. Mill, that is, knew what he lacked and where to find it prior to the crisis. He must, then, have already been well aware of the power of poetry; the new element was giving an importance to it. Before he had been "theoretically indifferent;" now he was interested. What had changed was not so much the feeling, as the theory.

The complexities of the temporal relationship of cause and effect suggest that Mill was over-simplifying, that the direction of the cause and effect relationship was, at the inception of the crisis, the opposite of the one he suggested. That is, that reading a new account of the theoretical importance of poetry directed his conscious attention to his own enjoyment of poetry. Now he went to art with one eye firmly on his reactions. Not surprisingly, while carefully watched, his emotions would not react. Convinced of the importance of the reaction, whereas

[37]*Ibid.*, pp.10, 14-15, 113.

before he had accepted it without special interest, Mill was horrified at his lack of feeling. He was a stick or a stone. Then the depression set in, a depression arising from a sense of inadequacy. It was only when he was reading casually, without the conscious attempt to stir his emotions that his feelings, released from a withering scrutiny, reacted. Reading Marmontel's *Memoires* he suddenly found himself weeping. He was as overjoyed at the release, as he had been depressed at his emotional impotence.[38]

From the experience he learnt two things. Firstly that excessive self-consciousness, too close a watch on spontaneous reactions, cheats and anaesthetizes those reactions. He learnt to aim, not for happiness itself, but at some other end, so that the happiness would come spontaneously. Secondly, he learnt that he must more consciously exercise his interest, which had always been there, in poetry and art.

The relationship between new theories of art and the crisis was probably two-way. Neither was the simple cause of the other, both grew together in a natural process of interaction. But the new theories were at least co-natal with the crisis, and some evidence might suggest that they were more cause than effect.

What were the sources of this new theory? Mill himself gives a list which includes nearly all the important English Romantic and post-Kantian influences of the time.[39] It was, initially, English Romanticism which was the source, however, and it was Romantic theories of poetry which provided the pattern of Mill's interpretation of the crisis. He was naturally a voracious and curious reader. He had evidently read Byron, traditionally the poet of violent feeling, for it was to Byron that he turned to remedy his emotional impotence at the time of the crisis.[40]
He must also have known Wordsworth at this time, and found him more suited to his taste. Wordsworth was the poet of "unpoetical natures."[41]Wordsworth's vehicle of expression was primarily, so it seemed to Mill, his thought, to which he added his feeling, whereas in Byron feeling was all. Wordsworth was therefore able to speak directly

---

[38]*Ibid.*, pp.140-141.
[39]*Ibid.*, p.161.
[40]*Ibid.*, p.146.
[41]*Ibid.*, p.149.

to Mill, and it was Wordsworth who "prepared" him for "the higher flights of Coleridge."[42]

But it was in Coleridge alone that Mill found the "only true description" of his state.[43] Thus the simplifications which enabled him to come to terms with the disturbing experience of growth to maturity came, not from his father, but from Romanticism and from Coleridge.

From Coleridge's poems Mill went on to read Coleridge's prose. Works like *Biographia Literaria* provided some of the material for his developing critique of Bentham. From then on the process was self-developing. Attracted initially, he soon found himself friendly with the Coleridgeans, the Positivists, and with Carlyle, and ideas suddenly became available on all sides in such profusion that the process was self-developing.

The account of Coleridge's share in these new ideas forms the substance of the following chapters. But it can be seen at this stage that Coleridge's importance was not the result of a sudden conversion to idealism. The crisis is evidently much inflated in Mill's account of it, and the real change must have occurred gradually and naturally. Mill's description is a dramatic one, and thereby gains a great deal in force and cogency, but it can be misleading. It was not any dramatic failure in his education, or any inevitable result of erroneous and narrow beliefs, which led Mill to his crisis.

Nor was it solely his new awareness of the value of feelings. It was a new theory. It would be pointless, even were it feasible, to claim that Mill was forced to read the Romantics by an urgent and insatiable need for a long denied fulfillment. Rather, he came to understand their ideas through a natural process of growth which was best described in terms of a 'crisis', although it was in reality gradual. The truth would seem to be that the crisis had been long prepared by an increasing awareness of new ideas, and that its cure was as much theoretical as its causes. The experience itself may have been as sudden as the effect of his first reading of Bentham, though one might detect a taste for melodrama in the accounts of both important stages of his education, but the surrounding circumstances were gradual and natural.

---

[42]Fox, I, 147.
[43]*Autobiography*, p.140.

This conclusion is a basis on which to build an account of the influence of idealism on Mill. A violent conversion, with all the imbalance and mental insecurity, might have been a source of influence, but might soon have led to a corresponding reaction. The real situation was different. Mill's use of Coleridge was based on a sensible realisation of the value of his ideas, and they became not suddenly, but carefully and gradually, part of a more comprehensive philosophy of life.

III

Mill's essay on "Coleridge" and the passages on Coleridge in the *Autobiography* are the classic statements of his debt. But the essay, for all its insight and generosity, is in parts severely critical of Coleridge. He is an "arrant driveller" in Political Economy,[44] and the conclusion is not really what the body of the essay would lead us to expect. Coleridge is finally praised only because he is a hidden liberal in the conservative ranks.

The expression of debt to Coleridge in the *Autobiography*, the public record of Mill's intellectual transactions, is short. It forms part of a general account of Mill's contact with the intuitionist schools which marked the period of his intellectual development and expansion after 1826.

> The influence of European, that is to say, Continental, thought, and especially those of the reaction of the nineteenth century against the eighteenth, were now streaming in upon me. They came from various quarters: from the writings of Coleridge, which I had begun to read with interest even before the change in my opinions; from the Coleridgeans with whom I was in personal intercourse; from what I had read of Goethe; from Carlyle.[45]

Coleridge is bound up with Maurice and "other German authors"[46] as part of the widened experience of the time, and little is made of his individual contribution. The early draft only adds that he "was now a

---

[44] *Mill on Bentham and Coleridge*, with an introduction by F.R.Leavis (London, Chatto and Windus, 1962), p.155. Subsequently referred to as *Bentham and Coleridge*.
[45] *Autobiography*, p.161.
[46] *Ibid.*, p.153.

frequent reader" of Coleridge.[47] Coleridge is seen as part of the general influence of the schools opposed to the Utilitarians.

The list of the main ideas which Mill derived from these new influences shows nothing characteristically Coleridgean; his belief in expediency, rather than absolute principle, in the fashioning of institutions, is included as part of the whole "European . . . reaction" against the eighteenth century.[48] But he does head the list of thinkers who influenced Mill, and the Coleridgeans, who transmitted the same ideas are second. In comparison Mill knew little of Goethe and saw nothing but "insane rhapsody" in Carlyle at a time at which he was reading Coleridge "with interest."[49]

The impression to be gained from the *Autobiography* is that Coleridge was the primary intuitionist influence on Mill, but that this influence, at least by the time the *Autobiography* was written was not of sufficient importance to be distinguished in any detail from the others. Indeed, the majority of Mill's attention is given to Wordsworth, Maurice and Sterling in the fields in which Coleridge might be expected to figure, and the reader of the *Autobiography* would not imagine Coleridge to be of more than very minor importance. This is the accepted position of Coleridge in Mill's thought; he is regarded as an early interest, who made a small, but not vital, contribution.

But an entirely different impression is given by a passage from a letter written to J.P.Nichol in 1834, and much closer in time to the events of the crisis than the *Autobiography*. Mill writes,

> I was wondering whether you were a reader of Coleridge, and should certainly have asked you the question very soon, when you unexpectedly wrote to me about him exactly what I think of him myself – except, by the way, when you say, 'as a politician he seems unprincipled.' I think he is not *unprincipled*, but *principled* – his views on politics are, I have reason to believe, systematic. Did you ever read his little work on Church and State? If not, read it; if you have tell me whether you agree with it in the main (I mean the Church part of it) as I do. Few persons have exercised more influence over my thoughts and character than Coleridge has; not much by personal knowledge of him, though I have seen and conversed with him several times, but by his works, and by the fact that several

---

[47]Stillinger, *op.cit.*, p.136n.
[48]*Autobiography*, p.161.
[49]*Ibid*.

persons with whom I have been very intimate were completely trained in his school. Through them, too, I have had opportunities of reading various unpublished manuscripts of his; and, on the whole, I can trace through what I know of his works, pieced together by what I have otherwise learned of his opinions, a most distinct thread of connection. I consider him the most systematic thinker of our time, without excepting even Bentham, whose edifice is as well bound together, but is constructed on so much simpler a plan, and covers so much less ground. On the whole, there is more food for thought – and the best kind of thought – in Coleridge than in all other contemporary writers.[50]

There is a great contrast between Mill's assessment of Coleridge's importance here and in the *Autobiography*. At first sight two factors might explain this. The letter is the work of a young man of twenty-eight whose opinions were still in a state of flux; The *Autobiography* comes from a man of nearly fifty, a man of settled outlook and broader experience. In 1834 Mill was not even familiar with Tocqueville and this fact alone puts the letter into perspective. It would be naive to accept Mill's assertion that "few persons have had more influence" as meaning any less than four or five thinkers.

The two accounts also had a very different audience and purpose. The letter is private, and written to a self-acknowledged admirer of Coleridge; the *Autobiography* is a public document, intended to remain as a considered record of Mill's opinions and education.[51] Mill's political allegiance was, and has been, the subject of argument, and he was writing in part to justify his place in the Utilitarian tradition.[52]But even with the subtraction imposed by these arguments the letter is a remarkable testimony. Mill is claiming Coleridge as a major influence at a time when such an influence must have been highly formative.

That Mill should defend a "system" in Coleridge's work indicates a rare familiarity and sympathy with it. A cursory reading of Coleridge does not disclose a "system". His system lies not so much in the ideas and concepts scattered through his writings, as in the spirit of enquiry

---

[50]*The Collected Works of John Stuart Mill*, ed. F.E.L.Priest;ey, Vols. XII and XIII, "The Earlier Letters, 1812-1848," ed. F.E.Mineka (University of Toronto Press, 1963), XII, 221. Subsequently referred to as *Works*, XII or XIII.

[51]Stillinger, *op.cit.*, p.15.

[52]*Correspondence of Henry Taylor*, ed. E.Dowden (London, Longmans, Green and Co., 1888), p.327; Courtney, *op.cit.*, pp.56-58.

which lies behind these ideas. Even Nichol did not see a system in
Coleridge. The belief that Coleridge's writings are systematic is
probably a modern one – the more typical opinion in the nineteenth
century, which persisted from Carlyle to Arnold, was that Coleridge
had wasted his genius in fragments.[53]

Mill's own training must have prepared him to expect intuitionism
to result in confusion; it would have been easy for him to share the
common opinion. Not only does he not share it, but his praise of
Coleridge is in the superlative. Coleridge is "the most systematic
thinker of our time, without excepting even Bentham." Mill was well
aware of the shortcomings of the Benthamite tradition by 1834 but he
usually, at this time and later, described the alien ideas which he added
to it as "widening" Utilitarianism, not as replacing it by something
more systematic. That he should feel the more extensive, but to most
of his contemporaries, more rambling edifice of Coleridge to be more
systematic, is remarkable.

Why then did Mill not give more allowance to Coleridge's
importance in the later *Autobiography* if he found him so vitally useful
in 1834? The answer may lie partly in the fact that Coleridge's was an
unhappy name to be associated with for moral, as well as political,
reasons. Equally, Coleridge was of most interest to Mill during his early
development. Coleridge's death in 1834 saw a sudden flow of praise
from a press which had been silent for years, and Mill's generosity may
also have been conditioned by the same desire to do posthumous
justice to a misjudged man. Even so, the letter to Nichol is a very
remarkable declaration of debt and admiration. Although Mill was
never to repeat it, it cannot be dismissed as the enthusiasm of a
moment.

IV

The letter to Nichol gives a lot of detail about Mill's debt to
Coleridge. Mill claims that he is a "reader" of Coleridge, and the status

---

[53]Thomas Carlyle, *The Life of John Sterling*, World's Classics, CXLIV (London,
Oxford University Press, 1933), p.58; Leon Gottfried, *Matthew Arnold and the
Romantics* (London, Routledge & Kegan Paul, 1963), pp.191-193.

of reader suggests habit; he insists that "few persons have exercised more influence over my thought and character;" and he is usefully explicit about the ways in which Coleridge's influence has reached him. These ways are through reading the published works, through direct personal contact, through the disciples, and finally through his access to Coleridge's manuscripts. These sources will be dealt with in detail in order to build up an accurate picture of Mill's knowledge of Coleridge and his ideas before examining the parallels between the two writers.

First in importance is Mill's reading of Coleridge. His claim in the letter suggests that his acquaintance with Coleridge's works was based on something more than a single, cursory perusal. Certainly he was "re-reading" Coleridge in 1839[54] in preparation for writing his essay on "Coleridge". In the *Autobiography* he claims that he had "begun to read with interest" the writings of Coleridge "even before the change in my opinions,"[55] and the early draft adds that he was "now a frequent reader."[56] Mill had even read some of Coleridge's manuscripts and the presupposition must therefore be that he had read at least once the majority of Coleridge's published output. This is supported by direct evidence.

There can be no doubt that Mill read *Church and State*. He admired it most of all Coleridge's works. He tells Nichol, for instance, that he "agreed with it in the main (I mean the Church part of it)." The earliest reference to the book in Mill's writings is 20-22 October 1831, little over a year after it was published,[57] and Mill's library contained two copies of it.[58] References and quotations from it occur in the essay on "Corporation and Church Property" of 1833, and in the "Coleridge" essay of 1840.[59] In 1839, when he re-read it for this essay, he still thought that it was "the best . . . of Coleridge's writings."

---

[54]*Works*, XIII, 406.

[55]*Autobiography*, p.161.

[56]Stillinger, *op.cit.*, p.136n.

[57]*Works*, XII, 75.

[58]Helen Taylor gave Mill's library to Somerville College, Oxford in 1905.

[59]J.S.Mill, "Corporation and Church Property," *Jurist*, IV (February, 1833), 1-26; reprinted in *Dissertations and Discussions*, 4 vols. (London, Longmans, Green, Reader, and Dyer, 1867-75), I, 1-41; subsequently referred to as *Dissertations and Discussions*; *Bentham and Coleridge*, pp.124n-125n, 142-145, 148-151, 155.

The *Lay Sermons* on the other hand, seem to have made little impression on Mill. He may not have read them until 1839, and they seemed to him "the worst of Coleridge's writings . . . though there are some excellent passages in them."[60] *Confessions of an Inquiring Spirit* Mill read at least six years before it was published. He wrote, in 1835,

> there will shortly appear a posthumous work of Coleridge (which I saw in manuscript before his death) altogether smashing the doctrine of plenary inspiration."[61]

Although the *Confessions* were not published until 1840, before Coleridge's death Sterling had taken a transcript of them, which he hoped to be allowed to edit.[62] It was probably this manuscript which Mill saw. There is also a copy of the first edition in Mill's library.

Did Mill read any other of Coleridge's manuscripts? He told Nichol that he had read "various manuscripts" and Coleridge's friends had, indeed, a number of works such as the *Theory of Life* and the lecture notes and fragments in their possession. Whether Mill saw them in manuscript or not, he read the *Literary Remains*, which contained a selection of these materials, when the volumes were published in 1836-39, and quoted from them in the Coleridge essay.[63] Mill also quotes from the *Aids to Reflection* in the "Coleridge" essay, and he probably read the copy of the first edition which is in his library.[64]

From similar evidence it would appear that the *Friend* was very important in Mill's reading of Coleridge. Many of Mill's concepts which can be related to Coleridge seem to come from this source. There is also direct reference to the *Friend*. Thus Mill remarks to Sterling, "yesterday I completed my task & reached a sort of landing place (vide

---

[60]*Works*, XIII, 409.

[61]*Ibid.*, XII, 265.

[62]Letter to James Dunn, May 2nd, 1828. Sterling says that he has "seen" Coleridge's *Confessions of an Inquiring Spirit* (National Library of Scotland, Ms 1765, 95). See also letter to Carlyle, September 8th, 1834, "I am familiar with his M.S.S. & conversations . . . I am in hope of being soon permitted to edit some of his theological M.S.S. among which are some most eloquent & striking letters for the purpose of preventing Bibliolatary." (National Library of Scotland, Ms. 1766, 27).

[63]*Bentham and Coleridge*, pp.147, 156, 161, 162, 164-5.

[64]See also an oblique reference, *Works*, XIII, 452.

the Friend)."[65] The copy of the *Friend* in Mill's library is frequently
marked in the margin. Several passages are marked with an (a) in the
margin, and the number of these passages is noted on the rear fly leaf.
Mill did not often mark his books, but if these are his markings they
suggest a thorough reading. The passages he marks would provide
interesting evidence of what Mill found memorable in Coleridge.

Curiously, in view of Mill's normally extensive and thorough
reading habits, there has been some controversy as to whether he
actually read *Biographia Literaria*. R.J.White scorns the idea that Mill
would be interested enough to read the *Lay Sermons*, or the
Biographia.[66] But Mill's writings on art clearly owe a great deal to
Biographia, and he makes direct references to it in the "Coleridge"
essay, in the early draft of the *Autobiography*, in a later letter, and in
the *Logic*.[67] It is likely that Mill read *Biographia Literaria* very early.
It contains the clearest statement of Coleridge's system to be found in
his published works, and must form the backbone of any real
knowledge of Coleridge's principles, such as Mill claimed to have by
1834. There were not many works of Coleridge's in print at this time
that Mill could have read, and if he was to describe himself as a
"reader", *Biographia Literaria* must have been one of them. The first
edition of it in Mill's library is, like the *Friend*, frequently marked in
the margin.

Coleridge's poetry was important in Mill's interpretation of his
"crisis". Mill "found a true description of what I felt"[68] only in
Coleridge. He comments that he had not read Coleridge during the first
depression of 1826, but, "in a later period of the same mental
malady."[69] Certainly he was soon acquainted with a range of
Coleridge's verse writing; he had even read Coleridge's translation of

---

[65]*Ibid.*, XII, 79; see also *Bentham and Coleridge*, pp.148, 161; see also *A System of
Logic*, 2 vols. (London, Longmans, Green and Co., 1879), II, 347-348. Subsequently
referred to as *Logic*.

[66]R.J.White, "John Stuart Mill," *Cambridge Journal*, V (1951-52), p.91.

[67]*Bentham and Coleridge*, pp.115, 160; Stillinnger, *op.cit.*, p.116n; *The Letters of
John Stuart Mill*, ed. Hugh S.R.Elliot, 2 vols. (London, Longmans, Green, and Co.,
1910), II, 224; *A System of Logic*, II, 342.

[68]*Autobiography*, p.140.

[69]*Ibid.*

Schiller's *Wallenstein*.[70] He greatly admired his verse, recognising the,

> power of making a few touches do the whole work, which excites our
> admiration in Coleridge. Every line suggests so much more than it
> says, that much may be left unsaid[71]

and he uses Coleridge as a standard by which to judge Tennyson's
early poems.[72]

Mill's reading of Coleridge thus appears, as his letter to Nichol
suggests, to be complete. He had read all the major works which had
been published, and read at least some of them again. This is the
central evidence of Mill's contact with Coleridge's ideas.

V

Mill's next source of Coleridge's ideas, after his reading, were his
visits to Coleridge, and friendship with the Coleridgeans, especially
John Sterling. How often the young Mill made the trek up Highgate to
visit London's popular intellectual curio, the now aging Coleridge,
shuffling and mumbling about "om-m-mject and sum-m-mject,"[73] but
still capable of energetic and impressive insight, cannot be known. It
was probably not often; Mill tells us it was "several times."[74] Two
references to visits to Coleridge remain, however. Mill met Edward
Irving there for the first time;[75] and Henry Taylor's letters record on
29th September 1831 that he, "went up to Highgate the other day with
Mill, Stephen, and Elliot, to pay an auscultatory visit to Coleridge."[76]

The Coleridge Mill saw in this visit was in the full flow of an
Indian summer. After the dark years of failure, poetic, domestic and
financial, the years of mammoth projects and little production, the
solicitous care of the Gillman's had enabled Coleridge almost to break
himself of the habit of opium, and to marshall his ideas into new
books. But the main feature of the last years was Coleridge's talk. It

---

[70] *Early Essays by J.S.Mill*, ed. J.W.N.Gibbs (London, G.Bell and Sons, 1897), 227.
[71] *Ibid.*, p.254.
[72] *Works*, XII, 245.
[73] Carlyle, *op.cit.*, p.57.
[74] *Works*, XII, 221.
[75] Fox, *op.cit.*, I, 150.
[76] Taylor, *op.cit.*, p.39.

became an institution. Coleridge, now permitted by age and respect to lecture rather than to converse, developed a habit of delivering his deepest thoughts in his wandering monologue. He came to believe that his talk would be his real bequest to posterity, his real claim to influence and fame. It was a curious situation. Coleridge talked, his visitors listened, both, apparently, believing that something great was being done in those long evenings at Highgate.

It was this talk that Mill heard. More importantly, perhaps, it was this talk that Coleridge's ardent young disciples heard, and transmitted through their own writings and friendships. Mill's contact with these disciples was considerable enough to be an important element in his knowledge of Coleridge, albeit at second hand. He claims in his letter to Nichol that one source of his knowledge was, "the fact that several persons with whom I have been very intimate were completely trained in his school."[77] These were the Coleridgeans, the teachers who had been taught by the "teacher of the teachers."[78] They were fulfilling Coleridge's prophesies of his influence[79] in transmitting the ideas which he himself had failed to popularise. Mill knew several of these disciples such as Henry Taylor, Julius Hare and Thomas Arnold, and was a close friend of others, such as F.D.Maurice and John Sterling.

Taylor, a minor disciple of Coleridge and a friend of Mill, is an interesting example of these transmitters of ideas. Taylor knew Mill for some years before he accompanied him on a visit to Highgate in 1831, and they continued their friendship through letters even after Taylor went out to govern the West Indies. It was at one of Taylor's London breakfast parties that Mill met Southey,[80] and he may have met Wordsworth there for the first time.[81] Although Southey and Wordsworth were part of the Coleridge circle, they were not

[77]Taylor, op.cit., p.39.

[78]Bentham and Coleridge, p.39.

[79]Collected Letters of Samuel Taylor Coleridge, ed. E.L.Griggs, 4 vols. (Oxford Clarendon, 1956-1959), I, 277.

[80]15th. November, 1830; see Taylor, op.cit., p.29.

[81]27 February, 1831; see Anna Jean Mill, "John Stuart Mill's Visit to Wordsworth, 1831," Modern Languages Review, XLIV (1949), 342; also Henry Taylor, Autobiography, 1800-1875, 2 vols. (London, Longmans, Green, and Co., 1885), I, 159-160, 83.

Coleridgeans; but Taylor was. He showed his debt to Coleridge even in the way he criticised Mill. Taylor judged that though Mill was,

> deficient in an essential portion of the knowledge of human nature and the constitution of human society [but] . . . the views of a philosophical mind, even when thus essentially defective, may be nevertheless valuable . . . though fallacious, may present matter worthy of consideration . . . A man may find truth mixed up even with the mud that is flung upon him.[82]

Taylor's pattern for this attitude is almost certainly Coleridge's emphatic belief in tolerant eclecticism, and understanding of the "half-truth" which is almost always found in the errors of opposing sects. It also coincides remarkably closely with Mill's attitude to Coleridge. Just as Taylor thinks that the opposite school can provide "matter worthy of consideration,"[83] so Mill felt that "you might be enriched even by the materials of his erroneous structure."[84]

Mill had made this comment to Taylor himself as they came away together from visiting Coleridge. Taylor told Southey that he "thought there was justice" in Mill's comments, and that he "made a mental application which you will not be at a loss to guess."[85] Thus, Taylor applied to Mill the apologia for eclecticism which Mill applied to Coleridge. They probably discussed this, and many other of Coleridge's ideas together.

Mill was only remotely acquainted with other Coleridgeans such as Hare and Arnold. The only reference he makes to Hare is to his "kindly & graceful biographical introduction"[86] to his life of their mutual friend, John Sterling. He wrote of Arnold that "I am not sufficiently acquainted with his turn of mind."[87] The influence of these men must therefore be discounted as slight compared to that of Sterling and Maurice, the Coleridgeans with whom Mill was most friendly. They first met at the London Debating Society, where Mill found his Benthamism opposed by a distinctively different philosophy which he soon came to recognise as Coleridgean. The crisis led him to seek their

---

[82]Taylor, *Correspondence*, pp.30-31.
[83]*Ibid.*, p.30.
[84]*Ibid.*, p.40.
[85]*Ibid.*
[86]*Works*, XIII, 726.
[87]*Ibid.*, XII, 92.

acquaintance, and a friendship sprang up.

He regarded Maurice as the thinker of the pair, "Sterling the orator, and impassioned expositor of thoughts which, at this period, were almost entirely framed for him by Maurice."[88] He had a great respect for Maurice, and,

> though my discussions with him were almost always disputes, I had carried away from them much that helped to build up my new fabric of thought, in the same way as I was deriving much from Coleridge.[89]

Maurice's ideas continued to ferment in Mill's mind, and in 1831, after they had ceased to meet, he wrote that "many things which have dropped from him . . . did not strike me at first but [have] . . . been a source of endless reflections since."[90] Later, Mill was to become very critical, but even so he continued to admire Maurice's ability. He felt his novel, *Eustace Conway*, to be a "remarkable production" of a "superior man".[91] Quoting from it in his 1836 essay on "Civilization" he comments, "nothing can be more just or more forcible than the description here given of the objects which University education should aim at."[92] Reading the *Kingdom of Christ* in 1842 only reinforced Mill's impression that this, too, was one of the "productions of a very remarkable mind."[93]

He regarded Maurice "as a disciple of Coleridge."[94] Indeed, Maurice himself explicitly records his debt to Coleridge in the introduction to the *Kingdom of Christ*. Mill's attitude to Maurice's ideas was very much an extension of his attitude to Coleridge's. He agrees with the criticism of the universities in *Eustace Conway*, and is "at issue with the writer, only on the proposition that these objects ever were attained, or ever could be so."[95] He felt Maurice's Coleridgean idea of the clerisy to be "much more successful in showing

[88] *Autobiography*, p.152.
[89] *Ibid*.
[90] *Works*, XII, 79.
[91] *Ibid*., 224.
[92] *Dissertations and Discussions*, I, 195.
[93] *Works*, XIII, 544.
[94] *Autobiography*, p.154.
[95] *Dissertations and Discussions*, I, 195.

that other people are wrong than that Churchmen or rather that an
ideal Churchman is in the right."[96] Mill's criticism reaches its clearest
formulation in the *Autobiograpy*.

> I have a deep respect for Maurice's character and purposes, as well as
> for his great mental gifts ... But I have always thought that there
> was more intellectual power wasted in Maurice than in any other of
> my contemporaries ... a wide perception of important and
> unobvious truths, served him not for putting something better into
> the place of the worthless heap of received opinions on the great
> subjects of thought, but for proving to his own mind that the Church
> of England had known everything from the first.[97]

In the eighteen-thirties Mill might not have felt that received
opinions were so totally worthless. His very limited final approval of
what Maurice stood for parallels the relative paucity of his treatment
of Coleridge in the *Autobiography*.

But Mill always admired Maurice's mind. However much he
differed from his "metaphysical doctrines," he told Maurice that "I
never voluntarily leave unread any of your writings,"[98] a tribute both
to Maurice's intellect and to his usefulness.

VI

Mill ceased to have much personal contact with Maurice soon after
they met, but John Sterling was to remain his close friend until
Sterling's death in 1844. Sterling, even more than Maurice, was a
fountain of Coleridgean ideas, but he was principally remarkable for
the brilliant and engaging way in which he could expound these ideas
in talk with his friends.

Sterling had a genius for friendship.[99] His own published work,
graceful and amusing, but minor, would not have preserved his name
as his biographers, Hare and Carlyle, have. Sterling's importance in
this context, however, lies in his close and eager contact with Coleridge
and his deep absorption of Coleridgean ideas at a time when he was

---

[96]*Works*, XIII, 544.
[97]*Autobiography*, p.153.
[98]Elliot, *op.cit.*, II, 29.
[99]John Tulloch, *The Movement of Religious Thought in Britain During the Nineteenth Century* (London, Longmans, Green and Co., 1885), p.38.

becoming John Stuart Mill's closest friend. Sterling became a strong
member of the Coleridgean school at Cambridge. He wrote in 1836,

> To Coleridge I owe *education*. He taught me to believe that an
> empirical philosophy is none, that Faith is the highest Reason, that
> all criticism, whether of literature, laws, or manners, is blind, without
> the power of discerning the organic unity of the object.[100]

Both Sterling's biographers agree that it was under Coleridge's
influence that he took orders, and in Sterling's writings many
essentially Coleridgean ideas can be found. Perhaps the most
convincing evidence of his Coleridgean affinities is his only novel,
Arthur Conningsby.[101] It tells the history of a young man at the time
of the beginning of the French Revolution. Fired by the ideal of a
perfect and free society, much like the young man in the preface to the
second volume of the Friend, and driven by revolutionary ardour, he
forsakes his true love, Isobel, and travels to France to help the
revolutionaries. After encountering Gothick terrors in a monastery on
his journey, he reaches Paris only to find it the scene of terror and
murder. Here he realizes that the old order is better than the new
anarchy, not because the old order is right, but because as Coleridge
put it, "a clothing of withered leaves is better than bareness."[102]

The parallel with the intellectual experience of Coleridge as he
passed from his early Godwinism to his later political theories is
remarkable. In the eighteen-thirties the climate of the age was turning
towards the new problems of reform and industrialisation. It is unusual
to find a novel written in 1833 so deeply immersed in the problems of
an earlier generation. Sterling's imagination is working as much in the
context of Coleridge's experience as of his own.[103]

But Sterling was not so much a direct source of Coleridgean

---

[100]John Sterling, *Essays and Tales*, ed. J.C.Hare, 2 vols. (London, John W.Parker, 1848), I,
xv; see also R.B.Ince, *Calverley and Some Cambridge Wits of the Nineteenth Century* (London,
Cayne Press, 1929), p.175.

[101]*Arthur Conningsby*, 3 vols. (London, Effingham Wilson, 1833); see also Susanne
Howe, *Wilhelm Meister and his Kinsmen, Apprentices to Life* (New York, Columbia
University Press, 1930), pp.210-220.

[102]*The Friend*, ed. Barbara E.Rooke, 2 vols. (London, Routledge & Kegan Paul,
1969), I, 48; subsequently referred to as *Friend*. See also *Philosophical Lectures*, ed.
Kathleen Coburn (London, Pilot Press, 1949), pp.159-160.

[103]*Friend*, I, 220-221, 224-225.

influence, as an indirect one. His importance is not his ability to express himself in print but his ability as a friend and talker. Carlyle gives a picture of Sterling as a vigorous talker, simple, enthusiastic, and energetic in character, and stubborn in argument. Caroline Fox also notes his determination to have his point understood and accepted. Her diary records the endless flow of references to Coleridge or Coleridgean ideas in this argumentative loquacity.[104]

One of the principal receivers of this talk was John Stuart Mill. After their first meeting they were drawn together when Mill championed Wordsworth against Roebuck. When they both resigned from the London Debating Club they became close friends. From the first Mill made it clear that he was glad of Sterling's "intimacy – which I value highly for this reason among many others, that it appears to me peculiarly adapted to the wants of my own mind; since I know no person who possesses more of what I have not, than yourself, nor is this inconsistent with my believing you to be deficient in some of the very few things which I have."[105] Their friendship became one of mutual respect and affection. Hare records that "Mr. John Mill [was] . . . one of the friends whom for many years he had most loved and esteemed and admired,"[106] and Sterling told Carlyle that whenever they could meet, "it was with the openness and freshness of schoolboy friends, though our friendship only dates from the manhood of both."[107] It was to Comte that Mill paid his last tribute to his friend after his death. He calls Sterling, "un du très petit nombre de ceux pour qui j'éprouvais une amitié vive et une estime parfaite."[108]

The two main periods of contact between Sterling and Mill were between their first meeting in 1828 and Sterling's voyage to the West Indies in 1831, and in the winters of 1838-9, and 1840. Sterling, wintering in Rome in 1838, saw

> a good deal of John Mill, whose society I like much. He enters heartily into the interest of the things which I most care for here.[109]

---

[104]Fox, *Op.Cit.*, I, 114-115, 118, 237, 249, 268.
[105]*Works*, XII, 29.
[106]Sterling, *Essays and Tales*, I, cxlvii.
[107]Carlyle, *op.cit.*, p.240.
[108]*Works*, XIII, 637.
[109]Carlyle, *op.cit.*, p.187.

The two men met again at Falmouth the next year, Mill joining the party in March 1840 for some weeks. Caroline Fox's journal records many of the events of these weeks. Sterling talked continuously, while Mill only added occasional comments. But he told Caroline privately how much he admired Sterling's talk.

> Though his writings are such as would do credit to anybody, yet they are inferior to his conversation; he has that rare power of throwing his best thoughts into it and adapting them to the comprehension of others.[110]

Sterling and Mill agreed on the deficiencies of the radicals[111] and, most conspicuously, they talked about the need for a non-sectarian spirit, and the need to accept the other half of the truth from sources other than one's own creed.

This close friendship gave Mill access to a fount of knowledge and ideas about Coleridge. There are numerous passing references in their letters, which could only make sense in the context of previous familiar discussions of Coleridge, to show how he used this opportunity.[112] One of the most important products of the friendship is the encouragement Sterling gave to Mill when he decided to write an essay on Coleridge. The closest point in the friendship coincides with the time at which Mill was writing the essays on "Bentham" and "Coleridge" to illustrate his new radicalism in detail. During this period Mill and Sterling wrote more frequently to each other than at any other time, and they discussed Mill's ideas for his essay at length. Mill told him,

> If I carry on the review to another number, it will be partly in order to publish in it an article on Coleridge ... It would be of most essential service to me to receive any suggestions or warnings from you, which may occur to you as needful.[113]

Mill subsequently, "set to work upon an article on Coleridge, partly in consequence of the encouragement you gave me."[114] He mentions that he had "always thought desirable"[115] an essay on

---

[110]Fox, I, 190.
[111]*Ibid.*, 151.
[112]E.g. *Works*, XII, 76, 79, 85; XIII, 411.
[113]*Ibid.*, XIII, 405-406.
[114]*Ibid.*, 411.
[115]*Ibid.*, 405.

Coleridge, but the conclusion of the essay as it was finally written suggests that Mill had passed the time when it would have been a natural outcome of his thoughts. It is an essay written in retrospect as the tensions between the importance Mill would seem to be preparing for Coleridge in his introduction, and the reality of his final assessment indicate. If chance had not thrown him into Sterling's company in 1838 the essay might never have been written.

VII

Mill's knowledge of Coleridge, his personality, his writings, his ideas and his influence was complete. Although he was the champion of the opposed school, he troubled to find out as much about Coleridge as any but his closest and most ardent disciples. Circumstances threw him into an energetic broadening of his mind at a time when Coleridge's renewed activity at Highgate was beginning to spread his ideas again; and circumstances also decreed that his close lifelong friend should be a Coleridgean. Coleridge is, of course, only one of many thinkers whom Mill chose to read and understand thoroughly. He was naturally inquisitive, and by training hard-working and exact. Few important books or ideas can have escaped his notice. In particular, certain of the major minds of the period struck Mill as worth close study. Come, Tocqueville, Carlyle, not to mention Bentham, were the major forces. Yet perhaps only Carlyle and Bentham were as close to Mill in so many ways as Coleridge was. Mill had read Coleridge's works, and re-read them; he had troubled to have a chance to read his manuscripts; he had visited him, and he was, for many formative years, closely friendly with ardent Coleridgeans. This is the basic evidence on which the study of Coleridge's relation to Mill will be built.

3 Platonist and Aristotelian: the contrasts

> Every man is born an Aristotelian, or a Platonist. I do not think it is
> possible that any one born an Aristotelian can become a Platonist;
> and I am sure no born Platonist can ever change into an Aristotelian.
> They are the two classes of men, beside which it is next to impossible
> to conceive a third. – S.T.Coleridge[1]

> Of their methods of philosophizing, the same thing may be said:
> they were different, yet both were legitimate and logical processes. In
> every respect the two men are each other's 'completing counterpart':
> the strong points of each correspond to the weak points of the other.
> Whoever could master the premises and combine the methods of
> both, would possess the entire English philosophy of his age. – John
> Stuart Mill[2]

Mill is an empiricist, Coleridge an idealist. This is the generally
accepted broad description of their thought; but the more the
description descends into the details the less clear cut the apparent
opposition of their epistemological foundations becomes. For though
Mill and Coleridge are commonly taken to be opposites, there are many
ways in which they do not fit such a simple description, for on some
issues they have much in common. The next three chapters set out to
expand this simple description into a detailed account, showing both
the underlying reality of the basic opposition, and some of the ways in

[1]S.T.Coleridge, *The Table Talk and Omniana*, ed.T. Ashe (London, G.Bell & Sons, 1923),
p.99. Subsequently referred at as *Table Talk*.
[2]*Mill on Bentham and Coleridge*, with an introduction by F.R.Leavis (London, Chatto and
Windus, 1962), p.102.

which these broad generalizations about them are inadequate. It will not do, however, merely to point to deficiencies in the common view. The curious fact is that this view is not just one which was imposed by the generalisations of later historians; it is one which Mill and Coleridge themselves accepted.   Coleridge believes that there is a radical distinction between Aristotelian and Platonist; Mill also thinks that irreconcilable principles have divided the two schools since the "first dawn" of thought.

> The one recognises no ultimate premises but the facts of our subjective consciousness; our sensations, emotions, intellectual states of mind, and volitions. These, and whatever by strict rules of induction can be derived from these, it is possible, according to this theory, for us to know; of all else we must remain in ignorance. The opposite school hold that there are other existences, suggested indeed to our minds by these subjective phenomena, but not inferable from them . . . which, however, we must, by the constitution of our mental nature, recognize as realities; and realities, too, of a higher order than the phenomena of our consciousness, being the efficient causes and necessary substrata of all Phenomena.[3]

The distinction between the two schools, often labeled empiricist and idealist in the broadest senses of those words,[4] rested on a supposed dichotomy between two radically opposed epistemologies, the associationist and the intuitionist. It was hardly novel in Mill or Coleridge, and it is still in use. Indeed, it might be possible to argue that the currency of the distinction owes a lot to the way in which Mill and Coleridge, and many others in the nineteenth century, applied it to themselves.

But of course the distinction, in this form, is a simplification. It would need to be qualified by a great deal of commentary on the foundations of post-Kantian idealism in eighteenth century English epistemology, and on the considerable Platonic elements surviving in English empiricism, if it were not to be misleading. It is essentially a schematic simplification, but such a generalisation can be illuminating not only in its truth, but also in its inadequacies.   Despite the complexity of philosophical opinions, Mill and Coleridge persistently

---

[3] J.S.Mill, *A System of Logic*, 2 vols. (London, Longmans, Green, and Co., 1879), II, 313-314. Subsequently referred to as *Logic*.

[4] See Norman Kemp Smith, *Prolegomena to an Idealist Theory of Knowledge* (London, Macmillan and Co., 1924), p.1.

saw philosophy in terms of two schools. Having established this polarity they both go on to claim that they individually have made some sort of bridge between the two opposites by arriving at new compromises.

In reality, none of their sources were purely idealist, or purely empirical, and the spirit of exploratory compromise has a long ancestry. There is also more in common between, say, J.S.Mill and T.H.Green, or between Mill and Coleridge, than division by this scheme would suggest. But in order to see the compromise working in Mill and Coleridge their scheme of the two schools must be accepted, and the nature of their opposition expounded, before examining what they have in common, and the way Coleridge influenced Mill.

II

Both Mill and Coleridge are important thinkers, but in very different ways. Coleridge is a metaphysician, whose greatest fame in the nineteenth century was as a theologian; Mill is a logician and reformer whose special achievement lay in his contribution toward the clarification and systematisation of the methods of the social sciences. The overlap between these two different concerns is slight. Mill was primarily interested in the analysis of cause and effect, Coleridge in the "homesickness of the soul."[5] In practice, too, philosophy is deliberate and, at least in formulation, rarely spontaneous. Romanticism, on the other hand, took spontaneity as its tap root to the poetic soul; it was infinite and idealistic, and, at least at first, bare of the ordering coherence of a philosophy.

But Coleridge has more in common with Mill than this would suggest. Coleridge was one of the few men in England in the early nineteenth century to combine the two attributes. He felt Wordsworth's spontaneity, and promptly set out to discover why. He was the only Romantic poet who was also, like Mill, a professional philosopher; and he is therefore the only representative of the other stream of thought who can be contrasted with Mill. Only in these two

[5]Novalis, quoted by John H.Muirhead, *Coleridge as Philosopher* (London, Allen & Unwin, 1954), p.30.

figures can two great movements of ideas in the early nineteenth century, Romanticism in literature and empiricism in sociology, be compared, only here can the roots of Tennyson and Beatrice Webb be examined.

The philosophical development of Coleridge and Mill also suggests some affinities. Thus Coleridge's early mental history is in certain respects strikingly similar to Mill's, and his change of opinions was brought on, like Mill's depression, by a spiritual "Sickness & some other & and worse afflictions, [which] first forced me into downright metaphysics."[6] Both men were left with wider insights and no longer fitted the simple categories of Platonist and Aristotelian, in the way the almost caricature Benthamite in John Mill's earlier writings had.

Mill's revolt from Benthamism had been in many ways a 'moral' one, that is, it was similar to Coleridge's revolt against empiricism, fed by a moral sense that was evolved by Romantic literature. In their years of philosophical wandering they both went largely along the same path. The Hartleian theory, to which they both adhered enthusiastically as young men, is at its worst in aesthetics. Hartley devotes only a few pages to imagination and dreaming,[7] just as James Mill was most unsatisfactory on literature and the creative mind.[8] It was this that made Coleridge look for a new theory, and it was the same thing that made Mill broaden his horizons. Since Coleridge had developed out of associationism, Mill, who was struggling with the same theory for the same reason, must have found Coleridge's experience relevant to his own.

There are differences, too, of course. They belonged to a different generation, Coleridge lived through the French Revolution of 1789, Mill through the revolutions of the 1840's. But the intellectual backlash of the French Revolution, the reassessment of eighteenth century empiricism, affected both Mill and Coleridge, though in different degrees. Equally, they are not so far apart in time as their dates of

---

[6]*Collected Letters of Samuel Taylor Coleridge*, ed. E.L.Griggs, 4.vols. (Oxford, Clarendon, 1956-1959), II, 814. Subsequently referred to as *Letters*.

[7]David Hartley, *Observations on Man, his Frame, his Duty, and his Expectations*, 2 vols. (London, S.Richardson, 1949), I, 383-389, 418-442.

[8]James Mill, *Analysis of the Phenomena of the Human Mind*, 2 vols. (London, Baldwin & Cradock, 1829), II, 191-208.

birth would suggest, for it is the late Coleridge, the philosopher of Highgate, writing in the 1820's, who was being read by the young Mill in the 1830's.

The role of religion in their early development was also different, as were the founding motives of their philosophies. All philosophies have a human cause, that is to say a foundation that is emotional as well as rational. We must in the end look beyond classification by the description of epistemologies to the forces that created these attempts to structure thought. Coleridge was driven by three basic factors, firstly, an individual and emotional desire for a personal religion, founded on 'friendship' with God, which became ever stronger; secondly, the development of philosophical curiosity in his chameleon, but critical, progress through available philosophies to one that suited his need; thirdly, a moral concern for the social conditions of men, vented by the preacher in his soul. The three paths conditioned, like co-ordinates, where Coleridge's thought wandered. Mill was also driven by political convictions and emotional needs to follow a wandering path between the boundaries of empiricism and intuitionism. Mill's and Coleridge's wanderings often overlap, sometimes unexpectedly; and between them they paced the whole field of thought in the early nineteenth century.

There are always very large differences between the two. Coleridge's aim in philosophy, what he meant by metaphysics, was the need to comprehend the world as a unity; Mill's aim was the rationalisation of man's social rather than his spiritual circumstances. But there are also overlaps. Both their epistemologies are limited as models of the mind which attempt to explain the mysteries of knowledge. Neither epistemology can answer the all important questions, and the choice between them seems, in the end, to lie in extra-rational criteria. In the case of Mill and Coleridge these are personal and political needs. In this sense both philosophies are an achievement of the imagination, of the creative mind.

III

It is best to start the formidable task of juxtaposing Mill's and Coleridge's fundamental assumptions with an attempt to pin-point the nature of Coleridge's philosophy. It is a dynamic panorama of changing ideas, and not a strategic line of positions held, and an account of Coleridge must be, at least in part, a history of his development.

Three simple classifications of Coleridge have emerged. The earliest, and most obvious, tradition was to see him as a post-Kantian intuitionist; the tradition of this century, starting with Muirhead, has been to see Coleridge as a figure of great and neglected importance in English Platonic Idealism, which runs from John Scotus Erigena, through the Medieval Platonists, The Cambridge Platonists, Berkeley, Coleridge, and T.H.Green to Bradley. Coleridge's quite explicit debts to the Cambridge Platonists are stressed, and his idealism and voluntarism are emphasized and expounded by this school of thought. Alongside both these traditions has run a third one, a typical recent expression of which is J.Pucelle, who writes,

> Coleridge est donc un vigoreux pionnier de l'idéalism . . . Il amorce des thèmes féconds; mais il ne sait ni les développer ni les coordonner.[9]

This tradition has perhaps the longest lineage, since Coleridge's immediate disciples belonged to it. It is, for instance, the basis of F.J.A.Hort's still quite admirable essay;[10] and even a man as antipathetic to Coleridge as Leslie Stephen can turn his severe judgement to praise on the ground that "he was stirring the thoughts which were to occupy his successors."[11] Many modern estimates also judge Coleridge by the complexity of,

> the dreamer [who] was also an acute and subtle thinker whose reason was always a little sceptical of his reveries[12]

rather than by his systematic achievements. Which of these three estimates can be safely taken as a real view of Coleridge, and more important for this study, which one did Mill himself take? A safe answer to the first question can only be that they all have some

---

[9]Jean Pucelle, *La Nature et L'Esprit dans le Pholosophie de T.H.Green* (Paris, Louvain, 1960), pp.31-32.

[10]F.J.A.Hort, "Coleridge," *Cambridge Essays* (London, J.W.Parker, 1856), pp.292-351.

[11]Leslie Stephen, "Coleridge," in *Hours in a Library*, 3 vols. (London, Smith, Elder & Co., 1899), III, 367.

[12]H.N.Fairchild, *Religious Trends in English Poetry*, 5 vols. (New York, Columbia University Press, 1949), III, 306.

validity, if only because it is impossible to give any description of Coleridge which is exclusive, and at the same time coherent.

But even this answer is becoming a tradition. Certainly the other traditions are all, by themselves, inadequate. The scholarship of Muirhead and Claude Howard[13] reveals how far Coleridge differs from Kant, and how much he owed to Platonism. They show how original he is at times, and how much he influenced British Idealism. But Muirhead's study presents too static a Coleridge; he misses the Coleridge who performed vast and unthinkable revolutions of thought,[14] and contradicted himself from year to year. Muirhead, indeed, recognises the force of,

> the unresolved conflict in his mind between what pressed upon him with the weight of tradition and what his own insight was constantly opening up to him,[15]

but his book stretches the claim for Coleridge as a solid worker in philosophy to the limits. Nor is Coleridge, the fragmentary genius, a sufficient explanation. Some areas of Coleridge's thought do form coherent and continuous accounts in a satisfactory way. But Coleridge's value is his influence, and this has declared him both part of a continuing and systematic tradition, and a thinker throwing off occasional sparks capable of inflaming very distant minds.

Finally, which was Mill's belief? In the end, the last one, but at the time of his early manhood, and first contact with Coleridge, it was different. Nichol believed Coleridge was a fragmentary genius, and Mill argued against him that Coleridge was "the most systematic thinker of our time, without excepting even Bentham."[16] Mill had, that is, run the gamut of attitudes to Coleridge, and perhaps ended with the more modern view. Certainly, Mill does not regard Coleridge as merely one of the intuitionist school.

[13]Claud Howard, *Coleridge's Idealism, A Study of its Relationship to Kant and to the Cambridge Platonists* (Boston, R.G.Badger, 1924).

[14]See J.A.Appleyard, *Coleridge's Philosophy of Literature* (Harvard University Press, 1965) pp.70-122.

[15]Muirhead, *Op.Cit.*, p.72.

[16]*The Collected Works of John Stuart Mill* ed.F.E.L.Priestley, Vols.XII and XIII, "The Earlier Letters, 1812-1848," ed. F.E.Mineka (University of Toronto Press, 1963), XII, 221. Subsequently referred to as *Works, XII* or *XIII*.

A different question is what the basis of Coleridge's thought was. The answer is, as with all thinkers, his intentions, his motives. These Coleridge declared to be,

> to support all old and venerable truths, to support, to kindle, to project, to make the reason spread light over the feelings, to make our feelings diffuse vital warmth through our reason.[17]

Or, as Deschamps puts it "un effort pour concilier la vision platonicienne du monde avec un système achevé et cohérent."[18] In many cases, Michael Moran remarks, when Coleridge appears to be "doing a piece of straight conceptual analysis" he is, in fact, "persuasively psychologising in an attempt to reorient contemporary philosophical attitudes into unison with contemporary Christian ideals."[19] It is this intention which is the key to his writings, and Coleridge's respect for needs of this sort was greater than his respect for logic.

Mill's reputation as a professional philosopher is quite different from Coleridge's. According to Bain, although "the *Logic* has been about the best attacked book of the time"[20] it became in the end the text-book of the nineteenth century universities, and held the field until it was replaced by the Hegelianism preached by T.H.Green in the 1870's.[21] It was "one of those books which captures the mind of a whole generation."[22] If Coleridge has most often been represented as a fragmentary genius, there has never been any doubt that Mill's philosophical achievement is the substantial and ordered result of disciplined labour. In this, as in everything else, Mill and Coleridge stand at opposite poles.

Yet curiously, if Coleridge is often criticized for incoherence, inconsistency, and obscurity, Mill has been criticized equally for the

---

[17]S.T.Coleridge, *Anima Poetae* (London, W.Heinemann, 1895), p.42.

[18]Paul Deschamps, *La Formation de la Pensée de Coleridge, 1772-1804* (Paris, Didier, 1964), p.379.

[19]Michael Moran, "Coleridge," in *The Encyclopedia of Philosophy*, ed.Paul Edwards, 8 vols. (New York, Macmillan & Co., 1967), II, 135.

[20]Alexander Bain, *John Stuart Mill, A Criticism* (London, Longmans, Green, and Co., 1882), p.67.

[21]Melvin Richter, *The Politics of Conscience; T.H.Green and his Age* (London, Weidenfeld and Nicholson, 1964), p.169.

[22]Noel Annan, *Leslie Stephen* (London, Macgibbon& Kee, 1951), p.141.

same fault. No writer has been more ingenuous about his doubts and uncertainties than Mill, no one makes it more clear that his hypothesis is a compromise when he is aware of uncertain foundations in his argument; and no one has been more bitterly and persistently attacked on charges of sleight of hand, and deliberate, or even pitifully naïve, inconsistencies.[23]

It is, of course, easier to characterize the main outlines of Mill's thought than it is of Coleridge's. With Mill, too, the motives of the work are simpler, at least superficially. They are declared to be the perennial and evident ones for any work of philosophy; the desire to find the truth through the discipline of even stricter logic, and the wish to disinherit the confused doctrines of the opposed school. Thus Mill objects to the low opinion of the powers of logic which was current, in particular to the doctrine that "with the exception of the rules of Formal, that is, of Syllogistic Logic, no other rules can be framed which are applicable to thought generally."[24]

His work proposes to remedy the deficiency. It is concerned with proof, and above all with canons of what constitutes evidence; a legalistic approach which derives from Bentham. But there is a political motive too. Mill wrote that:

> the authority of the Scotch philosophers (as Dr. Reid and his followers are termed), whose writings have been for the last fifty years the great stronghold of the enemies of Logic, has been for some time on the decline; and has at last fallen so low, that nothing, save the non-appearance of any worthy antagonist in the field of controversy, enables them to maintain any ground in public estimation.[25]

The *Logic* was fundamentally designed to fill this need.

[23]Charles Mackinnon Douglas, *John Stuart Mill, A Study of his Philosophy* (Edinburgh, W.Blackwood & Sons, 1895), p.205;*The Ethics of John Stuart Mill*, ed. with an introduction by C.M.Douglas (Edinburgh, W.Blackwood & Sons, 1897), pp.lix, lxxviii.

[24]J.S.Mill, *An Examination of Sir Williams Hamilton's Philosophy* (London, Longmans, Green, Reader, and Dyer, 1878), p.473. Subsequently referred to as *Hamilton*. Compare Mill's view in 1828, "Whatley's *Elements of Logic,*" *Westminster Review*, IX (1828), p.159.

[25]"Whatley's *Elements of Logic,*" pp.137-138.

IV

Perhaps the easiest route to the heart of the technical differences between Mill's and Coleridge's philosophy is to analyse their conclusions in an old philosophical dispute, the controversy of those who believed that universals had a real existence, the realists, against those who thought that universals were merely names, the nominalists. Although Coleridge's strictly philosophical writing is restricted and opaque, since he never gave himself time, or had the application, to write an extended analysis of his ideas,[26] everything he wrote about politics and history, the main concern of his prose works, shows his love of principle, and contempt for the mere, unconnected, fact. "After I had gotten my principles," he writes, "I pretty generally left the facts to take care of themselves."[27]

This love of principle is, indeed, essential to Coleridge. Principle, not custom or history, is the bed rock of his philosophy and politics, and a principle for Coleridge became not merely an epistemological, and then a moral universal, but a self-regulating and germinative idea, owing much to Plato and to Kant.

For Mill, too, principles are vital, but the extension of Coleridge's Platonism to a belief in the ontological reality of universals is so opposed to the temper of Mill's thought, that he directs the opening chapters of the *Logic* against this view in two cognate ways. Firstly, Mill wishes to establish that universals only exist as names. Secondly, he tries to re-argue the conventional distinction between induction and deduction, in order to dethrone the syllogism, and to show that it is an inferior form of inference, since all inference can only partake of one kind, reasoning about particulars.

Here Mill's philosophy is a direct antithesis of Coleridge's. As much as Coleridge starts with the rejection of facts for the sake of the

---

[26]Rene Wellek, "The Romantic Age," in *A History of Modern Criticism, 1750-1950*, 4 vols. (London, Jonathan Cape, 1955), II, 185.

[27]*Table Talk*, p.169; see also "The Statesman's Manual," in *Political Tracts of Wordsworth, Coleridge, and Shelley*, ed. R.J.White (Cambridge University Press, 1953), p.14, subsequently referred to as *Lay Sermons; Biographia Literaria*, ed. J.Shawcross, 2.vols. (Oxford, Clarendon, 1907), I, 9; II, 39, subsequently referred to as *Biographia Literaria; Letters*, I, 260.

more interesting principles, and a Platonic assertion that the principles
have real existence, so Mill, the Aristotelian, centres his *Logic* round
the argument that universals are purely linguistic devices, a sort of
'aide memoire', and only particulars have real existence. Mill believes
that "all which men can observe are individual cases."[28] It is therefore,
as he over-confidently asserts, an "unquestionable" maxim that the
concrete explains the general, "and not conversely."[29] Generals are, in
fact, merely a "valuable contrivance of language" for compressing
many particular statements "into one short sentence."[30]

Thus Mill destroys the idea of universals, as anything more than a
short-hand for the ultimately important facts, and sets up an
immediate and reasoned opposition to Coleridge's belief in the value of
principles, and their moral superiority to facts. In making this claim
Mill has to face the traditional criticisms of empiricism, which argue
that some generals at least must be real, the most notable of which are
mathematical concepts. He tried hard, if not always successfully, to
destroy the reality of number, and of the abstractions of geometry.
Geometers talk of lines which have no breadth, and any real line which
must have breadth would upset the exactness of their reasonings. But,
Mill urges,

> we can reason about a line as if it had no breadth; because we have a
> power, which is the foundation of all the control we can exercise over
> the operation of our minds; the power, when a perception is present
> to our senses or a conception to our intellects, of *attending* to a part
> only of that perception or conception, instead of the whole. But we
> cannot *conceive* a line without breadth.[31]

Mill is arguing that the abstractions of geometry, and he is to
argue later of mathematics too, are in point of fact only conveniences
of the mind. The ground of this rejection of universals is, of course, a
thoroughgoing empiricism. "Mine professes to be a logic of *experience*
only,"[32] Mill writes, and it needs no demonstration that he resolutely
clings to this epistemological empiricism throughout his work.

---

[28]*Logic*, I, 213.

[29]*Logic*, I, 213.

[30]*Logic*, I, 213; see also 227.

[31]*Ibid.*, p.259.

[32]*Works*, XIII, 412.

Mill tries hard to avoid admitting the need for something universal prior to the particular, and so introduces a number of logical inconsistencies, and difficulties.[33] The formal logic of Mill's empiricism starts with an analysis of the syllogism. Mill tries to discover if "the syllogistic process is, or is not, a process of inference," but he soon asserts that "nothing ever was, or can be, proved by syllogism."[34] He declares that the syllogism is not inference, but a process of defining names, one "purely verbal" which is only informative "respecting the name, not the thing."[35] Similarly, a definition is neither true nor false, being only about words and their usage, or declared intended usage.

Mill is in other words virtually a nominalist, and his 'propositions' are the ghost of nominalism.[36] He believes that the value of the syllogism lies in the fact that "the major is an affirmation of the sufficiency of the evidence on which the conclusion rests."[37] The syllogism is thus self-evident, in that it is entirely verbal.[38] But Mill's beliefs about the syllogism appear to be uncertain in the end. For he declares elsewhere that "generalisation is not a process of mere naming, it is also a process of inference."[39]

Mill is not contradicting himself, for he believes that the syllogism can also be one way of stating an inference, as well as merely a register of names.[40] But there does seem to be a lack of clarity in the ontological status Mill attributes to classification. At one point he asserts an extreme Nominalist position; at another he claims that real kinds exist in nature, and that certain sorts of definitions must conform to things.

Mill's epistemology requires a strict empiricism, yet subjected to the close analysis which he offers, any theory of classification reveals a

[33]Reginald Jackson, *An Examination of the Deductive Logic of John Stuart Mill* (London, Oxford University Press, 1941), p.5.

[34]*Logic*, I, 209.

[35]*Ibid.*, p.129.

[36]*Ibid.*, p.129.

[37]*Logic*, I, 235.

[38]Jackson, *op.cit.*, p.165-166.

[39]*Logic* (1887 edition), II, 141d-142a, quoted by A.O.Kubitz, "The Development of John Stuart Mill's *System of Logic*," *University of Illinois Studies in the Social Sciences*, XVIII (1932), p.132.

[40]See Jackson, *op.cit.*, p.84.

fundamental incoherence between the claim that classes are conveniences in the mind, and have no valid ontological status, and the claim that classes are real elements in experience. The first claim would probably lead Mill to an absolute scepticism in which the political conclusions he wished to draw from his empiricism would become unprovable; the second claim would jeopardize the relativism which was an equally important aspect of his criticism.

Mill's unhappy situation is inherent in the nature of what he is attempting, and no fault of his own. It is wrong to claim that Mill either disguised, or failed to recognise, his difficulties. No mind of Mill's power could remain ignorant of errors so obvious. We must look for the reasons for the 'errors' elsewhere than simple-mindedness. Mill, in fact, seems to be saying difficult things, in quite succinct ways, and trusting his readers to interpret fairly where the qualifications to guard against misrepresentation would be unwieldy and endless. It should rather be claimed, that Mill was aware of his difficulties and preferred to leave an ambiguity, rather than a false coherence.

It is interesting to see Coleridge, having faced the same dilemma of the ontological status of the major in the syllogism, preferring to rest in the same conclusion as Mill, and leave an ambiguity, rather than the philosophically neater dogmatism of one or other of the two possible firm answers. Like Mill, he sees that the syllogism is essentially a register for memory; he recognises that, if the analysis of the syllogism is all that logic means, it is but a "hollow science," and a thousand syllogisms amount merely to "nine hundred and ninety-nine superfluous illustrations of what a syllogism is."[41] But, he goes on,

> in every syllogism I do in reality repeat the same thing in other words, yet at the same time I do something more; I recall to my memory a multitude of other facts and with them the important remembrance that they have all one or more property in common.[42]

This "property in common" is an assertion about the ontological status of generals exactly parallel to Mill's belief that they are made in conformity to things. Coleridge makes his point more exactly when he remarks that,

---

[41]A.D.Snyder, *Coleridge on Logic and Learning* (New Haven, Yale University Press, 1929), p.81.
[42]*Ibid.*, p.143; see also *Table Talk*, p.110.

> it must be evident that . . . the whole force of the intellect must be exerted on the primary act, on the justification of the terms by which we seclude and of the fact implied in the predicate by which we include. Both of these, however, imply knowledges that are more than logical, that are real and not merely formal.[43]

The similarity of view of two writers of such opposed epistemologies is an initial indication of many fundamental similarities in outlook. For both of them the fundamental problem of the ontological status of classes is left unanswered, by declaring the syllogism to have value as a device for ordering thought, and leaving the relation between words and things unexplored.

We move now from the ontological dilemma to a discussion of Mill's and Coleridge's epistemologies. Once again, a traditional crux can provide the entry point for an analysis of their assumptions, the crux of the activity or passivity of the mind in perception. But here no identical compromise is reached, as on the syllogism. Rather the solution is that both retain the problem as an unsolved mystery at the periphery of the assertions they make, largely because of the pressure of their motives on their philosophy.

Love of principles was the first fundamental of Coleridge's thought, the second was a conviction of the independence of the human mind, which expresses itself after his early, and incomplete necessitarianism, as the belief that the mind plays an active role in perception; the insistence on 'moral will' as the ultimate truth; and the belief in inner self-development. All Coleridge's principles are based on his methodology, and his account of method starts with an epistemology which argues insistently for the a priori activity of the mind. He tells the reader that,

> a previous act and conception of the mind is indispensable even to the mere semblances of Method; that neither fashion, mode, nor orderly arrangement can be produced without a prior purpose, and 'a pre-cognition *ad intentionem ejus quod quaeritur*[44]

Associationism is overthrown and Coleridge's thought takes activity by the mind as its basis. The *Magnus Opus* itself was to be primarily a "strict analysis of those operations & passions of the

---

[43]*Ibid.*, p.82.
[44]S.T.Coleridge, *The Friend*, ed. Barbara E.Rooke, 2.vols. (London, Routledge & Kegan Paul, 1969), I, 475. Subsequently referred to as *Friend*.

mind."[45] Mill's account of the methods of perception is equally central
to his work, and the "*Logic* restates the classic empiricist theory in a
way which in many respects differs hardly at all from his father's
theories."[46] Indeed, although his work on classification seems to be
inspired by a nominalist outlook, it is in fact intended primarily as a
foundation for associationism.[47] His presentation of the laws of the
mind is close to the traditional one and without obvious uncertainty.
He reasserts the classic epistemology of associationism, and even the
organization of his argument follows his father's *Analysis of the
Phenomena of the Human Mind* quite closely, dealing first with
language, then with associationism.

Despite Mill's modification of his inherited tradition, the
epistemological foundations remained the same. Thus he summarizes
the laws of psychology in the *Logic*, though the very texture of Mill's
language there suggests that he is attempting to be thorough and
precise, in an area in which precision is bought by the sort of effort
which produces verbosity, not brevity.[48] Mill adds to these familiar
axioms two conclusions which form the prongs of all the attacks of
empiricism on intuitionism. Firstly, he claims that the fundamental
conceptions of the mind are not intuitive but have the same source in
early and forgotten associations as all our other ideas, since,

> the laws of association according to one class of thinkers, the
> Categories of the Understanding according to another – are capable
> of creating, out of those data of consciousness which are uncontested,
> purely mental conceptions, which become so identified in thought
> with all our states of consciousness, that we seem, and cannot but
> seem, to receive them by direct intuition.[49]

Secondly, he attacks the intuitionist belief in the identity of
mental reality and external reality. Mill points out that,

> an association, however close, between two ideas, is not a sufficient
> *ground* of belief; is not *evidence* that the corresponding facts are

---

[45]*Letters*, II, 947.
[46]But see A.O.Kubitz, *op.cit.*, p.185.
[47]Jackson, *op.cit.*, pp.66-67.
[48]*Logic*, II, 439-440.
[49]*Hamilton*, p.177.

united in external nature.[50]

In so far as he follows his father, there is little room to see him as anything but Coleridge's opposite, but some of James Mill's analyses were patently over-simplified. After Alexander Bain's work on associationism Mill modified his views, appending many footnotes to the new edition of the *Analysis*, though rarely solving the problems he now discovered in classic associationism. But Mill's ideas, like the English political system, seemed able to absorb any amount of radical opposition by a method of compromise which involved little real change.

What Mill did absorb, however, placed his associationism in an ambiguous position. He was thus involved in a continuous battle with the intuitionists, and Mill is at his most energetic and readable in this sort of controversy; in fact the clarity, and resultant brittleness, of much of his empiricism is the result of such conflicts of opinion. Perhaps, indeed, many of the over-statements which subsequent professional analysis has detected are due, not to Mill's inability, but to the exigencies of conflict.

All his life Mill had trained in the hard school of debate, and a certain cost to detached logical achievement is probably inevitable. But Mill was not dogmatic, indeed had he been so the controversies would have been, paradoxically, gentler. It was his apparent willingness to concede what looked like the main point, and then to deny it affected his argument substantially, which so led on, rebuffed (and thus incited) his opponents. For example, in the passage quoted above the apparent equation of "laws of association" with "Categories of the Understanding" seems to suggest a more conciliatory attitude to Kantianism than Mill could ever maintain for long.

V

Coleridge arrived gradually at his conviction that principles are

---

[50] James Mill, *Analysis of the Phenomena of the Human Mind*, a new edition, with notes illustrative and critical by Alexander Bain, Andrew Findlater and George Grote, edited, with additional notes by John Stuart Mill, 2.vols. (London, Longmans, Green, Reader, and Dyer, 1869), I, 407.

more important than facts, and that the mind has active priority in perception. though these ideas were undoubtedly latent from the beginning. He started, in contrast to Mill, with a mind "habituated *to the vast*,"[51] a strong religious sense from his education which was never really abandoned, and a love of Plato's "dear *gorgeous* nonsense."[52]

From this he went to Hartley, who had developed associationism, using it to explain complex ideas and beliefs in a way which made it a very attractive philosophy to the young minds of the time. It was specially attractive to Coleridge because it managed, with curious dexterity, to combine theology and empiricism.[53] From Hartley, Coleridge went to Berkeley, who at first appealed because he was an empiricist and an associationist, albeit a religious one. The later Berkeley was an idealist, believing in the sole and thoroughgoing reality of ideas. Coleridge probably absorbed both stages, for Berkeley is one of the hinges between empiricism and idealism in Coleridge's history.[54] The earliest plan for a great philosophical work, at this stage, was to end with "a bold avowal of Berkeley's system."[55] Spinoza was the next attraction. As Hegel remarked, every philosopher is sometimes a Spinozist.[56] But Spinoza denied the personal in God, and so Coleridge abandoned him after 1799.

At this stage Coleridge experienced two things, a disappointment, and an interest. The disappointment was in part an almost universal political experience of the age, and in part a personal one. The failure of Pantisocracy, and of the ideals of the French Revolution, brought in their wake the failure of his faith in empiricism. The new interest was a return to idealism, spurred on by his reading of Kant. March 1801 was Coleridge's "crisis" when he extricated the notions of time and

[51]*Letters*, I, 354.

[52]*Ibid.*, I, 295.

[53]Robert Marsh, "The Second Part of Hartley's System," *J.H.I.*, XX (1959), pp.264-273.

[54]Deschamps, *op.cit.*, p.426.

[55]*The Notebooks of Samuel Taylor Coleridge, 1794-1808*, ed.Kathleen Coburn, 4 vols. (London, Routledge & Kegan Paul, 1957), I, entry 174. Subsequently referred to as *Notebooks*.

[56]Quoted by Muirhead, *op.cit.*, p.47.

space,[57] a process which was heralded by the new and detailed intensity of philosophical study shown in his highly original critique of Locke and Descartes.[58] He also rejected Newton's idea of the passive mind at that time.

It was now that Kant "took possession of me as with a giant's hand."[59] But before Kant he had read the Cambridge Platonists, who prepared him for Kant as well as themselves contributing to Coleridge's ideas.[60] Many of the elements of Kant, and of his own later thought, are there in the Platonists.[61] Thus, they dissociated reason and faith, a distinction closely related to Kant's and Coleridge's distinction between Understanding and Reason. But there was an essential difference. Kant's epistemology limits the mind's ability to know, since for Kant God cannot be proved. The Cambridge Platonists' epistemology on the other hand *proves* that God is a rational necessity. Coleridge's aims were just those of the Cambridge Platonists,[62] that is, to prove the unity of faith and reason as the spiritual constitution of the universe, and to prove that Reason is a source of morals and religion.

Kant, despite this, was the turning point of Coleridge's life. But, typically, what sounds most Kantian in terminology is often not Kant's own opinion, and it is clear that Coleridge did not always fully understand the new thinking he so rapidly clasped to his heart.[63] English admirers of the time were not always Kantians in any real sense.[64] An example of Coleridge's limited understanding is his

[57]*Letters*, II, p.706.

[58]R.F.Brinkley, "Coleridge on Locke," *Studies in Philology*, XLVI (1949), pp.523, 528.

[59]*Biographia Literaria*, I, 99.

[60]Howard, *op.cit.*, p.24; see Deschamps, *op.cit.*, pp.402, 500.

[61]A.O.Lovejoy, "Kant and the English Platonists," in *Essays Philosophical and Psychological in Honour of William James*, by his Colleagues at Columbia University (New York, Longmans, Green, and Co., 1908), pp.301-302.

[62]Robert Preyer, *Bentham, Coleridge, and the Science of History*, Leipziger Beiträge zur Englishen Philologie, 41 Heft (Bochum-Langendreer, Verlag Poppinghaus, 1958), p.3.

[63]Graham Hough, "Coleridge and the Victorians," in *The English Mind, Studies in the English Moralists, Presented to Basil Wiley*, ed. Hugh Sykes Davies and George Watson (Cambridge University Press, 1964), p.179.

[64]S.Körner, *Kant* (London, Penguin Books, 1966), p.100.

conviction that Kant "in his Critique of the Practical Reason has completely overthrown the edifice of Fatalism, or causative Precedence as applied to Action."[65] Kant, in the sphere of phenomena, merely tied the knot of necessitarianism tighter.

The categories, far from liberating the mind, limit its freedom more completely. Coleridge, however, regarded freedom as a primary axiom of philosophy, and as a fact of the experience of creativity.[66] He thought he saw in Kant the opportunity to claim a sphere above necessity in Reason.[67] Coleridge may have been mistaken, but he did understand most of Kant, and he certainly used many of Kant's ideas. For instance, he argues for the existence of a synthetic a priori, following Kant's line of argument with very minor differences, in that he stresses the infinity and objectivity of 'universals' in this category.[68]

He takes mathematics as an example of the synthetic a priori; certain uniting elements in it, he claims, cannot be derived from experience alone.[69] He also follows Kant in his answers to Hume on the subject of causality.[70] Though many of Coleridge's comments suggest that his 'Ideas' derive from Platonic thought, they are also a type of the synthetic a priori. Other minor aspects of Kant Coleridge took over unaltered; a particular example is the ubiquitous and fertile distinction between person and thing. Kant writes that,

> man and every rational being *exists* as an end in itself, *not merely as a means* for arbitrary use by this will or that; but he must in all his actions . . . be regarded *at the same time as an end*[71]

Coleridge follows him when he writes,

> the distinction between person and thing consists herein, that the later may rightfully be used, altogether and merely, as a *means*; but the former must always be included in the [end], and form a part of the final cause.[72]

[65]*Letters*, III, 35.
[66]James Benziger, "Organic Unity: Leibnitz to Coleridge," *P.M.L.A.*, LXVI (1951), p.40.
[67]Hort, *op.cit.*, p.325.
[68]Muirhead, *op.cit.*, pp.78-79.
[69]Snyder, *op.cit.*, p.94.
[70]Snyder, *op.cit.*, p.94.
[71]Quoted by Körner, *op.cit.*, p.146.
[72]*Friend*, I, 190; see also *Lay Sermons*, p.106.

The distinction was subsequently taken over by Mill, who regarded the idea as Coleridge's.[73] Elsewhere Coleridge modified Kant's structure considerably to suit his own purposes.[74] Broadly, he seems to follow Kant in his constructive ideas, but differ from him on his negative criticisms of the ability of the mind to know.[75] This is most evident at the heart of Coleridge's system, on the question of the Reason.[76] Coleridge had accepted the categories of the Understanding, but not the regulative function of the Reason. Following Plato, he rejected this negative limitation on Reason, and claimed that reason, through 'Ideas' did have access to the Noumenal world.[77]

In this Coleridge was, of course, following the same path as all the post-Kantians, but his results were distinctive. It is assumed that Coleridge is in some sense faulty for not following Kant;[78] but he was neither an expounder nor a teacher of Kant's philosophy, but a thinker in his own right who had found a sympathetic mind but not a master.[79] In the end this is the only fair way to see the relationship between Coleridge and Kant.

From Kant, Coleridge went on to explore the neo-Kantians. He was quick to see the "contrast between what he called 'Kant's Aristotelianism' and the 'Platonism' of others like Schlegel."[80] Fichte was too anti-nature, but prepared him for dynamism; Schelling bridged the gulf between Noumena and Phenomena that Kant left as the distinctive, and substantial mark of his philosophy. But Coleridge was disillusioned with Schelling between 1817 and 1818. He felt that Schelling's system made the world a part of God, and no more, though in fact he had learnt a great deal from Schelling's more sympathetic

[73]See Bentham and Coleridge, p.157.

[74]R.L.Brett, Reason and Imagination (London, Oxford University Press, 1960), p.86.

[75]Muirhead, op.cit., p.82.

[76]D.G.James, "The Thought of Coleridge," in The Major English Romantic Poets, A Symposium in Reappraisal, ed.Clarence D.Thorpe, Carlos Baker and Bennet Weaver (Carbondale, Southern Illinois University Press, 1957), p.110.

[77]Muirhead, op.cit., p.91.

[78]E.g. René Wellek, Kant in England (Princeton University, 1948).

[79]Moran, op.cit., 134.

[80]Shirley R.Letwin, The Pursuit of Certainty (Cambridge University Press, 1965), p.229.

Platonism.[81]

Coleridge did not develop so rapidly after 1821, and he stood at the end nearer Fichte than Hegel.[82] Beyond Jacobi, Fichte and Schelling, Coleridge hardly went. He was, he said, "no Zealot or Bigot for German Philosophy taken without comparison,"[83] and he regarded "most Germans" as "not altogether wrong, and . . . never altogether right."[84] His knowledge of the German transcendentalists seems, in fact, to have been limited.[85] Despite his reputation as a German scholar, Coleridge's reading outside the favourite and plundered few was apparently slight.[86]

He returned in the end, as he tells us, to a purer Platonism. The "prior and better Lights"[87] proved to be the ultimate guides of Coleridge's thought. He found *Biographia Literaria* an inadequate expression of his ideas, and increasingly he abandoned post-Kantianism, and became an eclectic. And it was, of course, the later Coleridge which was the inspiration of the talk which Sterling passed on to Mill. Ultimately, then, Coleridge's thought might be described as a mixture of Kant, post-Kantianism, and Platonism.

This is to describe its affinities and origins. What of its philosophical content? Coleridge is, of course, essentially an intuitionist in the sense that his aim in "the referring of the mind to its own consciousness for truths indispensable to its own happiness",[88] and he believed that,

> the knowledge of *spiritual* Truth is of necessity immediate and *intuitive*[89]

and that,

---

[81]*Letters*, IV, 874.

[82]Muirhead, *op.cit.*, pp.58-59.

[83]*Letters*, IV, 793.

[84]*Table Talk*, pp.163-164.

[85]Preyer, *op.cit.*, pp.2-3.

[86]F.W.Stokoe, *German Influence in the English Romantic Period, 1788-1818* (Cambridge University Press, 1926), pp.128-129.

[87]*Letters*, IV, 874.

[88]*Friend*, I, 108.

[89]S.T.Coleridge, *Aids to Reflection* (London, G.Bell and Sons, 1884), p.104. Subsequently referred to as *Aids to Reflection*.

all Truth is a species of Revelation.[90]

Coleridge's 'system' arises out of the distinction between 'Reason' and 'Understanding'. A large proportion of his philosophical writing is designed to teach this distinction, for using it he was able to solve his greatest philosophical problems. The distinction was, he said, "pre-eminently the *Gradus ad Philosophium.*"[91] He made many attempts to define the distinct natures of Reason and Understanding, and the different aims and successes of these attempts are a study on their own. A typical statement is,

> by the *Understanding,* I mean the faculty of thinking and forming *judgements* on the notices furnished by the sense ... By the pure *Reason,* I mean the power by which we become possessed of principle,[92]

or, again,

> Supreme Reason, whose knowledge is creative, and antecedent to the things known, is distinguished from the understanding, or creaturely mind of the individual, the acts of which are posterior to the things it records and arranges.[93]

What the eighteenth century called religion, and included in the ideal and visionary hopes of man, Coleridge following Kant christened the Reason. What the eighteenth century had called 'reason' became 'understanding' in Coleridge. The understanding is the representative and whipping boy of what is characteristic of eighteenth century thought,[94] and Coleridge's Reason is not rational in the normal sense of being discursive or analytical.

In this way, Coleridge, to one way of thinking, merely abdicated the real problems of the argument between philosophy and religion, between logic and inspiration, by a verbal confusion. To another, more sympathetic, way of thinking his nomenclature was asserting, to great polemical advantage, that religion was fully rational, if not logical.[95] Coleridge recognized that the distinction between Understanding and

[90]*Letters,* II, 709; also *Lay Sermons,* p.46.
[91]*Table Talk,* p.75.
[92]*Friend,* I, 177n.
[93]*Lay Sermons,* p.18.
[94]Wellek, *A History of Modern Criticism,* II, 164.
[95]Muirhead, *op.cit.,* pp.108-109.

Reason was a conceptual tool, and not an absolute disjunction in the mind, and he also recognized that the usefulness of the distinction depended on the prior assumption, which he states quite explicitly, "of a *one* as the ground and cause of the Universe."[96]

Reason is a faculty of unity, and unity is a hypothesis, a hypothesis which enables us to unify our knowledge. Here we return to a basic assumption from which all philosophers set out, and to which they ultimately return for their sanction. The assumption in Coleridge's case is the need for knowledge, and the conviction that the world is so constructed as to make this possible; constructed as a unity. This conviction is a response to a need, and is not in the province of logic. It was Kant's dualism which most offended this original and ineradicable sense of unity in Coleridge. The Trichotomic logic of thesis, antithesis, and synthesis, Coleridge believed, offered the solution to this dualism, a solution which elegantly required the existence of a dichotomy in order to function; the necessity was thus the explanation.

Coleridge was following the well-beaten path of post-Kantian idealism, though the sources of the Trichotomy are rather obscure.[97] He appears to be the first Englishman to attempt to grapple with the dialectical logic, but he was not successful in many ways, and his attempts to explain the idea remain the most elusive and mysterious part of his work, and the most tenuous part of Muirhead's reconstruction. Without a broad previous knowledge of the history of post-Kantian idealism in Germany, Coleridge's attempts are the most aloof and incomprehensible passages in a writer who often seems to use obscurity with casual contempt for his reader. Coleridge tells us,

> The *Identity* of Thesis and Antithesis is the substance of all *Being*; their *Opposition* the condition of all *Existence* or Being manifested; and every *Thing* or Phaenomenon is the exponent of a Synthesis as long as the opposite energies are retained in that Synthesis.[98]

The ideas are familiar from the German tradition, and not perhaps incomprehensible to the initiated, but the English language will not bear the weight of the distinction between 'Being' and 'Existence' that Coleridge's translation of the German terms puts on it. Coleridge's

---

[96] *Aids to Reflection*, p.110.
[97] Muirhead, *op.cit.*, pp.84-85.
[98] *Friend*, I, 94n.

philosophy of contradiction is often used in trivial, as well as complex and vital, matters. But it always has one purpose, to enable him to explain the strange and contradictory nature of the world. It was, that is, an offshoot of the same sense of wonder which produced the great poems; a sense of the inexplicable complexity and diversity of things which in the poet yoked up images both uncanny and reverberant, and in the philosopher produced a theory of synthesis. The theory was intended to record wonder, and so some obscurity was an appropriate accompaniment.

The most superficial use of the idea was in a persistent tendency to see extremes meeting, which has been described as a "constitutional malady."[99] "My favourite proverb," Coleridge remarks, superfluously, is "extremes meet."[100] But besides his quaint discoveries of exemplars of this proverbial truth, the concept of synthesis had many profound uses in Coleridge's thought, and it became a potent tool of explanation. Thus his epistemology rests on,

> the remarkable fact [which] forces itself on our attention, viz. that the material world is found to obey the same laws as had been deduced independently from the reason.[101]

He explains this by pointing out that, to know anything for certain is to have a clear insight into the inseparability of the predicate from the subject (the matter from the form), and *vice versa*, since,

> the truth is universally placed in the coincidence of the thought with the thing, of the representation with the object represented ... During the act of knowledge itself, the objective and subjective are so instantly united, that we cannot determine to which of the two the priority belongs.[102]

Coleridge adventures in many directions with this concept; not often successfully, but always stimulatingly. Thus he reconciles the duality of body and mind,

> for since impenetrability is intelligible only as a mode of resistance;

[99]A.D.Snyder, *The Critical Principle of the Reconciliation of Opposites as Employed by Coleridge*, Contributions to Rhetoric, No.9 (Ann Arbor, University of Michigan Press, 1918), p.20.

[100]*Friend*, I, 529; also 110, 205; *Notebooks*, I, entry 1725 and note; *Aids to Reflection*, p.1; *Letters*, II, 857; *Table Talk*, p.31.100

[101]*Friend*, I, 462.

[102]*Table Talk*, p.57.;*Biographia Literaria*, I, 174.

its admission places the essence of the matter in an act of power, which it possesses in common with *spirit*; and the body and spirit are therefore no longer absolutely heterogeneous, but *may* without any *absurdity* be supposed to be different modes, or degrees in perfection, of a common substratum.[103]

Coleridge also explains the paradoxes of religion by the same means.

Revealed religion is in its highest contemplation the unity, that is, the identity or coinherence, of Subjective and Objective. It is in itself, and irrelatively, at once inward Life and Truth, and outward Fact and Luminary. But as all Power manifests itself in the harmony of corresponding Opposites, each supposing and supporting the other, – so has Religion its objective, or historic and ecclesiastical pole, and its subjective, or spiritual and individual pole.[104]

Coleridge, who knew little of Hegel, rarely goes further than the act of synthesis to see the process as part of a longer chain of dialectic growth. Growth is another vital element in Coleridge's thought, but it is more the growth of the Platonic idea, than the growth derived from the struggle of opposites. It is the organic, "ab intra, *evolved* generation, and not the "ab extra, *impressed* fabrication of mechanism.[105]

Hope, a dynamic antecedent of growth, is essential to Coleridge's idea of humanity, it is what distinguishes man from animals, by arousing the desire for 'permanent' moral good, and it thus "facilitates that grand business of our Existence – still further, & further still, to generalize our affections, till *Existence* itself is swallowed up in *Being.*[106] The terminology sounds Hegelian, but it would be wrong to confuse what is essentially Christian, a Platonic hope of future beatitude, with a Hegelian concept of dialectic, even though the hope has become clothed in the language of Absolute Idealism. "Christianity," Coleridge tells us, "is a growth, a becoming, a progression. . . .History, therefore, and history under the form of moral freedom, is that alone in which the Idea of Christianity can be

---

[103]*Ibid.*, p.88.

[104]*Confessions of an Inquiring Spirit*, ed H.St.J.Hart (London, A. & C.Black, 1956), p.79. Subsequently referred to as *Confessions of an Inquiring Spirit*.

[105]*Notebooks*, II, entry 2444.

[106]*Letters*, II, 758; also *Friend*, I, 223.

realized."[107] Throughout Coleridge's philosophy of synthesis one aim is
clear, the desire to bring together the experienced diversity of thought
and things into an explanation of the apprehended need for unity.

VI

Coleridge's work was one of pilgrimage in search of a fountainhead
which he ever circled with his logic. But the logic that was to ensnare
the dream was, at least in part prepared – a logic of Reason versus
Understanding, of Trichotomy, and of Organic Growth. Mill's logic in
total contrast is primarily a logic which redefines the relationship
between deduction and induction, and makes a detailed analysis of the
canons of inductive inference. Mill is concerned to analyse the rules of
reasoning, which he defines as synonymous with inference in inductive,
deductive, and syllogistic processes.[108] He argues that "every step in
the Deduction is still an Induction,"[109] in the sense that it is a register
of past inductions, for,

> though in many particular investigations the place of the induction
> may be supplied by a prior deduction; but the premises of this prior
> deduction must have been derived from induction.[110]

In the social sciences Mill argues for the use of the deductive
method on this basis, since although,

> the more complex laws of human action, for example, may be
> deduced from the simpler ones; but the simple or elementary laws
> will always and necessarily have been obtained by a directly inductive
> process.[111]

Having placed deduction as a subordinate form of inductive
inference, Mill then proceeds to develop his canons of induction. It is
not part of the present purpose to discuss these, but two observations
are important. Firstly, that they are canons of 'proof' and not of
discovery. Their undoubted success in this seems to have blinded Mill
to the fact that the methodology of the discovery of initial hypotheses

---

[107]Quoted by Muirhead, *op.cit.*, p.247 from MS.c., p.112.
[108]*Logic*, I, 185.
[109]*Ibid.*, 252.
[110]*Ibid.*, 529.
[111]*Ibid.*, 530; see also Jackson, *op.cit.*, p.58.

might be very different from the methods of verification, and indeed that there is no reason from an a priori logical inspection why they should not be. Certainly Mill himself failed to give such a reason. This oversight is the root of much of the confusion in his discussion with Whewell,[112] and is still a source of controversy.[113]

Secondly, Mill himself cannot deny that induction is not a process which can claim absolute certainty, since it is a generalisation about both observed instances and "an indefinite number of cases which we have not examined."[114] The canons of induction are, of course, designed to increase the certainty of the inductive process. But Mill has pointed out that most inferences are only "apparent", not valid, and has discarded any possibility of self-evidence in the basic axioms of a reasoning process. He is therefore in need of some "real inference" to base his "proofs" on. This Mill cannot now find, and it seems in the end that his failure to provide real inference in either syllogism or induction is linked to the same problem as faced his epistemology, that of the reality of universals.[115]

This uncertainty is significantly expressed in Mill's querulousness over the problem of new truths. Thus, Mill's analysis of the syllogism convinces him that "in all these cases there is not really any inference; there is in the conclusion no new truth, nothing but what was already asserted in the premises."[116] This argument contradicts what he said above about universals. If the criticism of the syllogism is to be that it produces no "new truth", it might be fairly expected that the virtue of the inductive method would be that it did produce "new truth". That is, the logical conclusion of Mill's criticism of the syllogism is that induction must create universals. In fact, Mill would certainly not allow this. The ambiguity over the ontological status of general reasoning which can thus be diagnosed is similar to that which his

[112]E.W.Strong, "William Whewell and John Stuart Mill: Their Controversy about Scientific Knowledge," *J.H.I.*, XVI (1955), 209-231.

[113]See P.B.Medawar, *Induction and Intuition in Scientific Thought* (London, Methuen and Co., 1969), p.45; K.R.Popper, *The Logic of Scientific Discovery* (London, Hutchinson, 1959), p.419.

[114]*Logic* (1887 edition), 126a; quoted by A.O.Kubitz, *op.cit.*, 143.

[115]Jackson, *op.cit.*, p.61.

[116]*Logic*, I, 183.

earlier discussion of the syllogism disclosed.

Mill's difficulties are well illustrated by some of his speculations about deduction. He gives deduction a surprisingly large place in his methodology, despite his apparently inductive ideal of proof. Indeed, he argues that ultimately deduction will become the main process in science. He speculates on the "ultimate laws" which may be found, and considers the,

> interesting question whether there are any necessary limits to this philosophical operation, or whether it may proceed until all the uniform sequences in nature are resolved into some one universal law.[117]

His belief that final deductions can be found is typical of nineteenth century scientific certainty. It is of course open to question, whether all these incoherences, whether of classification, induction or deduction, spring from the fundamental uncertainty in Mill's mind as to the ontological status of logical operations. They may rather be in a real sense trivial, that is easy to produce and difficult to dissolve, and of passing interest to a seriously motivated criticism.

VII

Coleridge's poetic and trichotomic logic result, intermittently but persistently, in two firmly held positions which are in many ways original and represent the essence of the distinctively Coleridgean. These are his doctrine of Ideas, and his attempts to construct a philosophy of voluntarism. An 'Idea' Coleridge defines as,

> that conception of a thing which is not abstracted from a particular state, form or mode, in which the thing may happen to exist at this or that time; nor yet generalized from any number or succession of such forms or modes; but which is given by the knowledge of its ultimate aim.[118]

Ideas can unite the Noumena and Phenomena, whereas Kant divides them. Ideas are also creative, they originate in the Reason and the will, that is they are Noumenal and moral; they are, like Kantian

[117]*Ibid.*, II, 3.

[118]S.T.Coleridge, *On the Constitution of Church and State* (London, Hurst, Chance and Co., 1830), p.3.

Categories, the basis of conceptions. The other distinctive facet of Coleridge's thought is his voluntarism. The free will became so much the basis of Coleridge's later thought as to be at times suggested as the constitutive factor of experience. How much it was postulate, and not proven, he was well aware.

> This, therefore I repeat, is the final conclusion. All *speculative* Disquisition must begin with Postulates, which the conscience alone can at once authorize and substantiate: and from whichever point the Reason may start, from the things which are seen to the One Invisible, or from the Idea of the Absolute One to the things that are seen, it will find a chasm, which the Moral Being only, which the Spirit and Religion of Man alone can fill up.[119]

And again, "freedom must be assumed as a *ground* of philosophy, and can never be deduced from it."[120] Coleridge fought against "the vicious habit of assigning the precedence to the intellectual instead of the moral,"[121] and tried to show that Will is prior to Being.[122] But his voluntarism failed to achieve systematic exposition, despite Muirhead's attempts to show that it did, and it had to wait two generations until it became fashionable.[123] But Coleridge's arguments do demonstrate more clearly than anything else how much the fundamental assumptions of Coleridge's philosophy, in summary, can only be regarded as a highly individual form of idealism, confused with bold, and sometimes foolish experiments, but driven throughout by his overriding sense of the unity of the world, and the duality of philosophical explanations; driven that is, by a human, and not a logical motive.

VIII

The characteristic conclusions at which Mill arrives are, in the

---

[119]*Friend*, I, 523n.

[120]*Biographia Literaria*, I, 185.

[121]Quoted by Muirhead, *op.cit.*, p.146. Muirhead refers to Snyder, *Coleridge on Logic and Learning*, p.133, but this version does not contain this sentence. Neither do other versions of the passage, e.g. *Literary Remains*, 4 vols. (London, William Pickering, 1836-1839), I, 297.

[122]Muirhead, *op.cit.*, p.227.

[123]*Ibid.*, p.117.

occasions of their appearance, similar to Coleridge's. Coleridge's idealism and voluntarism appear as ultimate positions beyond which he believes argument cannot go. But they are in no way translucent to the inquiring mind; they are the harbingers of mysticism, not the lamp-holders of discovery. Mill's relativism fulfills a similar role. He insists that logic can go no further, and he seems to prefer the blank and closed door of mystery to the speculations of hypothesis. They both, that is, display a curious opacity in their final positions.

Mill deliberately aimed to "keep clear" of problems such as "the controversy respecting the perception of the highest Realities by direct intuition."[124] He thus insists that "for logical purposes, the sensation is the only essential part of what is meant by the word" attribute,[125] in this way laying aside the question of the reality of attributes. In the *Logic* Mill regards the ultimate laws of the mind, and the ultimate facts of consciousness as mysteries beyond the possibility of investigation. The law of association is founded on likeness, but,

> likeness and unlikeness, therefore, as well as antecedence, sequence, and simultaneousness, must stand apart among relations, as things *sui generis*. They are attributes grounded on facts, that is, on states of consciousness, but on states which are peculiar, unresolvable, and inexplicable.[126]

Mill feels that these ultimate laws are too intricate, and after suggesting a reason why they are so, prefers not to try to solve them.

> To determine what it is that happens in the case of assent or dissent besides putting two ideas together, is one of the most intricate of metaphysical problems. But whatever the solution may be, we may venture to assert that it can have nothing whatever to do with the import of propositions; for this reason, that propositions (except sometimes when the mind itself is the subject treated of) are not assertions respecting out ideas of things, but assertions respecting the things themselves.[127]

The simplest aspects of association came into this category of the "ultimate laws of our minds" which no one could "analyse or explain."[128] Mill seems to have meant by an ultimate law only

---

[124]*Works*, XIII, 406.
[125]*Logic* (1887 edition), 59a. Quoted by A.O.Kubitz, *op.cit.*, p.81.
[126]*Logic*, I, 75.
[127]*Ibid.*, 97.
[128]*Works*, XII, 237.

something which could not be explained any further, although he did
discuss the possibility that there might eventually prove to be only one
set of ultimate laws. He was, undoubtedly, therefore, aware of the
unsatisfactoriness of the partial 'ultimates' of which consciousness
itself, and many of its laws, are examples. But he was even more
acutely aware of the unsatisfactoriness of the alternative, intuitionist,
explanations. He was anxious, therefore, to leave the problem before it
became unmanageable. He evidently and explicitly felt that these
concepts were beyond analysis, and the meagre explanations which had
been thrashed out between his father, Bain and himself should be left
as the best possible, or perhaps the best current, it is not clear which
he means, hypothesis.

Ultimately, then, when faced with the problem of the real nature
of consciousness, Mill again leaves an uncertainty, as he did over the
ontological status of classification. Consciousness, the very problem of
epistemology, he declares is the "final inexplicability."[129] Both the
strength and unsatisfactoriness of James Mill or Hartley lies in their
firm belief that they can explain consciousness. Yet John Mill slackens
his grip at that very point on which the whole fabric of his thought
will rest. Thus Mill relegates the uncertainties about the empirical
model of the mind which he left dangling in his footnotes to his edition
of his father's *Analysis* to the area beyond the limits of logic. He thus
placed logic within the clearly defined boundaries, which are the source
and protection of the whole coherence of his system.[130] Logic became
for Mill a,

> collection of precepts or rules ... concerned only with Forms, since,
> being rules for thinking, it can have no authority but over that which
> depends on thought.[131]

But although Mill's formal logic contained itself within these
strictly set limits, he probed deeply into the problems of associational
psychology and at times ends in clear disagreement with his father.
The will to disagree, though not perhaps the analysis which forced the
disagreement, reached its peak during his close friendship with Carlyle

[129] *Hamilton*, p.248.

[130] J.B.Schneewind, "Mill," in *Encyclopedia of Philosophy*, ed.Paul Edwards, 8 vols.
(New York, Macmillan & Co., 1967), V, 316.

[131] *Hamilton*, p.462.

in the 1830's. Mill did not, of course, pursue the half formed ideas of translating mysticism into logic.[132] But certain doubts remained, and were to remain, although they were obscured by party political struggles at the time, and the exigencies of a political climate that, for the first time, genuinely promised reform in reward for effort. Mill told Sterling while he was writing the *Logic*,

> I am very far from agreeing, in all things with the 'Analysis,' even on its own ground . . . I can understand your need of something beyond it & deeper than it, & I have often bad moods in which I would most gladly postulate like Kant a different ultimate foundation 'subjectiver bedürfnisses willen' if I could.[133]

But they were only the 'bad moods', and Mill did not, and could not, make such a postulate. But, none the less, the doubts were there, and something of the tone which haunts the querulous and uncertain rationalism of the *Three Essays on Religion* is here too. The importance of these doubts was not, however, that they made Mill change any essential part of the epistemological foundations of Utilitarianism, but simply that they made him doubt.

The effect of this was to relax that tight logicality and conclusiveness which characterized Bentham and James Mill. The degree of tolerance he developed was to have much magnified consequences in the subsequent superstructure this incomplete epistemology bore, in the essays on *Utilitarianism* and on *Liberty*. It also gave him access to Coleridge. Mill explicitly placed these uncertainties outside the limits of his logic, and plausibly claimed that this limitation did not detract from his system. To criticise these speculations is not therefore to criticise that system. But it is to point out the area of uncertainty in Mill, in order to compare it with a similar area in Coleridge.

Aristotelian and Platonist in their initial assumptions, divided from the outset by their aims and by the texture of their style of thought, Mill and Coleridge were, broadly speaking, philosophical opposites. Coleridge believed in the reality of universals, and in broadly intuitive ideals; Mill verged on nominalism and maintained a circumspect, but persistent, empirical associationist model of epistemology. But they

[132]*Works*, XII, 219.
[133]*Ibid.*, XIII, 406-7.

were both dealing with the relation etween the logical and the real in a manner which respected its complexity sufficiently to allow unsolved problems to remain within easy access of the surface of their argument. They both recognized more possibilities than they could synthesize and they were both left with uncertainties which proscribed dogmatism, and enabled Mill to read Coleridge with more than sympathy.

4 Crossfire: conflicting criticisms

It deeply concerns the greatest interests of our race, that the only mode of treating ethical questions which aims at correcting existing maxims, and rectifying any of the perversions of existing feeling, should not be borne down by clamour. — John Stuart Mill[1]

This is the philosophy of death, and only of a dead nature can it hold good. . . .But these men have had their day: and there are signs of the verging to its close. — S.T.Coleridge[2]

In this chapter Coleridge's criticisms of the "mechanico-corpuscular" philosophy are placed beside Mill's criticism of the intuitionists. Mill's and Coleridge's opposition is reinforced by the persistent criticisms which they make of the other school, but the similarities also stand out. The criticisms are based on personal, inner knowledge of these systems. Both Mill and Coleridge in their early twenties almost adopted the other system. So the criticisms are informed, reasonable, and experienced, and very different from the näive obtuseness of many lesser contemporaries in the sectarian battle. Equally, the criticisms, for all their force, are tempered by a relativism which places them above sectarianism and makes them tolerant in their own affirmations.

Neither simply offers a critique of the position of the other, but rather attacks the cruder contemporary versions of the opposite

---

[1] J.S.Mill, *Dissertations and Discussions*, 4 vols. (London, Longmans, Green, Reader, and Dyer, 1867-1875), I, 159. Subsequently referred to as *Dissertations and Discussions*.

[2] S.T.Coleridge, "The Statesman's Manual," in *Political Tracts of Wordsworth, Coleridge and Shelley*, ed. R.J.White (Cambridge University Press, 1953), pp.44-46.

doctrine.   Thus   the   "mechanico-corpuscular"   utilitarianism   that
Coleridge attacks is a long way from the strict relativism of Mill's real
thought, and the intuitionism which Mill attacks is not that of
Coleridge, but of Hamilton.

I

Coleridge's criticisms of associationism are so strong because of his
own close personal involvement with the philosophy of the eighteenth
century. Coleridge's thought, and this is a well recognized part of his
greatness, was the very stuff of his emotional and personal life.
Wrestling with, and throwing off, Hartley was a personal victory, and
naturally induced triumph. It was very much a personal and private
Odyssey, and the perils of his soul on the journey account for the force
of his warnings to others on the same road. From the promised land
Coleridge was approaching – the oasis of his soul – the land he had
scrambled over looked unforgivably parched and rocky.

Mill also had more than a speculative interest in the defeat of the
other party. He was an intellectual in politics, and it is clear that he
sees intuitionism not so much as an alternative metaphysics, as an
alternative politics. The very considerable sectarian energy that goes
into his attacks on it can only be explained in this way. Intuitionism is
for him primarily "the great intellectual support of false doctrines and
bad institutions,"[3] and the quarrel with intuitionism is thus, "not a
mere   matter   of   abstract   speculation;   it   is   full   of   practical
consequences".[4] Intuitionism, Mill explains, is really only a form of
systematization of customary feeling, "an apparatus for converting
those prevailing opinions, on matters of morality, into reasons for
themselves."[5] Mill thinks that the success of this philosophy is due to a
common delusion of the mind for, he argues, we believe to be intuition
what is really the result of a long forgotten inference.

Just how far Mill's resistance to intuitionism is political, rather

[3]J.S.Mill, *Autobiography*, 3rd ed. (London, Longmans, Green, Reader, and Dyer,
1874), p.225. Subsequently referred to as *Autobiography*.

[4]*Ibid.*, p.273.

[5]*Dissertations and Discussions*, II, 453.

than speculative, can be shown by analysis of his arguments. Thus Mill supports the argument from forgotten inference by repeating that,

> what we are said to observe is usually a compound result, of which one-tenth may be observation, and the remaining nine-tenths inference,"[6]

and this inference is unconscious. Where the one-tenth direct observation is missing we believe the inference to be intuition. When Mill says that the mind's own previous inferences condition what we see, he is saying something superficially similar to Kant. Kant and Mill agree that the mind does condition perception, but Mill argues that this conditioning itself is only the product of experience, whereas Kant claims that this is just what it cannot be since it must in all cases, however far we regress, be logically prior to experience. Kant and Mill would agree, however, following the tradition of Locke and Hume, that this conditioning of the mind is called into play by experience, that is, it is synthetic.

Mill, was aware (though it is difficult to guess how clearly) of his predicament in this, and tried to reduce the basic categories of knowledge to a minimum number of inferences.[7] Thus he deliberately left the definition of what he means by the 'pristine' state uncertain. Consciousness is the ultimate mystery. But association appears to depend on the idea of time, which is a part of the concept of memory. The ability to retain an after-image is the prior requirement for the theory that after-images can associate to form ideas. But Mill has left as a final mystery the fact that the mind can be aware of its past and future, *i.e.* be conscious of itself as a state of mind as a term in a series of states, or as a whole series. He merely regards the laws of association as empirical laws. In other words he has nothing to say about what he calls the "Intuitionist" doctrine from the logical point of view, and he has only claimed against it that simple experience would not seem to confirm it. Indeed, all that he does say is confined to the effect of the doctrine on political matters, and is not about intuitionism as a competitive epistemology.

---

[6] J.S.Mill, *A System of Logic*, 2 vols. (London, Longmans, Green, and Co., 1879), II, 186. Subsequently referred to as *Logic*.

[7] J. Schneewind, "Mill," in *The Encyclopedia of Philosophy*, ed. Paul Edwards, 8 vols. (New York, Macmillan & Co., 1967), V, 318.

Mill, then, is concerned firstly with the political implications of intuitionism, which for him is a broad term covering all ethical and political philosophies other than the strictly empirical. The value of associationism, he insists, is that it is a practical instrument for change, not that it is a thorough logical analysis of the problems of epistemology. He thus believed himself to have a special mission to provide not only an attack, but an alternative to this school of thought; "jusqu'ici, personne n'est venue se planter en face de cet ennemi"[8]. Mill hoped that his system would provide this alternative and help banish the philosophy which he saw clearly and disastrously ascendant.

The *Logic* was to be a "text book of the opposite doctrine."[9] Mill wrote to Comte at some length, explaining his hopes for his *Logic*.

> Je ne crois pas être trompé par l'amour-propre en croyant que si mon ouvrage est lû et accueilli (ce qui me parait toujours très douteux) ce sera le premier coup un peu rude que l'école ontologique aura reçu en angleterre, au moins de nos jours, et que tôt ou tard ce coup lui sera mortel.[10]

He was to be proved right, although not till many years later. For all their speculative guise, Mill's criticisms of intuitionism are at root political in motive. Mill's struggle to free himself from his early closeness to intuitionism must also have added some personal bias.

Thus there was strong motivation for both critiques of the opposing school. On Coleridge's side there was the long habit of theology and the passion for personal salvation, and on Mill's the equal passion for political reform and the history of tangled loyalties.

II

When Coleridge passed beyond his early attraction to the philosophy of the eighteenth century he only did so gradually and he never abandoned it entirely; the process was rather one of adding the

---

[8]*Collected Works of John Stuart Mill*, ed. F.E.L.Priestley, Vols.XII and XIII, "The Earlier Letters, 1812-1848," ed. F.E.Mineka (University of Toronto Press, 1963), XIII, 575. Subsequently referred to as Works, XII or XIII.

[9]*Autobiography*, p.225.

[10]*Works*, XIII, 530.

new truths of intuitionism to what was valuable in associationism. In 1801 Coleridge made the famous announcement that he had "overthrown the doctrine of Association" and this was to be the gateway to great solutions. He now hoped "to evolve all the five senses . . . & in this evolvement to solve the process of Life & Consciousness."[11] He was thus hoping to master the problem which both Mill and Hamilton were to agree to leave as the final mystery. A bold hope indeed.

In reality, Coleridge at first seems to have merely altered the mode of association to make feeling, and not temporal conjunction, the operative force.

> I hold, that association depends in a much greater degree on the recurrence of resembling states of Feeling, than on Trains of Idea/ that the recollection of early childhood in latest old age depends on & is explicable by this – & if this be true, Hartley's System totters. . . . I almost think, that Ideas *never* recall Ideas, as far as they are Ideas – any more than Leaves in a forest create each other's motion – The Breeze it is that runs thro' them/ it is the Soul, the state of Feeling.[12]

But the implied distinction between these two – that time is a matter of external chance occurrence and that feeling is an inner and directing force – is not explored. He merely insists on the supremacy of feelings. Coleridge's half-formed new theory is strikingly similar to Mill's at the same stage of transition between two systems. When Mill was unable to explain the creative powers of the mind by association he developed a second type of association, by feeling, to help. Coleridge, faced with a similar inadequacy in associational theory for the similar problem of explaining creativity, finds a similar solution. But the solution was a contradictory one. Association by feeling is no longer association, so Coleridge dropped association for all but simple aspects of mental activity, and Mill dropped his struggles with the problems of creativity. Coleridge continued to unravel the phenomena of association in his journals, but his philosophy considered it no longer

---

[11]*Collected Letters of Samuel Taylor Coleridge*, ed. E.L.Griggs, 4 vols. (Oxford, Clarendon, 1956-1959), II, 706. Subsequently referred to as *Letters*.

[12]*Ibid.*, 961.

an adequate explanation of mental activity.[13]

Mill's acquaintance with the intuitionist school other than the English Coleridgeans, was not extensive. He had explored post-Kantian German philosophy to some extent, partly at Sterling's insistence, He had learnt some German as early as 1825, and he was, at the time of the crisis, deriving much "from the writings of Goethe and the other German authors which I read during those years."[14] He wrote to Comte in 1843 summarizing the effect of this reading on his thought in typically generous terms, though admitting that his knowledge of the school was limited,[15]

> n'ayant moi-même lu ni Kant ni Hegel ni aucun autre des chefs de cet école, que je n'ai d'abord connu que par des interprètes anglais et français. Cette philosophie m'a été, à moi, fort utile; elle a corrigé ce qu'il y avait de trop exclusivement analytique dans mon esprit nourri par Bentham et par les philosophes français du 18me siècle: ajoutez à cela sa critique de l'école négative, et surtout un sens réel quoique trop incomplet des lois historiques et de la filiation des divers états de l'homme et de la société, sens qui est, je crois, le plus développé chez Hegel.[16]

John Sterling tried to persuade Mill to read the 'Germans' before revising his *Logic*. Although Mill considered the force of Sterling's urgings carefully, he decided against a major study of German logic before completing his own work, on the grounds that "their way of looking at such matters is so very different from mine."[17] But he must have subsequently given in, for he writes to Fox three weeks later, "here is Sterling persuading me that I must read all manner of German Logic which though it goes much against the grain with me, I can in no sort gainsay."[18]

But whatever Mill did read at the time did not increase his sympathy with the general temper of the contemporary German school

---

[13]S.T.Coleridge, *The Notebooks, 1794-1808*, ed. K. Coburn, 4 vols. (London, Routledge & Kegan Paul, 1957), I, entry 1770; see also Paul Deschamps, *La Formation de la Pensée de Coleridge, 1772-1804* (Paris, Didier, 1964), pp.420, 516.

[14]*Autobiography*, p.153.

[15]Charles Mackinnon Douglas, *John Stuart Mill, A Study of his Philosophy* (Edinburgh, W.Blackwood and Sons, 1895), p.157.

[16]*Works*, XIII, 576.

[17]*Ibid.*, 459.

[18]*Ibid.*, p.455.

of philosophy. After a brief period when their contrast to Benthamism was a useful aid to him in balancing his mind, he invariably regarded them as "injurious influences."[19] The reason was, he explained,

> that philosophy of this cast admitted of easy adaptation, and would bend to the very Thirty-nine Articles; as it is the essence of a philosophy which seeks its evidence in internal conviction, that it bears its testimony with equal ease for any conclusions in favour of which there is a predisposition.[20]

The German school, he felt, had been marked by a dangerous geometrical spirit from the time of

> Spinoza, who gave to his system the very forms as well as the entire spirit of geometry; through the mathematician Leibnitz, who reigned supreme over the German speculative mind for above a generation; with its spirit temporarily modified by the powerful intellectual individuality of Kant, but flying back after him to its uncorrected tendencies, the geometrical spirit went on from bad to worse, until in Schelling and Hegel the laws even of physical nature were deduced by ratiocination from subjective deliverances of the mind.[21]

It was Hegel whom Mill singled out in particular as the representative of all that was bad in his version of the German tradition. He,

> found by actual experience of Hegel that controversy with him tends to deprave one's intellect. The attempt to unwind an apparently infinite series of self-contradictions not disguised but openly faced, really, if persisted in, impairs the acquired delicacy of perception of false reasoning and false thinking which has been gained by years of careful mental discipline with terms of real meaning.[22]

It is hardly surprising that Mill was no pioneer in the study of German logic. The irritation of a mind proud of its lucidity dominates his responses.

Mill picks on Hegel's concept of 'being' as an example of the misuse of language he regards as common to all intuitionism. Hegel's confusions he thinks come from

---

[19]*Logic*, II, 446; see also J.S.Mill, *Three Essays on Religion* (London, Longmans, Green, and Co., 1885), p.163. Subsequently referred to as *Three Essays on Religion*.

[20]*Dissertations and Discussions*, II, 456-457.

[21]*An Examination of Sir William Hamilton's Philosophy*, 5th ed. (London, Longmans, Green, Reader, and Dyer, 1878), p.628. Subsequently referred to as *Hamilton*.

[22]*The Letters of John Stuart Mill*, ed. H.S.R.Elliott, 2 vols. (London, Longmans, Green, and Co., 1910), II, 93.

overlooking this double meaning of the word *to be*; from supposing
that when it signifies *to exist*, and when it signifies to *be* some
specific thing . . . it must still, at bottom, answer to the same idea
. . . It was from overlooking this that Hegel . . . arrived at the self-
contradictory proposition on which he founded all his philosophy,
that Being is the same as nothing.[23]

It is interesting that Coleridge, who like Mill found that he had
soon to put Hegel down unfinished, diagnosed the same wanton
confusion between the meanings of the word to be.[24] Here the English
inheritance of both Mill and Coleridge came into contact with Hegel,
and both alike rejected him for the same reason.

Thus Mill's acquaintance with intuitionism led in the end to its
rejection. Coleridge's acquaintance with associationism had also ended
in rejection. Here then, are two thinkers whose criticisms of what they
saw as the opposing doctrine are based on experience.

III

The criticisms of Hartley which Coleridge formulated after his
disentanglement from associationism are trenchant indeed. Had
Hartley's theory been a true one, he tells us,

the consequence would have been, that our whole life would be
divided between the despotism of outward impressions, and that of
senseless and passive memory. Take his law in its highest abstraction
and most philosophical form, viz. that every partial representation
recalls the total representation of which it was a part; and the law
becomes nugatory, were it only for its universality. In practice it
would indeed be mere lawlessness . . . If therefore we suppose the
absence of all interference of the will, reason and judgement, one or
other of two consequences must result. Either the ideas, (or reliques
of such impression,) will exactly imitate the order of the impression
itself, which would be absolute *delirium*: or any one part of that
impression might recall any other part . . . without a cause present
to determine *what* it should be.[25]

Coleridge's argument is hardly sympathetic. Nor is its analytic

[23]*Logic*, I, 86, 113n.

[24]A.D.Snyder, *Coleridge on Logic and Learning* (New Haven, Yale University Press,
1929), pp.162-163.

[25]S.T.Coleridge, *Biographia Literaria*, ed. J.Shawcross, 2 vols. (Oxford, Clarendon, 1907), I,
77.

stance successful. The associated memory which exactly imitates the order of experience would be the very opposite of delirium. For delirium might be defined as sensations in a chaotic, or nonsensical order. But the idea of 'chaos' or 'nonsense' means in an empirical context, 'an unusual order' or an order never found in primary experience. That is, delirium is experience in the order in which it has never occurred, whereas memory is the order in which experience did occur and is, on this analysis, equivalent to non-delirium. Hume similarly concludes that the uniformity which we come to assume in the operation of the 'laws' of cause and effect consists merely of a constant conjunction, or sequence; thus coherence in the external events of nature depends on invariable sequence. Therefore, it might be argued against Coleridge, coherence is merely invariable sequence, in this coherence is created purely by memory, which is the faculty which enables us to experience invariable sequence.

Coleridge, however, argues on, ignoring the possibility of such a retort, "thus, as materialism has been generally taught, it is utterly unintelligible, and owes all its proselytes to the propensity so common among men, to mistake distinct images for clear conceptions."[26] He determines to, "apply the plain rules of common logic to the existing Theories of the Corpuscular Philosophy . . . and expose its unimaginable images, and all the blind-work of its mere verbiage."[27]

Typically, he ignores the contemporary exponents of the doctrine and returns to its fountainheads, Locke and Berkeley, for the substance of his attack. He first formulated his ideas in an extended criticism of Locke, to whom he was rather unfair.[28] Coleridge argued that Locke was in no way original.

> Ask what Locke did, & you will be told if I mistake not, that he overthrew the Notion, generally held before his time, of Innate Ideas, and deduced all our knowledge from experience . . . these Innate Ideas were Men of Straw . . . Locke's *System* existed in the writings of Descartes; not merely that it is deductible from them, but that it

---

[26] *Ibid.*, 91.

[27] *Letters*, IV, 807.

[28] D.G.James, "The Thought of Coleridge," in *The Major English Romantic Poets, A Symposium in Reappraisal*, ed. C.D.Thorpe, Carlos Baker and Bennet Weaver (Carbondale, Southern Illinois University Press, 1957), p.107.

exists in them, *actually*, and *explicitly*.[29]

The three long letters to Josiah Wedgewood complete the destructive criticism, proving firstly that there is nothing in Locke that was not previously, and better, expressed in Descartes; and secondly that Locke's work did not, in fact, explain sensation, and is often mere verbiage.

Coleridge also developed a critique of Berkeley's sensationalism, which applied to all similar forms of the doctrine. He argues that Berkeley confuses sensation and developed perception[30] and demonstrates that in empiricism the 'perception' is taken as the 'thing' which results in just that insecurity with respect to the real ontological status of the perceived which we noted was inherent in almost all Mill's discussions. The perceived becomes,

> a strange *ens hybridum* betwixt real and logical, and partaking of both; namely, it *is*, yet it is not as this or that, but as sensation per se; i.e. the *perceptum*, surviving its annihilation, borrows the name by which, in its least degree, it has been distinguished and commences a new genus without species or individual. . . .The error here noted is only one of a host that necessarily arise out of having only *one* starting point, viz. the lowest.[31]

It is a criticism which is still respectable.

The result of all philosophy of mechanism, then, is that it is ultimately incoherent and explains nothing, that it "leads, as we have seen, to its own confutation, and scorpion like destroys itself while the tail, turning round in its torture, infixes the poisoned sting in its head."[32]

IV

If Coleridge's critique of associationism, mixes rhetorical attacks with pin-points of accurate insight, Mill's critique of intuitionism, is, by contrast, made of the steady questions of common sense and clarity. His attack starts with the traditional complaint of the empiricist about

---

[29]*Letters*, II, 686.

[30]J.H.Muirhead, *Coleridge as Philosopher* (London, Allen & Unwin, 1954), p.76.

[31]Quoted by *Ibid.*, p.77 from MS C., p.10.

[32]Snyder, *op.cit.*, p.130; see also *Biographia Literaria*, I, 80-88.

the absurdities of the language the idealist uses. "Metaphysics," he calls, "that fertile field of delusion propagated by language."[33] These delusions are understandable, since words and things are so continually associated as to endow words with apparently self-evident reality,[34] but they are not excusable. It is the profession of the philosopher to analyse and avoid such delusions, and the intuitionist who, not content in failing in his duty of precision exploits the common credulity, is unforgivable. As Mill remarks, with evident irritation, the result is that,

> an error which seemed finally refuted and dislodged from thought, often needs only put on a new suit of phrases, to be welcomed back to its old quarters, and allowed to repose unquestioned for another cycle of ages.[35]

A good example of this is his criticism of Hamilton's concept of the absolute, which uses the term 'absolute', properly only an adjective, as a noun. "The word is devoid of meaning," Mill writes,

> unless in reference to predicates of some sort. What is absolute must be absolutely something; absolutely this or absolutely that ... If we are told therefore that there is some one Being who is, or which is, The Absolute – not something absolute, but the Absolute itself, – the proposition can be understood in no other sense than that the supposed Being possess in absolute completeness *all* predicates; is absolutely good, and absolutely bad; absolutely wise, and absolutely stupid; and so forth.[36]

Mill also cites Hegel as an example of the same error, which, in Mill's view, he exacerbates until it reduces his philosophy to an absurdity. Hegel's whole philosophic edifice is but, "a good example of the bewildering effect of putting nonsensical abstractions in the place of concrete realities."[37] The sort of dialectical paradox, so dear to Coleridge, which seeks to explain the sense of unity in diversity, is given scant respect by Mill.

> If there is any meaning in the words, must not Absolute Unity be Absolute Totality, which is the highest degree of Plurality? There is no escape from the alternative; the Absolute either means a single

[33] *Logic*, I, 143.
[34] *Ibid.*, II, 251.
[35] *Ibid.*, I, 200.
[36] *Hamilton*, p.59.
[37] *Ibid.*, p.62.

atom or monad, or it means Plurality in the extremest degree.[38]

And in this logical prison with no escape Mill hopes to suffocate Hegel, and all the post-Kantian intuitionists.

The supposed attributes of the deity are equally alluring targets for this sort of comment. If Mill had little time for the absoluteness and unity of God, the goodness attributed to him is the butt of some of Mill's most eloquent derision, and is the occasion for one of the proudest and most famous outbursts of the enraged reason. Mill writes,

> That we cannot understand God, that his ways are not our ways; that we cannot scrutinize or judge his councils – propositions which, in a reasonable sense of the terms, could not be denied by any Theist – have often been tendered as reasons why we may assert any absurdities and any moral monstrosities concerning God, and miscall them Goodness and Wisdom.[39]

The problem of evil forced Mill into Manicheanism, and the proud assertion that "I will call no being good, who is not what I mean when I apply that epithet to my fellow-creatures; and if such a being can sentence me to hell for not so calling him, to hell I will go."[40] Mill probably thought this assertion a safe one. What he is really trying to say, however, would seem to be that metaphysics should be abandoned as an impossible science.

The diagnosis of absurdity which Mill makes was to become, during the century, the common one; and before Mill wrote his proud challenge, Kierkegaard was answering for him. In some sense, Coleridge with his less rigid, and more human mind, perceived emotionally that this paradox had to be accepted. But Mill's bravery, social if not supernatural, stood as a beacon for many, just as Coleridge's verbal entanglements quieted and guided many of the other school.

The result of the misuse of language which led to meaningless absurdities like the 'goodness of the absolute' was that, in Mill's view, almost all the premises of the more sophisticated intuitionist arguments depended on their conclusions. He thus analyses Whewell's ethics into three "vicious circles", each one more vicious and "wonderful" than the last, and concludes that, "every attempt to dress up an appeal to

---

[38]*Ibid.*, p.65.
[39]*Ibid.*, pp.112-113.
[40]*Ibid.*, p.129.

intuition in the form of reasoning, must break down in the same manner. The system must, from the conditions of the case, revolve in a circle.[41]

The crucial circularities of intuitionism, are the ethical theories which

> first take for their standard of moral truth what, being the general, they deem to be the natural or instinctive sentiments and perceptions of mankind, and then explain away the numerous instances of divergences from their assumed standard, by representing them as cases in which the perceptions are unhealthy.[42]

This circle is indeed a vicious one from the reforming sociologist's viewpoint. The argument, supposedly deriving custom from nature is, in reality, equating nature to custom, and providing an apparently unbreakable rationale for conservatism.

Circular arguments in ethics are, Mill concludes, a mark of what he calls intuitionism. There is, he realizes,

> all too strong a tendency to mistake mutual coherency for truth; to trust one's safety to a strong chain though it has no point of support ... All experience bears testimony to the enthralling effect of neat concatenation in a system of doctrines, and the difficulty with which people admit the persuasion that anything which holds so well together can possibly fall.[43]

Mill's irritation seems to be softened by his understanding of the familiar plight.

Another aspect of intuitionist assumptions, which Mill believes to be a mistaken foundation to much of their thinking, is the belief that there is a relation of whatever sort between the conceivable and the real. This belief, at various levels of sophistication, is characteristic of many forms of idealism, from the time of Berkeley to Fichte and Hegel's complex systems of dialectical digestion of the real by the conceived. Mill's answers, if they avoid the brutality of Johnson's kick at the all too solid stone, still take the familiar line of the common sense reply of empiricism. Many of the errors of philosophy, he claims, are a result of assuming that the relationships between our own mental events correspond to relationships in external events, or, to express the

---

[41]*Dissertations and Discussions*, II, 490; see also *Hamilton*, pp.167-168.
[42]*Logic*, II, 408.
[43]*Ibid.*, 403.

idea in a common, and to Mill "most undistinguished", form, "Things which we cannot think of together, cannot coexist; and Things which we cannot help thinking of together, must coexist."[44]

It is these fallacies which Mill finds pervading all forms of idealism from Descartes and his disciples to Spinoza, Leibnitz and the subsequent German school of his own time. The fallacy is so common that it,

> has been the cause of two-thirds of the bad philosophy, and especially of the bad metaphysics, which the human mind has never ceased to produce. . . . mysticism is neither more nor less than ascribing objective existence to the subjective creations of our own faculties.[45]

The sweeping generalisation, right or wrong, is an index of Mill's annoyance at the prevalence of a doctrine so fundamentally opposed to his own assumptions.

Even in the methodology of science, Mill finds the same belief at work in the common criterion that "'nature always acts by the simplest means', *i.e.* by those which are most easily conceivable."[46] Mill's distinction between conceptual elegance and real simplicity is an important aspect of his scientific methodology and one which still represents a formidable crux in the analysis of any hypothesis.[47]

But as well as these simpler, almost instinctive forms, there were, of course, a large variety of ways in which the belief in a relation between the conceivable and the real was held. Even if the cruder claim that the mind immediately knows the truth is abandoned – and some intuitionists were aware of the force of Mill's objection that this would and did merely tend to consecrate prejudice – there were many lesser claims.

Mill takes Hamilton as the exponent of one of the more sophisticated versions of the belief. Hamilton's assertions, he believes, whatever the care of their formulation, in the end destroy the distinction between belief and knowledge.[48] In any case, "as beings of

---

[44]*Ibid.*, 319.

[45]*Ibid.*, 320, 326.

[46]*Ibid.*, 324.

[47]See K.R.Popper, *The Logic of Scientific Discovery* (London, Hutchinson, 1959), pp.136-145.

[48]*Hamilton*, p.151.

limited experience, we must always and necessarily have limited conceptive powers."[49] Thus this universal assumption of intuitionism, which is, Mill believes, "the foundation (among others) of the systems of Schelling and Hegel" is both illogical and over-confident. "An assumption more destitute of evidence could scarcely be made,"[50] he concludes.

Mill's own philosophy asserts what is a fundamentally opposite doctrine. The whole problem of the relation between subject and object is collapsed by the assertion that the relation is of no concern because it cannot be explored in the framework of an empirical epistemology. Experience merely informs us of the existence of mental events, and of no more. Mill thus takes refuge from the metaphysical problems of idealism in ever stricter empiricism. His epistemology here reaches the totality of the claim that,

> the existence, therefore, of a phenomenon, is but another word for its being perceived, or for the inferred possibility of perceiving it.[51]

Matter, Mill ultimately claims, can be defined, and only defined as "a Permanent Possibility of Sensation,"[52] a formulation which he claims to be consistent with a correct interpretation of Berkeley and to represent the strongest claim to an ontology of which developed psychological empiricism is capable.

Behind these, the logical objections to intuitionism, there lay also a personal objection to the belief in the unity of the world and the human spirit. Thus, in the *Three Essays on Religion*, Mill argues that nature, far from being the measure of the good and 'natural', is often morally bad.[53] Mill's sense of the discrepancy between the human mind and the world was very strong. At the time of the crisis he even seems to have believed that his misery was due, not to his own difficulties in the process of adjustment, but to the "flaw in life itself,"[54] the imperfection of the world; a reversal of associationism and adoption of

---

[49]*Logic*, II, 321; see also Reginald Jackson, *An Examination of the Deductive Logic of John Stuart Mill* (London, Oxford University Press, 1941), p.184.

[50]*Hamilton*, p.85.

[51]*Logic*, II, 143.

[52]*Hamilton*, p.233.

[53]*Three Essays on Religion*, pp.18-21, 46, 62.

[54]*Autobiography*, p.145.

characteristically Romantic attitudes.

This declaration of independence for the ideals of the mind was the emotional obverse of the rational face of Mill's objection to intuitionism. Mill recovered from those depths of despair, but his stringent empiricism remained as much a temper of mind, as a philosophical conviction. It contrasts very sharply with Coleridge's instinctive sense of unity, deeply religious idealism, and Romantic love of all natural phenomena.

Mill's criticisms of the language and epistemological assumptions of intuitionism take the common line of a reduction of the opposing arguments to a simple form which displays any absurdities they contain, followed by a re-assertion of an opposite epistemology which avoids these pitfalls. But he is curiously, and perhaps indicatively, concerned not to discuss the question of the activity or passivity of the mind in perception, which would appear to be one of the main cruxes separating him from intuitionism. It is, after all, the stumbling block of the epistemology he claims to hold that it does not seek to explain the activity of the mind, as it is the success of Kant's that it does. Mill, however, rejects the problem as not his concern, since he is dealing with logic; he regards the ultimate questions of consciousness as for the time being insoluble, and maintains, outside areas where his politics require assertions to be made, the strictest relativism. He regards the intuitionists' distinction between active and passive as "elaborately" drawn and insists that, for the purpose of logic, they are both "states of mind" and the difference is of "secondary importance."[55]

In fact, Mill had available a conceptual tool which might have made light work of this distinction, though he does not seem to have taken advantage of it. In discussing cause and effect he points out the deficiency of the common view which distinguishes between the active, causative factor and the passive, affected factor. The distinction depends, he claims, on a false wish to locate the effect exclusively in one or other of the interacting factors. The cause and its location can be, as in the cases of gravitational or magnetic attraction, equal and opposite. This model of gravity could have been applied to epistemology. Only custom locates the activity exclusively in the

---

[55]*Logic*, I, 58-59; see also *Hamilton*, pp.466-467.

perceiver or the perceived. Mill could have argued on the analogy of gravity that such an exclusive location was erroneous.[56] The argument has been developed in more recent times with considerable success for the empiricist cause, and, despite a superficial resemblance to the Schellingean-Coleridgean idea of the unity of subject and object in perception, it would have been for Mill a useful stage in the process of discrediting such a metaphysics.

But Mill did not develop this argument, and contented himself merely with a dogmatic insistence on the unimportance of the problem. He thus brushes aside the difficulty in epistemology on which Coleridge's thought pivoted and on which his own hesitated. It had cost him considerable effort to reconcile his father's *Analysis* with his own scrupulous enquiries, and in some areas his queries were never to be resolved. He had taken a position, indeed, which was based on the claim that they never could be solved, but might be safely assumed. But it is open to us to doubt if the reason was perhaps that here the real danger to empiricism lay, and Mill's overriding political concerns persuaded him to declare the question unanswerable, since he could not answer it.

There were other problems which Mill did face. He dealt with the delusion of language and the belief in the reality of mental ideas which he found ready targets. He also attacked the problem of the activity of the mind in method which he found impregnable, for he had to face the more sophisticated arguments for intuitionism which had been born out of Hume's empiricism. From Mill's point of view, coming to Kant's synthetic a priori categories after Coleridge, they were both extensions and refinements of Coleridge's belief in the activity of the mind. Mill realised in his treatment of intuitionism in the extended essay on Hamilton, that he must face and find some answer to the structure which Kant had erected on the grave of Hume's empiricism.

Kant claims that certain abstractions are synthetic a priori categories through which the world is interpreted by the mind. The main examples are the forms of sensibility, space and time, and the categories of the understanding such as causation and certain

---

[56]Robert McRae, "Phenomenalism and J.S.Mill's Theory of Causation," *Philosophy and Phenomenological Research*, IX (1948-49), 240.

mathematical truths. Mill sets out to claim that each of these are not a priori but empirical in origin. He wishes to prove that there is not,

> any necessity to assume . . . a peculiar fundamental law of the mind to account for the feeling of infinity inherent in our conceptions of space and time; that apparent infinity is sufficiently accounted for by simpler and universally acknowledged laws.[57]

Causation, for instance, he agrees to be "coextensive with human experience,"[58] but, he says, this does not endow it with any special status as a universal. Maintaining his usual strict relativity of knowledge, he attempts to prove that the concept of causation is derived solely from experience. Whatever its status, he insists that this category cannot be used to adduce a metaphysical origin for the world, since "it is *events*, that is to say, *chance*, not substances, that are subject to the law of Causation."[59]

Mill deals at great length with the ontological status of mathematical generalisations, which is one of the key examples of the synthetic a priori in Kant. Mill argues that,

> this character of necessity, ascribed to the truths of mathematics and even . . . the peculiar certainty attributed to them, is an illusion; in order to sustain which, it is necessary to suppose that those truths relate to, and express the propensities of purely imaginary objects.[60]

Mill explains the reason for this illusion by talking about geometry.[61] He tries to argue that mathematical ideas are merely generalisations, built up from experience of particulars in the normal way. They are, however, more precise than other generals, and less open to modification. They thus appear, in rather the same way as accustomed inferences in morals, to be intuitive truths. But their superior certainty is a matter of quantity, not a difference of quality. But Mill's arguments of this point are among his least satisfactory achievements, and have led commentators to claim that his

[57] *Logic*, I, 277.
[58] *Ibid.*, 376.
[59] *Hamilton*, p.366; see also *Logic*, II, 95.
[60] *Logic*, I, 258.
[61] *Ibid.*, 259.

understanding of mathematics was severely limited.[62]

Mill's main argument against Kant is contained in his more general argument against the reality of universals and the function of the mind in method. Kant's system depends on a conception of method, familiar through Coleridge, in which the mind's initial contribution is an a priori universal, which is subsequently modified by a sensation. Mill insists on an opposite interpretation of method.

> The conceptions, then, which we employ for the colligation and methodization of facts, do not develop themselves from within, but are impressed upon the mind from without; they are never obtained otherwise than by way of comparison and abstraction, and, in the most important and the most numerous cases, are evolved by abstraction from the very phenomena which it is their office to colligate.[63]

Considerable space is devoted to this point in the *Logic*, and Mill sets out in detail how he believes this method yields generals.

> Our conceptions, though they may be clear, are not *appropriate* for our purpose, unless the properties we comprise in them are those which will help us towards what we wish to understand . . . We cannot, therefore, frame good general conceptions beforehand. That the conception we have obtained is the one we want, can only be known when we have done the work for the sake of which we wanted it . . . Yet such premature conceptions we must be continually making up, in our progress to something better. They are an impediment to the progress of knowledge, only when they are permanently acquiesced in. When it has become our habit to group things in wrong classes. . . when, in the belief that these badly-made classes are those sanctioned by Nature, we refuse to exchange them for others. . . This is what. . . the world in general does in morals and politics to the present day. It would thus, in my view of the matter, be an inaccurate mode of expression to say, that obtaining appropriate conceptions is a condition precedent to generalization.[64]

Mill's model of generalization leaves open to question just what forms the original purpose or motive. The work is done only when what "we wanted" – and the past tense in Mill's account is important

---

[62]Ernst Cassirer, *The Problem of Knowledge; Philosophy, Science, and History since Hegel*, trans. W.H.Woglom and C.W.Hendel (New Haven, Yale University Press, 1950), p.55; see also John Watson, *Comte, Mill and Spencer* (Glasgow, James Maclehose & Sons, 1895), p.47.

[63]*Logic*, II, 199; see also 202.

[64]*Ibid.*, 208-209.

evidence – is achieved, and this "want" can only be prior to the initiation of the work. Equally, it is evidently Kant's idea also that the generalizations should be modified by experience; this is what Kant himself means when he says that they are synthetic, and not analytic, a prioris. The point which can be best attacked in Kant's argument is the possibility of the synthetic a priori as such. The central criticism that this may be a contradiction in terms itself, Mill does not make.

Mill's own statements about generalization, here and elsewhere, are also open to some uncertainties. Thus Mill claims that there are some generals which are exactly true, though they originate by induction.[65] The exact status implied by "exactly true," particularly with regard to its proof is uncertain. It is doubtful whether Mill in fact regarded the ultimate laws of nature as open to complete certainty, as he in some places seems to be suggesting. The deductive method, Mill claims, is fully applicable to these perfect generalizations, but he seems to be ignoring the fact that all inductions must be incomplete, if they are of a general nature, and that perfection can only be claimed if a different sanction than induction, which would have to be a priori, is claimed for it. Thus Mill's criticisms of Kantian thought cannot be said to be conclusive.

V

The ethics of Mill and Coleridge follow the same outlines as their epistemologies. Coleridge however, although his opposition to utilitarianism can be presumed, did not devote the energy and space to a criticism of the ethics of empiricism that he had given to its methodology. Undoubtedly this was in part due to the relative crudity of the utilitarianism he knew. It is the ethics of Paley and Godwin, not the refinements of Mill, which Coleridge criticises. Thus, although what he has to say is at times pointed, it is not sustained, and although he presents what he regards as insurmountable objections to the "greatest happiness" principle, he provides no concrete alternative system, such as Kant's analysis of duty. Indeed in practice he even seems to employ a utilitarian principle as his criterion.

[65]*Ibid.*, I, 265.

Coleridge's technique in attacking utilitarianism is to demonstrate that the original proposition is a truism in so far as it is loosely understood; and, if analysed closely, reveals a fundamental incoherence in its main terms. Thus the "greatest happiness" principle is one accepted by "every one of us." But the word "happiness" is totally uninformative in this context.

> Don't you see the ridiculous absurdity of setting up *that* as a princple or motive of action which is, in fact, a necessary and essential instinct of our very nature – an inborn and inextinguishable desire? How can creatures susceptible of pleasure and pain do otherwise than desire happiness? But, *what* happiness? That is the question.[66]

It is then easy for Coleridge to show that concepts of happiness present a diversity so bewildering that no practical prescriptive morality could ever come from the axiom. He is perhaps too quick to claim that "there is no escaping this absurdity, unless you come back to a standard of reason and duty," but substantially he has shown that the vagueness of the concept of "happiness" is a weak point in utilitarianism.[67]

In a similar manner Coleridge produces destructive criticisms of the common notions of "self" and of "motive." The utilitarian self was merely "the semblance produced by an aggregate on the mind of the beholder."[68] But if there is a real self it must be anterior to all the perceptions which go to make it up. Coleridge argues that body is neither the first, nor the ultimate location of the real self. Body is a location of sensations, but the child's self included his mother, and our self includes society. Thus the concept of "self" shows an instability under analysis which renders it a difficult foundation for any system of ethics.

He deals similarly with the idea of "motive."

> For what is a motive? Not a thing, but the thought of a thing. But as all thoughts are not motives, in order to specify the class of thoughts we must add the predicate, 'determining' and a motive

[66]S.T.Coleridge, *The Table Talk and Omniana*, ed. T.Ashe (London, G.Bell and Sons, 1923), pp.134-135.

[67]S.T.Coleridge, *The Table Talk and Omniana*, ed. T.Ashe (London, G.Bell and Sons, 1923), pp.134-135.

[68]Quoted by Muirhead, *op.cit.*, p.143.

must be defined a determining thought.[69]

Thus the concept of "motive", as with that of "self" and "happiness" proves to be unhelpful. Utilitarianism in Coleridge's view has merely changed the names without explaining the meanings. Very often, of course, it was Godwin who was the butt of this attack on rationalistic morality. Coleridge had in fact planned a small volume,

> to shew not only the absurdities and wickedness of *his* System, but to detect what appear to me the defects of all the systems of morality before & since Christ. . . \My last Chapter will attack the credulity, superstition, calumnies, and hypocrisy of the present race of Infidels.[70]

But the volume – it hardly surprises us – and the attacks remained fragments. There are similar fragments of a criticism of Paley, whom Coleridge disliked with added fervour because of his attempts to subsume Christianity under an infidel ethics. Interestingly, Mill rejected Paley's ideas as vigorously as Coleridge did, although Mill is essentially in Paley's tradition. A dislike of the tradition in extreme forms is one of the ambiguities which troubled Mill's utilitarianism.

Coleridge's critique of Paley, and any morality which depends on external effects to make moral judgements, is drawn from a distinction between morality and law. Morality is the inner, law the outer criterion. We cannot judge by consequences and not inner causes, because the effect depends on the talent of the agent as well as his intentions, because "Providence" modifies the effects, and because some of these effects are inner, that is the total consequences include the effects on the psychology of the agent. Finally, Coleridge argues that to separate the agent from his act, the subject from the object, in the artificial manner of the Utilitarians is philosophically indefensible. Schelling had taught Coleridge to believe that there was a unity between subject and object which he now applied to morality.[71]

---

[69]Snyder, *op.cit.*, p.132.

[70]*Letters*, I, 267-268.

[71]S.T.Coleridge, *The Friend*, ed. Barbara E.Rooks, 2 vols. (London, Routledge & Kegan Paul, 1969), I, 317-318.

VI

Coleridge's critique of utilitarianism, and his criticism of epistemological empiricism, form the two main strands of his dislike of what he lumped together under the undignified epithet of "mechanico-corpuscular"; an epithet as undignified as (and perhaps the model for) Mill's own description of Coleridge's thought as "Germanico-Coleridgean." Some of Coleridge's criticisms are beyond doubt serious ones that tear destructively at the fabric of mechanism. But his positive ideas are few and the program which he attempted to carry out in the *Friend* of rejecting the mechanico-corpuscular philosophy, and inculcating the intuitionist one is not successful. Coleridge, indeed, explains why this should be so. "It is the Intuition, the direct Beholding, the immediate Knowledge, which is the *substance* and true *significance* of all – But to *give* or *convey* to another the *Immediate* is a contradiction in terms." Thus the correct philosophy cannot be taught, and,

> all that a Teacher can do is, 1. to demonstrate the hollowness and falsehood of the Corpuscular Theory and of every other scheme of Philosophy which commences with matter as a *jam datum* . . . 2. to excite the mind to the effort, and to encourage it by sympathy.[72]

Coleridge, then, because of the nature of his subject, can only offer criticisms of the wrong philosophy, and cannot offer to teach proofs of the right one. It is perhaps curious that the young Mill should have felt that this partial and fitful stimulus was a system better than Bentham's. But Coleridge's criticisms do perhaps to a sympathetic interpretation add up to an impressive, if sometimes cloudy, display of insight.

By contrast Mill's criticism of intuitionism is much more systematic. But political motivation made him base it on a crude view of intuitionism. Intuitionism may claim that ideas are inner givens, but it does not necessarily claim that humanity lives up to these insights. Mill's claim that it would always discover the ideal to be the existing in morals is simply not borne out in practice. His attack on intuitionism was due more to its historical and contemporary

[72]*Letters*, IV, 768.

association with conservatism, than to any prior distaste for its purely philosophical principles.

VII

Any community of aim between Mill and Coleridge may seem difficult to claim after a discussion of their energetic critiques of the opposing schools. But the real targets of this critique in both were the cruder versions of the opposite doctrine, not the eclectically refined versions held by Mill and Coleridge themselves.

Coleridge's ideas were largely formulated if not published in the decade before Mill's ideas started to be widely heard. Coleridge wrote against Paley, Godwin, and the eighteenth century tradition of rational empiricism. That he would not have liked Mill's version of that tradition seems likely enough, although his increasing radicalism may have given such un-sectarian documents as *On Liberty* a sympathetic audience on Highgate Hill.

Mill on the other hand could well have chosen Coleridge as his butt. His criticisms of intuitionism however were directed not against Coleridge, and rarely against Kant, but against Hamilton. Partly this is because Mill believed the roots of intuitionism to lie with "Reid among ourselves" and with "Kant for the rest of Europe;"[73] Coleridge is not mentioned as a leader of the intuitionist school. There are further reasons why it was Hamilton, and not Kant or Coleridge that Mill chose to attack, despite the fact that he recognized Kant as the major thinker, and probably knew Coleridge's writings more completely. Kant, he realized, had considerable elements of the Aristotelian in him, and was in many ways a corrective to the "German spirit." Equally, perhaps Mill's sensitiveness to the role of language in metaphysics prevented him from depending on his knowledge of German by criticising Kant's work.

If Kant was a difficult target because of his considerable subtlety, Coleridge was an impossible one for the sort of public declaration Mill had in mind, because of the difficulty of obtaining a consistent doctrine to attack. Mill also probably avoided Coleridge's work because it was

[73]*Hamilton*, p.1.

an unhappy name to be associated with for a number of reasons. Mill
had also recognized in Coleridge something more than a fragmentary
intuitionism, an original eclecticism, for otherwise there was still good
reason to attack the one who was, at least in the circles Mill knew, one
of the most influential of all the opposing leaders.

Most of Mill's arguments are directed against two epistemological
doctrines, intuitionism and pseudo-relativism. Coleridge held neither of
them in any pure form. He believed in the innate Idea, but Coleridge's
Idea, firmly based in Plato rather than in Fichte and Hegel, acquired
an "organic" element and an English empiricism which placed it close
to Mill's own ideas of self-development. Equally Coleridge's lack of
clarity and system had great value as a defence. Hamilton's system
invites criticism of Mill's carefully marshalled type.[74] Political reasons
also pointed to Hamilton as the butt. He was most likely to affect the
minds of the new generation of young men at the Universities, and so
delay the reforms Mill lived for.

Mill does on rare occasions criticize Coleridge, but only in passing,
and he never turns his criticism into a general one. Thus, talking of
"fallacies of simple inspection" Mill writes,

> I have given a variety of instance in which the natural prejudice, that
> causes and their effects must resemble one another, has operated in
> practice so as to give rise to serious errors ... Coleridge in his
> *Biographia Literaria* (note, Vol.i, chap.8) affirms as an 'evident
> truth' that 'the law of causality holds only between homogeneous
> things, *i.e.* things having some common property,' and therefore
> 'cannot extend from one world into another, its opposite:' hence, as
> mind and matter have no common property, mind cannot act upon
> matter, nor matter upon mind. What is this but the *à priori* fallacy
> of which we are speaking?[75]

But Mill is only using Coleridge as a convenient example. It is not
intended to be a condemnation of Coleridge's method, but only of one
instance of its application. For Mill, at another time, quotes Coleridge
as a critic of this very fallacy of "simple inspection." Thus, in the
Friend in discussing the proverb "Fortune favours fools" Coleridge
"very happily sets forth the manner in which, under the loose mode of
induction which proceeds *per enumerationem simplicem* ... opinions

---

[74]*Logic*, II, 412-413.
[75]*Ibid.*, 341-342.

grow up with the apparent sanction of experience, which have no foundation in the laws of nature at all."[76]

Mill was aware of Coleridge's example and sometimes turned to him when discussing the intuitionism chiefly exemplified by Hamilton or Whewell. But Mill saw in Coleridge more of an eclectic spirit than a dogmatic intuitionist.

VIII

Both Mill and Coleridge had sufficient motive and insight, personal as well as professional, to make perceptive critiques of the opposite systems. Coleridge's early associationism in particular, because it was a more complete commitment to what was to become the other sect, left him as he moved away by stages with a fundamental and experienced knowledge of its defects. Coleridge tries to show that passive association would be mere delirium, and that materialism stands on the gulf of an infinite regress. Sensationalism is shown to be a curiously hybrid philosophy, and utilitarian ethics to depend on uninformative uses of incompletely analysed common words, and an inadequate view of human psychology.

Mill for his part has evidently a less extensive if in all probability more systematic acquaintance with the other school. From this knowledge he seizes on the ungrammatical, and hence in his view illogical, use of adjectival words as nouns in intuitionism. He then attacks the belief that any relation subsists between concept and reality, and finally attempts in one of his least successful arguments to irreparably damage the Kantian system of categories by questioning the a priori nature of such judgements as mathematical statements.

Both claim that the other side survives in popular esteem simply because of its superficial clarity. Thus for Coleridge the mechanico-corpuscular philosophy "owes all its proselytes to the propensity so common among men, to mistake distinct images for clear conceptions."[77] Similarly, Mill claims that the success of intuitionism is merely due to the common "tendency to mistake mutual coherency for

---

[76]*Ibid.*, II, 347-348.
[77]*Biographia Literaria*, I, 91.

truth."[78] Both Mill and Coleridge seem to regard depth of analysis a better quality than clarity of surface.

[78]*Logic*, II, 403.

5 Communities of ideas

I looked forward, through the present age of loud disputes but generally weak convictions, to a future which shall unite ... convictions ... firmly grounded in reason and in the true exigencies of life. — John Stuart Mill[1]

The strongest argument for Xstianity, the weak Argument that do yet persuade so many to believe – i.e. it fits the human heart. — S.T.Coleridge[2]

Mill and Coleridge have opposed epistemologies, and support them by well directed attacks on the opposing systems. It is hardly a promising circumstance for the discovery of communities of ideas. Yet the relation between the two thinkers is not a simple one of opposition. Mill's criticisms were not directed at Coleridge and there were some important parallels. Both, despite their concern with epistemology and the methods of logic, seem to regard logic as a tool, and not an ultimate arbiter. They are both prepared to lay this tool aside when its usefulness seems in doubt. It is not difficult to show that Coleridge relied on feelings and not logic in his "proofs" of religion. The task is, in his case, rather to defend him as a rational thinker at all against the charges of commentators such as Wellek, who believe him to be merely a weak and emotional disciple of Jacobi.[3] Mill was also prepared to

---

[1]J.S.Mill, *Autobiography*, 3rd ed. (London, Longmans, Green, Reader, and Dyer, 1874), p.166. Subsequently referred to as *Autobiography*.

[2]S.T.Coleridge, *The Notebooks, 1794-1808*, ed. K.Coburn, 4 vols. (London, Routledge & Kegan Paul, 1957), I, entry 1123.

[3]René Wellek, *Kant in England* (Princeton University Press, 1931), p.132.

admit evidence which displaced the analysis of reason. The resultant difficulties in *Utilitarianism* and *Liberty* have been philosophers' training grounds for over a century.

I

Coleridge's philosophy has been defined as an urgent desire to know God, and a Platonic love of the general principle. But, although he is anxious to reduce everything to principles and rational forms, he is, in many ways, an anti-rationalist. There seems to be a paradox in his writings between his love of principles and his rejection of rationality in favour of the 'needs' of the total human spirit. He tells us that he,

> laboured at a solid foundation on which permanently to ground my opinions in the component faculties of the human mind itself,[4]

and that the *Friend* was written to show,

> the nature and importance of *Principles*. The blindness to which I have long regarded as the Disease of this discussing, calculating, *prudential* age.[5]

"I write," he insisted, "to found true *principles*, to oppose false *principles* in Legislation, Philosophy, Morals, International Law."[6] But Coleridge's insistence on principles, in politics at least, is partly a reaction to Cobbett and other political writers of the day. It has a negative and critical emphasis. He is incensed at the inconsistency and want of principle he finds around him.

> How strange and sad is the laxity with which men in these days suffer the most inconsistent opinions to lie jumbled lazily together in their minds . . . What are these men's minds but a huge lumber-room of *bully*, that is, of incompatible notions brought together by a feeling without a sense of connection?[7]

But when he comes to setting out his own ideas, he is against what

---

[4] S.T.Coleridge, *Biographia Literaria*, ed. J.Shawcross, 2 vols. (Oxford, Clarendon, 1907), I, 14. Subsequently referred to as *Biographia Literaria*.

[5] *The Collected Letters of Samuel Taylor Coleridge*, ed. E.L.Griggs, 4 vols. (Oxford, Clarendon, 1956-1959), III, 129. Subsequently referred to as *Letters*.

[6] *Ibid.*, 141.

[7] S.T.Coleridge, *The Table Talk and Omniana*, ed. T.Ashe (London, G.Bell and Sons, 1923), p.402. Subsequently referred to as *Table Talk*.

he calls 'Jacobinism,' the excessive reliance on principle. Beyond the negative and critical insistence, he regards principles as a means, never an end. The end of philosophy for Coleridge is not the coherence of through-going principles, but rather "to *think*, and by thought to gain Tranquillity!"[8] And this is achieved by making "the reason spread light over our feelings, to make our feelings, with their vital warmth, actualize our reason."[9] The aim, that is, is a unity of our whole being, not just a unity of principle; the aim is to achieve the tranquillity of satisfactory answers.

But in Coleridge, the urgent importance of the end is so emphasized that it eclipses and contradicts the means. The end can be summed up in the word 'reason;' the means is knowledge, but Coleridge warns,

> not that knowledge can of itself do all! The light of religion is not that of the moon, light without heat; but neither is its warmth that of the stove, warmth without light. Religion is the sun.[10]

The light of knowledge cannot of itself achieve the end. That is, perhaps, the whole message of his criticism of utilitarianism. Mill writes in a letter,

> I have known some who have been *rationally* educated, as it is styled. They were marked by a microscopic acuteness; but when they looked at great things, all became blank & they saw nothing – and denied *very illogically* that any thing could be seen; and uniformly put the negation of a power for the possession of a power – & called the want of imagination Judgement, & the never being moved to Rapture Philosophy![11]

Coleridge's philosophy is a philosophy of great things, of Imagination, and of rapture, and where 'logic' conflicts with this Coleridge is, himself, illogical. Thus his belief in religion is closely and proudly grounded on human need, and not on logic. His famous outbursts have a splendour of spirit which is only matched by the horror they must inspire in the logical mind.

Evidences of Christianity! I am weary of the word. Make a man feel

---

[8]S.T.Coleridge,*The Friend*, ed. Barbara E.Rooke, 2 vols. (London, Routledge and Kegan Paul, 1969), I, 56. Subsequently referred to as *Friend*.

[9]*Ibid.*, 108.

[10]*Ibid.*, 106.

[11]*Letters*, I, 354-355.

the *want* of it; rouse him, if you can, to the self knowledge of his *need* of it; and you may safely trust it to its own Evidence.[12]

And, again,

Friend! The truth revealed through Christ has its evidence in itself and the proof of its divine authority in its fitness to our nature and needs.[13]

Coleridge's true evidence for Christianity is "the inward feeling . . . of its exceeding *desirableness* – the experience that he *needs* some-thing."[14] The role of the discursive understanding in all this is real, but subordinate, for, he tells us, "the energies of the intellect . . . are necessary to keep alive the substantial faith in the heart. They are the appointed fuel to the sacred fire."[15]

Mill's reaction to this can be presumed – and yet it may be rash to assume too quickly, for Mill himself could cast aside logic where the needs, in his case politics rather than of religion, conflicted with it. These needs are, in both thinkers, the needs of humanity. Coleridge's outbursts are firmly centered on human needs, not on divine needs; he is far from a religion of sacrifice. An analysis of his more discursive statements of this theme illustrates the complexity of his attitude.

Let the believer never be alarmed by objections wholly speculative, however plausible on speculative grounds such objections may appear, if he can but satisfy himself, that the *result* is repugnant to the dictates of conscience, and irreconcilable with the interests of morality. For to baffle the objector we have only to demand of him, by what right and under what authority he converts a thought into a substance, or asserts the existence of a real somewhat corresponding to a notion not derived from the experience of his senses. It will be of no purpose for him to answer, that it is a *legitimate* notion. The *notion* may have its mould in the understanding; but its realization must be the work of the *Fancy*.[16]

Coleridge is suggesting not an irrational reaction, but a more exact analysis of the arguments used against what the heart needs. In other

[12]S.T.Coleridge, *Aids to Reflection* (London, G.Bell and sons, 1884), p.272. Subsequently referred to as *Aids to Reflection*.

[13]S.T.Coleridge, *Confessions of an Inquiring Spirit*, ed. H.StJ.Hart (London, A.& C.Black, 1956), p.64.

[14]*Biographia literaria*, II, 215.

[15]S.T.Coleridge, "A Lay Sermon," in *Political Tracts of Wordsworth, Coleridge and Shelley*, ed. R.J.White (Cambridge University Press, 1953), p.89.

[16]*Aids to Reflection*, p.111.

passages the foundations of this analysis become clearer. "All motives of hope and fear from invisible powers, which are not immediately derived from, and absolutely coincident with, the reverence due to the supreme reason of the universe, are all alike dangerous superstitions."[17] In *Aids to Reflection* he writes, "my object has been to establish a general rule of interpretation and vindication applicable to *all* doctrinal tenets . . . to provide a *Safety-lamp* for religious inquirers. Now this I find in the principle, that all Revealed Truths are to be judged of by us, as far as they are possible subjects of human conception, on grounds of practice, or in some way connected with our moral and spiritual interests."[18] The "reverence due to the supreme reason" in the first passage is not only fear of God – though it is that – it is also fear of the absurd, of the 'nonsensical'. Coleridge is saying that logic must be constantly checked against real needs.

This rather unstable criterion of 'truth' frequently led Coleridge into absurdities, as when he claims, "I find it wise and human to believe, even on slight evidence, opinions, the contrary of which cannot be proved, & which promote our happiness without hampering our intellect."[19] This, as Wellek is quick to point out, is unworthy. But, on the other hand, Coleridge is sometimes saying what is both modest and wise:

> Tho' the Reason denounces the notion as *superstitious*, & indeed arrogant . . . yet the feeling remains – neither greater or less – common to all men, whatever their opinions may be, and amid all differences of knowledge & understanding. It must therefore be right at the bottom; & probably needs only a wiser interpretation to appear so.[20]

Coleridge's limitations on reason were part of a more general trend in philosophy. He is merely repeating Kant[21] when he claims that, "to set about *proving* the existence of a God by such means is a mere circle, a delusion. It can be no proof to a good reasoner, unless he

---

[17]*Table Talk*, p.369.
[18]*Aids to Reflection*, p.114.
[19]*Letters*, I, 479.
[20]*Ibid.*, II, 1132.
[21]D.G.James, "The Thought of Coleridge," in *The Major English Romantic Poets, A Symposium in Reappraisal*, ed.C.D.Thorpe, Carlos Baker and Bennet Weaver (Carbondale, Southern Illinois University Press, 1957), p.102.

violates all syllogistic logic, and presumes his conclusion."[22] He takes Kant's point that it is as important to know what the understanding "*cannot* do" as what it can, but then goes on to draw the un-Kantian, but very Coleridgean, conclusion that,

> though we are incompetent to give a scientific proof of any other and higher sources of knowledge, it is equally true that no Logic requires us to assert the negative, or enables us to disprove that a position which is neither theoretically undeniable nor capable of being logically *concluded*, may nevertheless be morally *convincing* or even philosophically *evident*.[23]

What Coleridge was, in the end, doing that was different, was to use Christianity as the weapon to make the same point that Kant had made using his critical reason. "Now I do not hesitate to assert, that it was one of the great purposes of Christianity, and included in the process of our Redemption, to rouse and emancipate the soul from this debasing slavery to the outward senses, to awaken the mind to the true *criteria* of reality."[24] He is not, of course, doing anything as common and retrogressive as waving the authority of religion to chase away rationalism. He has his own technical arguments to support his position.

One of them is a philosophy of voluntarism which systematizes the link between ethical religion and motives, or emotions. In *Biographia Literaria* Coleridge describes how,

> I became convinced, that religion, as both the corner stone and the key stone of morality, must have a moral origin; so far at least, that the evidence of its doctrine could not, like the truths of abstract science, be wholly independent of the will.[25]

But René Wellek, one of the least sympathetic of all the scholars who have studied Coleridge deeply, feels that this philosophy is no more than a mystification. "Coleridge's pusillanimity, his lack of confidence in speculative Reason led him to deny to Reason communicability which brings it even more dangerously near to private

---

[22]*Table Talk*, p.274.

[23]A.D.Snyder, *Coleridge on Logic and Learning* (New Haven, Yale University Press, 1929), p.100.

[24]*Aids to Reflection*, p.272.

[25]*Biographia Literaria*, I, 135.

mystical intuition."[26]

Wellek's charges are pinpointed in his assertion that Coleridge is essentially of a kind with Jacobi, and shares the same faults of vague and dangerous irrationalism.[27] It is thus of relevance to see to what extent the question "metaphysician or mystic?" which Muirhead proposes, can be arbitrated in Coleridge's favour. Muirhead believes that the real test of importance is a writer's relation to the real problem of his time, and not his borrowings. He defends Coleridge by analysing what he believes to be the "problem of the age" and the two solutions to it, and tries to show that Coleridge and Jacobi took divergent solutions.[28] Coleridge does, however, sometimes appear to be following Jacobi. But he gives no evidence of hoping to solve his problems by returning to dogmatic faith – his wrestlings with metaphysics are more purposeful than that.

Wellek's and Muirhead's arguments serve to illustrate, as much as anything, the diversity of Coleridge's thinking – a diversity which is, as so many scholars have recognized, merely the obverse of his fragmentary and inconclusive formulations. But what conclusions can be drawn from this? Coleridge, at the least, values the satisfaction of certain real human needs above the satisfaction of the intellect alone. But he is not prepared, as was Jacobi, to abandon the intellect totally, and tries rather to forge a path between the felt needs of conscience, and the dangers of irrationalism. Thus he criticises Jacobi and applies Kant's more subtle argument that the ability to conceive God implies a closer relation than intuition between mind and Noumenon. Coleridge refuses, throughout his writings, to accept a simple intuitionism, basing his ideas on Kant's criticism of perception, which he applies to intuition as well as to sense perception.

Ultimately, undoubtedly, Coleridge gave up reasoning. "Omnia Exeunt In Mysteria," including Coleridge's ethical theory. Love is the root of all, and love must remain "one of the five or six *magna*

---

[26] Wellek, *op.cit.*, p.110.

[27] Elizabeth Winkelman, *Coleridge und die Kantische Philosophie*, Palaestra, 184 Heft (Leipzig, Mayer & Müller, 1933), pp.230-239.

[28] J.H.Muirhead, "Metaphysician or Mystic?" in *Coleridge: Studies by Several Hands*, ed. E.Blunden and E.L.Griggs (London, Constable and Co., 1934), p.185.

mysteria of human nature."[29] But, on his way to this conclusion, he does at least avoid extremes of irrationalism. Although the nearest category for his thought is undoubtedly idealism, he is not an absolute idealist; thus he follows, ultimately, Kant, and not Fichte, in that the idea, for Coleridge, rises from the contact of the mind and the world, not from the mind alone. The aim, he once said, was to unite Plato and Aristotle.[30] He cannot, of course, do it, but he prefers to maintain the tension of both, rather than to adopt a solution which his personal experience feels to be inadequate. He wants to accept and systematize Locke, Hume and Hartley and their conclusion in Kant, as well as Plato, and Schelling. This is, indeed, difficult. But Coleridge, with the eclecticism which is the most lasting characteristic of his mind, is at pains to show that it is not impossible to make a start.

Coleridge claims that although religion is irrational, it is only so in a 'reasonable' way, and with a rational purpose. That this claim involves him in some rather dubious playing with the word 'reason' is easy to show; but 'rational' can have the meaning of useful as much as the idea of consecutively coherent. Coleridge's aim, that is, is descriptive and empirical, in the sense of empiricism which implies insight and not just observation. He leaves it to his reader to decide whether this confusion over the use of the word 'reason' is deliberate sleight of hand, as Wellek would argue, or whether it is a metaphor to express an important perception. Coleridge perhaps means that the transparency of religious enlightenment has the quality of something suddenly and well understood, but incomparably greater, and that this experience partakes both of supreme rationality, and also goes beyond and denies reason. If the vagaries of this belief are disturbing, its successes are elating and contribute as much as anything to his present stature.

One would expect Mill to be opposed to this sort of justification for irrationalism. Nevertheless, he often says things about the limits of reason and the needs of humanity which are very close in spirit to Coleridge. It is, of course, not easy to point to echoes of Coleridge's

---

[29]Quoted by J.H.Muirhead, *Coleridge as Philosopher* (London, Allen & Unwin, 1954), p.159.
[30]Snyder, *op.cit.*, p.125.

irrationalism in Mill. He was the author of what was to become the standard text-book on logic in the nineteenth century British universities. But he has the same pragmatism about means as Coleridge. Mill asserts that system should be abandoned when it is in conflict with our wants and needs, with the "true exigencies of life."[31] And his arguments against Comte that "there is no necessity for an universal synthesis"[32] tend in the same direction. A "universal synthesis" is an unwarranted extrapolation of merely logical coherence, when the real necessity is for what is useful, that is, what satisfies our needs. Mill's standard of the desired certainty in logic is that of a "human purpose."[33]

Mill's logic is marked by his great care never to assert more than is strictly warranted by his premises and critics find Mill confused because he prefers to stop with a statement that is true if logically incomplete.[34] His analysis of the syllogism might be one example.[35] Similarly, his empiricism, for all its dogmatism in political applications, is carefully sceptical.[36] But his readiness to break the chain of argument is nowhere more clearly seen than in his ethics. The central example is the controversial introduction of "qualities" of pleasure in *Utilitarianism*. He is aware that simple utilitarianism cannot explain certain moral experiences, and so he introduces a proviso which is as inconsistent with his premises as it is practically exact. Thus Mill was prepared to tailor his logic to the dictates of more fundamental needs. Like Coleridge, he used logic as a tool and not a master.

The logic and methodology of Mill and Coleridge also have some

---

[31]*Autobiography*, p.166.

[32]E.L.Priestley, Vol.X, "Essays on Ethics, Religion and Society," ed. J.M.Robertson (University of Toronto Press, 1969), 359.

[33]J.S.Mill, *A System of Logic*, 2 vols. (London, Longmans, Green, and Co., 1879), I, 372. Subsequently referred to as *Logic*.

[34]Charles Mackinnon Douglas, *John Stuart Mill, A Study of his Philosophy* (Edinburgh, W.Blackwood & Sons, 1895), pp.10-11; see also W.Stanley Jevons, "John Stuart Mill's Philosophy Tested," in *Pure Logic and Other Minor Works* (London, Macmillan & Co., 1890), p.201.

[35]Reginald Jackson, *An Examination of the Deductive Logic of John Stuart Mill* (London, Oxford University Press, 1941), p.193.

[36]O.A.Kubitz, "The Development of John Stuart Mill's *System of Logic*," *University of Illinois Studies in Social Science*, XVIII (March-June, 1932), 169.

similarities. Thus the initial analysis of the syllogism, in both thinkers, produced the assertion that "all logical reasoning is simply classification."[37] But whereas the device for Mill was fundamentally a register for memory or, for Coleridge, a technique for recalling "to my memory a multitude of other facts,"[38] yet both Mill and Coleridge finally declared that the logic of the syllogism is more than a series of identical propositions. For Mill, the new general is, in some sense, a new truth; for Coleridge, the syllogism recalls to mind not only the facts but also "the important remembrance that they have all some one or more property in common."[39]

They also have a common attitude toward the Hegelian dialectic of 'being' and 'not being,' which both believe to rely on a confusion due to failure to analyze the difference between the disparate functions of the various forms of the verb 'to be.' Another parallel is the belief that it is in an analysis of "the component faculties of the human mind itself,"[40] whether the result confirms the conclusions of associationism or of intuitionism, that the fundamental philosophical answers are to be found.   Similarly, it is the experience of both that the most important single element in the errors of other thinkers is the improper use of language.

A minor parallel is Mill's use of the term "unconditional" in his *Political Economy* in a sense close to Coleridge's, and which may have been derived from him. Coleridge talks of the desire of philosophy to find *"for all that exists conditionally . . . a ground that is unconditional and absolute."*[41] As Kubitz observes, "the manner in which Coleridge phrases the necessity of having unconditional propositions as a basis for conditional truths, as well as the similar use of these terms by others, may have led Mill to apply the term 'unconditional' to the type of law he needed for deductive purposes."[42]

[37]Snyder, *op.cit.*, p.142.
[38]*Ibid.*, p.143.
[39]*Ibid.*
[40]*Biographia Literaria*, I, 14.
[41]*Friend*, I, 461.
[42]Kubitz, *op.cit.*, 175.

II

There are more important similarities in political methodology. Mill's desire to advance the theory of methodology was stimulated early by Macaulay's reply to his father's essay on Government.[43] James Mill's essay set out with rigid and barely examined premises, and proceeded to deduce simplified regularities which he unwisely claimed to be universal laws of human social behaviour. It was not difficult for Macaulay to challenge this argument; he did so on two counts. Firstly, he claimed that Mill had failed to verify the conclusions of his deductions. In practice, Macaulay showed, a man applies his experience of affairs to modify his reasonings. The conclusions Mill had arrived at were, in Macaulay's view, wide of the truth by a considerable margin. Secondly, he pointed out that Mill's premises were wrong, or at least too limited. Man is not only motivated by the cruder manifestations of self-interest. Many examples point to the real force of considerations of honour, of tradition, of social custom and of altruism.[44]

Macaulay's criticisms made a great impact on the younger Mill at a time when his mind was already beginning to look beyond the simple outlines of the system he had grown up with. For a time, he developed a criticism of Benthamism which closely followed the lines Macaulay had laid down. Gradually, though, he developed a more exact methodology which took these criticisms into account, instead of merely opposing them. Mill had the choice of answering either of Macaulay's objections. He could alter the premises, but leave the method, or he could accept the premises, and devise a new method of inference from them which would yield more reliable results.[45]

In the end, he chose to devise a new methodology, capable of taking into account more premises. He had, at an earlier stage, accepted Macaulay's implicit method in which practice differed from

---

[43] T.B.Macaulay, "Mill's Essay on Government," *Edinburgh Review*, XCVII (March, 1829), 159-189. Reprinted in *Critical and Miscellaneous Essays*, 5 vols. (Philadelphia, Carey & Hart, 1841-1844), V, 328-367.

[44] See Fred Kort, "The Issue of a Science of Politics in Utilitarian Thought," *American Political Science Review*, XLVI (1952), 1144.

[45] Kubitz, *op.cit.*, 34.

theory in so far as allowances were made by the man experienced in the art of politics for practical deviations from theoretic conditions. But as a child he had been severely reprimanded for distinguishing in this way between theory and practice[46] and he was soon to take up the slack in his early compromise as he developed his analysis of scientific methodology in the *Logic*.[47]

He now used the theory of counteracting causes to explain the action of complex and contradicting premises on the final inferences of sociology. But he rejected induction as a method of sociology because of the impossibility of conducting experiments on social phenomena, and decided on a method of deduction which he elaborated into the 'inverse deductive method.'[48] The soundness of this method lay in his realization that a purely empirical experimental method was inapplicable because of the unusual complexity of the composition of causes in social phenomena.[49] Its weakness lay in failing to realize that all science must be empirical and that inductive inference is a vital element in the construction, and not merely the verification, of hypotheses.[50] If Mill believed that social and physical phenomena were not essentially different, he should have been prepared to apply the same methodologies, whatever the complexity of the causes. His inverse deductive method of sociology has been heavily criticised for this reason.[51]

In the last part of the *Logic*, Mill describes three stages in the history of political methodology, the 'geometrical' method, the 'chemical' method, and his own inverse deductive method which he regards as a culminating development. Both the 'geometrical' and 'chemical' methods in politics are suspect. The 'geometrical' method is used by those,

> who deduce political conclusions not from laws of nature, not from
> sequences of phenomena, real or imaginary, but from unbending
> practical maxims. Such, for example, are all who found their theory

---

[46]*Autobiography*, p.32.
[47]Kubitz, *op.cit.*, 35.
[48]*Logic*, II, 508-530.
[49]Kubitz, *op.cit.*, 251-252.
[50]Kort, *op.cit.*, 1151-1152.
[51]*Ibid.*, 1150.

of politics on what is called abstract right, that is to say, on universal precepts.[52]

Examples of this method are not only Hobbes, Bentham and James Mill, but also Paine and Godwin, against whom Coleridge argues in the *Friend* in terms similar to Mill's.[53]

Mill borrows an example of the failure of the 'geometrical' method from Coleridge. "One of the conditions oftenest dropped, when what would otherwise be a true proposition is employed as a premise for proving others, is the condition of *time*. It is a principle of political economy that prices, profits, wages, &c. 'always find their level'; but this is often interpreted as if it meant that they are always, or generally, *at* their level; while the truth is, as Coleridge epigrammatically expresses it, that they are always *finding* their level, 'which might be taken as a paraphrase or ironical definition of a storm'."[54] Coleridge is, as usual, the source for an occasional insight which pinpoints one particular argument with an accuracy which no other writer could match. Mill wisely does not try. But Coleridge is not the source of a system, and in discussing the other inadequate method of politics, the 'chemical' one, Mill includes Coleridge as an example of this erroneous method.

The chemical method combines causes in a simple sum of additions and subtractions. More sophisticated than the geometrical method, it is still imperfect. One variant is the method of residues, which Mill regards as more plausible than most, though he believes himself to have made an advance on it. This method "appears, on the first view, less foreign to this kind of inquiry than the other three methods."[55] His example of this method is Coleridge.

> Something similar to this is the method which Coleridge (*Biographia Literaria*, i, 214) describes himself as having followed in his political essays in the *Morning Post*. 'On every great occurrence I endeavoured to discover in past history the event that most nearly resembled it. . . .Then fairly subtracting the points of difference from those of likeness, as the balance favoured the former or the latter. I conjectured that the result would be the same or different. . . .' In

---

[52] *Logic*, II, 481.

[53] *Friend*, I, 30n, 31n, 32, 165-168.

[54] *Logic*, II, 386.

[55] *Ibid.*, 475-476.

this enquiry he no doubt employed the Method of Residues; for, in 'subtracting the points of difference from those of likeness,' he doubtless weighed, and did not content himself with numbering, them: he doubtless took those points of agreement only, which he presumed from their own nature to be capable of influencing the effect, and, allowing for that influence, concluded that the remainder of the result would be referrable to the points of difference. Whatever may be the efficacy of this method, it is, as we long ago remarked, not a method of pure observation and experiment; it concludes, not from a comparison of instances, but from the comparison of an instance with the result of a previous deduction. Applied to social phenomena, it presupposes that the causes from which part of the effect proceed are already known; and as we have shown that these cannot have been known by specific experience, they must have been learnt by deduction from principles of human nature; experience being called in only as a supplementary resource, to determine the causes which produced an unexplained residue.[56]

Mill finds Coleridge's method inadequate, if interesting enough to quote at length, an honour which he accords to no other method. The honour is an important one. Mill has characterised Coleridge's methodology as the most advanced form of the 'chemical' method, in turn the most advanced of the previous methods. Although Mill's inverse deductive method is a further advance, it is possible to argue that Mill's achievement is more a refinement than a radical re-thinking of Coleridge's method.

Coleridge also rejected the 'geometrical' method in politics and criticised empirical systems strongly. Thus Hobbes's mistake was to believe that fear could ever be a principle of order. Theories of reason, of the rights of man, and of the General Will, Coleridge declares, all fail to provide any guide to the technique of government. But there must, none the less, be principles to give a firm footing to political methodology. The need for these principles is the major message of The Friend. Thus Coleridge sets out coherently the principles of the positive and negative ends of government. As well as protection, it should guarantee subsistence, means of self-improvement, and hope, for the country. These principles are not rules, but "Ideas," and Coleridge's favourite word enables him to combine empirical and a priori elements in a way which bears comparison with Mill's mixed method of sociology. An "Idea" is a regulative principle whose working

[56]Ibid., 476-477.

out in the contingent world must be decided empirically. It is perhaps this element in Coleridge's thought, which is closest to Mill's.

Clearly, Mill's method with social and political questions is not the same as Coleridge's. But Mill's claim that sociology is deductive is in part a claim that it must proceed from fixed principles. This is close to Coleridge's argument, though the two men reached the similar conclusion by different roads. Fundamentally, the difference is that Mill's method takes the factors involved into account in a strictly methodical way, whereas Coleridge relied on political instinct. Coleridge's approximations allow so much personal bias to enter the calculation that Mill's exact formulations appear of a totally different order of detachment. But it is a difference with common roots. Coleridge's typically incomplete analysis of methodology is a vital link in the preparation of the more advanced formulations of Mill's 'inverse deductive method.'

The sources of both methodologies are identical. They lie in a dissatisfaction on the one hand with the abstract rationalism of Bentham, Godwin, Paine and Adam Smith, and on

> the other hand with, the vulgar notion, that the safe methods on political subjects are those of Baconian induction – that the true guide is not general reasoning, but specific experience ... Nothing can be more ludicrous than the sort of parodies on experimental reasoning which one is accustomed to meet with, not in popular discussions only, but in grave treatises, when the affairs of nations are the theme.[57]

From this dissatisfaction, Mill's and Coleridge's analyses follow cogent lines. They both set up a tripartite structure in which the major predisposing evidence of their own theories lies in a critique of the two previous theories.

The result is a parallel balance between principle and practice. This balance in Coleridge is capricious and personal in contrast to Mill's careful methodology. But in both it is born of the same compromise between the deficiencies of previous theories. The practical effects of this balance are sometimes unexpected. Thus Mill argues for a leisured class because it is the only way to ensure that the ideal of culture is upheld, and Coleridge argues against the individual

---

[57] *Ibid.*, I, 526.

possession of capital, although he has argued for unhindered possession of land, because it interferes with human self-development, in the exploiter as much as in the exploited.

Coleridge's attitude to land and capital is an example of the flexibility of his methodology. His political theory is largely based on the concept of a landed society. When talking of land and its tenure he is a conservative, although he does reassert the principle that property is not absolute, but in trust. The trust is, however, for practical purposes, absolute. But when he comes to deal with questions of the tenure and distribution of capital he becomes the radical. He is in favour of strict factory acts. He talks of what is "ironically called *Free Labour*," and is prepared to dare to "prohibit Soul-murder and Infanticide on the part of the Rich, and Self-slaughter on that of the Poor."[58] Had Coleridge lived to see the coming struggle for political power between worker and industrialist, rather than between labourer and estate owner, he would have been as radical as any.

The evidence of these politically heterogeneous social recommendations suggests that the intentions of Mill and Coleridge are closely cognate. They were often on the same side in the real political battles – both those of their own age, and those that were to come. The real political opposition of the early nineteenth century can be characterized as that between the planners for an improved society, and those who sought merely to preserve, or procure, the maximum of privilege. In these broad terms Coleridge and Mill were both planning for a society void of the ills of unearned privilege; Mill saw it in electoral reform, Coleridge was opposed to such reform until the last.[59] He hoped, instead, for spiritual regeneration. But both wanted to change the current situation, and both wanted to preserve privilege where they saw it to be earned, among their own middle-class intelligensia.

Their community in the face of the political battles to come is even more striking. The area of conflict swung, after the reform of electoral distribution, to the reform of economic distribution. Mill

---

[58]*Letters*, IV, 855; see also S.T.Coleridge, *Two addresses on Sir Robert Peel's Bill, (April 1818)*, ed. Edmund Gosse (London, Printed for Private Circulation, 1913), p.20.
[59]*Table Talk*, p.156.

remained, however, curiously unaware of the new movement represented by Marx.[60] He continued, late into the nineteenth century, to think in terms Coleridge would have understood.

Mill and Coleridge also have much in common in their concepts of historiography. Mill first saw the Germanico-Coleridgeans as a new "historical school," and Coleridge's subsequent influence was probably more on the writing of history, theological and secular, than on the making of politics – an appropriately theoretic achievement for one of the century's great dreamers. Eighteenth century philosophy was inadequate, in Mill's view, because it failed to take historical forces into account. The change heralded by his crisis was, as much as anything, a decision to take the historical circumstances and trends of human society as seriously as its theoretical needs.[61]

Mill's early blindness to history was not solely due to Bentham. The fault was partly James Mill's, and partly a lack of experience in John Mill himself. Certainly Bentham's annoyance with some eighteenth century historiography did not preclude an appreciation of its importance.[62] Mill and Coleridge both opposed the linear idea of progress of the eighteenth century with a more subtle account of historical trends. The final estimate of their similarities can be made in an analysis of the influence each thinker's historiography had over their disciples. Thus Preyer's account of Thirlwall and Grote[63] shows that their theories of history correlate very closely, and illustrates the strong convergence of Mill's and Coleridge's concepts of historiography.[64]

In the continual struggle between rich and poor Mill was most often on the side of the workingman, Coleridge most often on the side of the landowner. Yet both would rather have seen either side

[60]Lewis S.Feuer, "John Stuart Mill and Marxian Socialism," *J.H.I.*, X (1949), 297-304.

[61]Clark W.Bouton, "John Stuart Mill: On Liberty and History," *Western Political Quarterly*, XVIII (1965), 569.

[62]R.Preyer, *Bentham, Coleridge, and the Science of History*, Leipziger Beitrage zur Englishen Philologie, 41 Heft (Bochum-Langendreer, Verlag Poppinghaus, 1958), p.3.

[63]Cannop Thirlwall (1797-1875), historian and clergyman; George Grote (1794-1871), banker, M.P., and historian of Greece.

[64]Preyer, *op.cit.*, p.78.

absorbed into the triumph of the middle class. It is thus in politics
that Mill and Coleridge were, paradoxically, closer than anywhere. In
the last chapter of the *Logic* it is Coleridge to whom Mill turns more
than to any other writer as an example both to support and sharpen
his own arguments.   Mill certainly went beyond Coleridge in
systematizing a methodology of political analysis, but Coleridge's
example, which so closely echoes the negative aspects of Mill's
criticisms of previous methods, helped in the initial stages of Mill's
progress from the 'geometrical' method of Bentham to his own
deductive method.   In 1834 Mill thought Coleridge was more
systematic than Bentham, because at that time, having experienced the
errors of the purely geometrical method of analysing human affairs, he
was seeking another method.   Coleridge's sophisticated version of the
'chemical' method filled his needs. That Mill went beyond this method
in no way reduces its importance as a stage in the history of his ideas.

6 New ideals: utilitarianism, liberty, religion

> He spoke of Mill with evident contempt as a renegade from philosophy, *Anglicé* – a renouncer of Bentham's creed and an expounder of Coleridge's. – Caroline Fox on John Bowring[1]

In *Utilitarianism* Mill sets out to redefine the "greatest happiness" principle, and defend it against its intuitionist critics.[2] In doing this he faces and probes the difficulties of the system with an honesty which has curiously been regarded not as admirable but as indefensible. The least objectionable part of the essay is its last chapter, "How connected with Justice," where the connection between utilitarian-type criteria and the public administration of morality is amply defended. Here even Coleridge would agree. It is earlier that he faces the controversial problems. The initial statement on which his whole argument depends is that, "our moral faculty . . . is a branch of our reason, not of our sensitive faculty."[3] This, as he formally recognizes, is a controversial position, so, although he has claimed morals to be reasonable, he immediately goes on to admit that, "questions of ultimate ends are not amenable to direct proof. Whatever can be proved to be good, must be so by being shown to be a means to

---

[1] *Memories of Old Friends, Being Extracts from the Journals and Letters of Caroline Fox from 1835 to 1870*, ed.H.N.Pym, 2 vols. (London, Smith, Elder & Co., 1882), I, 216.

[2] Charles Mackinnon Douglas (ed.), *The Ethics of John Stuart Mill* (Edinburgh, W.Blackwood and Sons, 1897), p.xvi.

[3] J.S.Mill, *Utilitarianism, Liberty, Representative Government*, introduction by A.D.Lindsay (London, J.M.Dent & Sons, 1962), p.2. Subsequently referred to as *Utilitarianism*, or *Liberty*.

something admitted to be good without proof."[4] None the less, he believes that, "considerations may be presented capable of determining the intellect either to give or withold its assent to the doctrine; and this is equivalent to proof."[5] Mill's point has provoked many hostile comments. It constantly requires sympathetic insight to follow his meaning between the absolute desire to reason about morals and the absolute realization that ends cannot be proved.

The greatest happiness principle founders, as Coleridge earlier pointed out[6] and Mill was aware, on the difficulty of defining happiness. Mill rests his utilitarianism on the declaration that, "by happiness is intended pleasure, and the absence of pain; by unhappiness, pain, and the privation of pleasure."[7] He further defines the concept of happiness which he is to defend by emphasizing that,

> the happiness which forms the utilitarian standard of what is right in conduct, is not the agent's own happiness, but that of all concerned. As between his own happiness and that of others, utilitarianism requires him to be as strictly impartial as a disinterested and benevolent spectator.[8]

Mill's critics claim that he commits the fallacy of composition, in transferring the same concept of happiness from personal pleasures and pains to a general social application.

Mill also makes two other statements which have proved to be the storm centres of controversy. In his discussion, "Of What Sort of Proof the Principle of Utility is Susceptible," he claims that,

> the only proof capable of being given that an object is visible, is that people actually see it. The only proof that a sound is audible, is that people actually hear it; and so of the other sources of our experience. In like manner, I apprehend, the sole evidence it is possible to produce that anything is desirable, is that people do actually desire it.[9]

But by almost universal acceptance, the most damaging statement

---

[4]*Ibid.*, p.4.

[5]*Ibid.*

[6]S.T.Coleridge, *The Table Talk and Omniana*, ed.T.Ashe (London, G.Bell and sons, 1923), pp.134-135. Subsequently referred to as *Table Talk*.

[7]*Utilitarianism*, p.6.

[8]*Ibid.*, p.16.

[9]*Ibid.*, p.32.

is Mill's claim that, "it is quite compatible with the principle of utility to recognize the fact, that some *kinds* of pleasure are more desirable and more valuable than others."[10]

These, then, are the crucial points for both defence and criticism of Mill's form of utilitarianism. The difficulty of defining happiness is inherent in utilitarianism itself. The maintenance of the distinction between utilitarianism and ethical hedonism depends on overcoming this difficulty. But the other two difficulties are peculiarly Mill's own, and spring from his modifications of the ideals of Benthamism. The attempt to discuss proof in discursive terms, in which the limitations and characteristics of proof are the main focus of attention, is as typical of the author of *A System of Logic* as it is alien to the habits of mind of the author of *An Analysis of the Phenomena of the Human Mind*. Similarly, the qualities of pleasure, the ideal of nobleness and the self-denying cultivation of higher sensibilities, while they may owe much to his father's example, owe nothing to his philosophy. It is this, in particular, which demands explanation.

What, first, do Mill's commentators say? There is a fair division between those, recently more numerous, who feel that "it is most unfair to charge Mill with elementary logical blunders and obvious verbal confusions,"[11] and those who, like C.D.Broad, learnt to criticize "Mill at our mother's knee,"[12] and could not break the habit. They regard him as a fundamentally confused writer,[13] and whatever the individual defences offered, feel that there still remain logical errors "which cannot possibly be explained away," although his "ambivalent attitude" towards his father's philosophy gave him "very good psychological reasons for being less clear and consistent"[14] in *Utilitarianism*.

Many of Mill's critics among professional philosophers have charged him with the fallacy of composition, among them Mackenzie,

---

[10]*Ibid.*, p.7.

[11]Carl Wellman, "A Reinterpretation of Mill's Proof," *Ethics*, LXIX (1958-59), 274.

[12]C.D.Broad, *Five Types of Ethical Theory* (London, Kegan Paul, Trench, Trubner & Co, 1934), p.174.

[13]*Ibid.*, p.232.

[14]Morgens Blegvad, "Mill, Moore, and the Naturalistic Fallacy," in *Philosophical Essays Dedicated to Gunnar Aspelin* (Lund, 1963), p.19.

Sorley, Dewey and Sidgewick.[15] Mill is commonly defended on the grounds that he did not intend the "common happiness" in any other sense than that of the aggregate of individual happiness.[16] But it is far from indisputable that this really is what he meant, since this defence collapses the distinction between ethical hedonism and utilitarianism. But it is also arguable that Mill failed to grasp the different implications of these disparate ethical principles. Thus he confuses the practical effect of tradition in adding force to the personal sanction of altruism, with the more exact calculations of unimpeded hedonism.[17] In other words he is not distinguishing between pursuit of sympathetic pleasure, and acquired moral associations, both of which he seems to use in estimating the effect of the pleasure of others on the individual. To clarify his aggregation of individuals into the "greatest number" he would need to clarify this point.

His treatment of the martyr, on the other hand, suggests that he did distinguish between egoistical hedonism and utilitarianism. But, unfortunately for Mill, the criterion of this distinction is extra-utilitarian.   Thus, he tells us, refuting the charge of egoistical hedonism,

> unquestionably it is possible to do without happiness . . . it often has to be done voluntarily by the hero or the martyr, for the sake of something which he prizes more than his individual happiness. But this something, what is it, unless the happiness of others, or some of the requisites of happiness? It is noble to be capable of resigning entirely one's own portion of happiness, or chances of it: but, after all, this self-sacrifice must be for some end; it is not its own end; and if we are told that its end is not happiness, but virtue, which is better than happiness, I ask, would the sacrifice be made if the hero or martyr did not believe that it would earn for others immunity from similar sacrifices?[18]

[15] A useful summary is in James Seth, "The Alleged Fallacies in Mill's Utilitarianism," *Philosophical Review*, XVII (1908), 469-472; reprinted in his *Essays in Ethics and Religion*, ed.A.Seth Pringle-Pattison (Edinburgh, W.Blackwood & sons, 1926), pp.22-25.

[16] See Seth, *op.cit.*, 27; also Peter Zinkernagel, "Revaluation of J.S.Mill's Ethical Proof," *Theoria*, XVIII (1952), 70; Wellman, *op.cit.*, 273.

[17] Henry Sidgewick, *The Methods of Ethics* (London, Macmillan and Co., 1893), pp.498n-499n.

[18] *Utilitarianism*, pp.14-15.

Thus the impulse to self-sacrifice is explained because it is "noble", but not purely "virtuous". The nobility is, one is justified in concluding, exactly that nobility which distinguished Socrates from the pig – a nobleness which is induced, indeed, from a broad empirical observation of how men do, in fact, behave, but is deductively at odds with the premises of utilitarianism.

An attempt has been made to relieve Mill of this difficulty with the idea of martyrdom by arguing that he allowed himself to be misled by a "verbal ambiguity" between "the verb 'to please' and the phrase 'to be pleasant'."[19] Thus a martyr may be more *pleased* with his sacrifice than with a life of egoistical hedonism, though the former is undoubtedly less *pleasant* than the latter. The point turns, once again, on the definition of happiness. Utility is for the greatest happiness, but so, said Coleridge, is "every one of us."[20] But is happiness pleasure in things pleasant, or is it being pleased by a noble humanity? Some other criterion is needed than utility to make the distinction, and it is here that Mill introduced the concept of qualities of pleasure. Thus this attempt to rescue Mill cannot be said to have succeeded.

It is Mill himself, however, who makes his own best defence. Herbert Spencer made the criticism which is being discussed when he claimed that, "the principle of utility presupposes the anterior principle, that everybody has an equal right to happiness."[21] Mill replies in a footnote to *Utilitarianism,*

> it may be more correctly described as supposing that equal amounts of happiness are equally desirable, whether felt by the same or by different persons. This, however, is not a *pre*-supposition; not a premise needful to support the principle of utility, but the very principle itself.[22]

The reply is more sensible than it might, at first, appear. For Mill's initial assumptions define morality as a social, and not an individual, matter. To be moral is to help others, and the only expansion of "to help others" which is empirically defensible is to give

---

[19]Broad, *op.cit.,* p.186.

[20]*Table Talk,* p.134.

[21]Herbert Spencer, *Social Statistics* (London, Williams and Norgate, 1868), p.367. Quoted in *Utilitarianism,* p.58.

[22]*Ibid.*

them happiness. Therefore it is a logical deduction from the premises of an empirical ethics that the happiness of others is as important as our own.

The initial assumptions are however unprovable, and hence the major part of Mill's essay is concerned to discuss questions of proof, and not, it must never be forgotten, simply to prove. To this question of the possible proofs of utility philosophers have, appropriately, devoted much of their time. It makes the assessment of these discussions easier to remind ourselves of the orientation of the essay on utilitarianism. It is to a large extent polemical. It is directed against intuitionism, and it tries to defend utilitarianism against common attacks and misunderstandings. The extent to which it is a defence and not an exposition may relieve some of the difficulties due to deficiencies in Mill's explanations of the finer points. Mill did not always make himself scrupulously clear in areas where he did not sense a contemporary reaction, and the quality of proof he wishes to establish is primarily that which would show utilitarianism to be more sensible than intuitionism. He is not concerned to establish proofs aimed at satisfying professional philosophical analysis, even were that possible on ethical subjects.[23]

Mill is commonly charged with having been misled in the passage quoted above by the verbal similarity between "visible" and "desirable" into drawing an analogy between them. The error, it is said, is a result of failing to distinguish between what "ought" to be, and what "is", a failure common in empirical ethics. Once again, Mill has defenders.[24]It is pointed out, very justly, that Mill uses the word "proof" only about "visible" and uses the word "evidence" in the partly analogous case of "desirable."[25] Apart from this defence, it is maintained that on Mill's premises the analogy is complete. If "desirableness" and "desiredness" are not distinguished in an ethical system, then to say "the desirable just is the desired" is not a logical error.[26]

---

[23]Everett Wesley Hall, "The 'Proof' of Utility in Bentham and Mill," in *Categorical Analysis* (Chapel Hill, University of North Carolina Press, 1964), p.115.

[24]E.g.Wellman, *op.cit.*, 272.

[25]D.Daiches Raphael, "Fallacies in and about Mill's *Utilitarianism*," *Philosophy*, XXX (1955), 347.

[26]Hall, *op.cit.*, pp.106-109.

There are also good common sense reasons for claiming that "desires" and the fact that something is desired are beyond analysis and therefore desirableness is equally a fact, and not an inference.[27] To envisage an ethical good which "nobody ever desires is just being academic and unrealistic."[28] But a more subtle adjudication points out that the premise "happiness alone is desired" changes its logical status during the essay. At first it is an empirical statement, that is it is "synthetic"; later it is stated as a logically undeniable proposition, that is it is "analytic".[29]

Mill is, then, in difficulties with his analogy, but in difficulties of a different logical order to the näivities he has often been charged with. Similarly, it is obviously misguided to charge him with ignoring the transition from "is" to "ought". In the last chapter of the *Logic* he himself warns of the difference. "A proposition of which the predicate is expressed by the words *ought* or *should be*, is generally different from one which is expressed by *is*, or *will be*."[30] Indeed, even Bentham, whom John Mill apparently did not regard as perceptive of these problems, did in fact make a distinction between "censorial" and "expository" ethics.[31] Bentham's distinction was based on an understanding of the difference between "ought" and "is", and though his ethics asserts that the only standard for what ought to be is what is, it is "another kind of 'is' than the 'is' of already existing 'oughts'."[32] A thorough-going empirical ethics cannot recognize an absolute disjunction between desirableness and the fact of desire, between 'ought' and 'is', though it may recognize that they should not be näively equated. Mill did not solve these problems; clearly he was in difficulty, and his wish to avoid the dogmatism he disliked in intuitionism left his argument inconclusive.[33] His excuse must be that

---

[27]Zinkernagel, *op.cit.*, 71.

[28]Hall, *op.cit.*, p.118.

[29]Atkinson, *op.cit.*, 164.

[30]J.S.Mill, *A System of Logic*, 2 vols. (London, Longmans, Green, and Co., 1879), II, 553. Subsequently referred to as *Logic*.

[31]David Baumgardt, "Bentham's 'Censorial' Method," *J.H.I.*, VI (1945), 461.

[32]*Ibid.*, 464.

[33]J. Schneewind, "John Stuart Mill," in *The Encyclopedia of Philosophy*, ed. Paul Edwards, 8 vols. (New York, Macmillan & Co., 1967), V, 320.

he was offering not a proof, but a defence. To try to offer that proof for him is doomed by the very complexity of his position.

This complexity springs, in large measure, from the distinction between qualities of happiness he introduced into Bentham's system. The distinction between utilitarianism and hedonism rests with this concept of nobility, and many of the obscurities of what is or ought to be desired could have been made more transparent by a simpler system of valuation of pleasures. But Mill's utilitarianism is outstandingly and disturbingly based on a belief that pleasures differ in quality, and not only in quantity. This new foundation has been extensively regarded as disastrous. It introduces, many believe, insurmountable contradictions,[34] and it has been explained as the result of the entrance of a new and totally different aim.

> John Mill carelessly knocked down the barricades piled up by Bentham against the tyranny of those who claimed to know how their neighbours should live. But then Mill's purpose ... in everything else written after his crisis, was exactly contrary to Bentham's. He meant to secure the leadership of those who knew better, otherwise the human race could not progress to its ultimate perfection.[35]

There is, of course, much truth in this. The simplicity of Bentham's system was intended to deny any opportunity to the special pleading of privilege. Mill's system is based on a need to establish and protect the right, if not the privilege, of those who know over those who do not know.[36] The conclusion cannot be escaped, but Cowling, who presses it energetically,[37] makes the error of mistaking Mill's reason, which is the benevolent aim of extending the privilege of education, rather than the conservative wish to restrict privilege.

Mill's introduction of qualities of pleasure is not, however, solely the result of new aims. He has been defended by a judicious exploration of the latent distinction between capacity for pleasure and contentment. On this argument pleasure is not satisfaction, but capacity, and unfulfilled desire does not detract from happiness. Thus

[34]Douglas, op.cit., p.lxxviii

[35]Shirley R.Letwin, The Pursuit of Certainty (Cambridge University Press, 1965), p.306.

[36]Utilitarianism, p.9.

[37]Maurice Cowling, Mill and Liberalism (Cambridge University Press, 1963), pp.104-105.

the small capacity for pleasure of the animal, easily fulfilled, does not in summation offer as much happiness as the larger, but only partially satisfied, capacities of Sophocles.[38] But this argument is tenuous. Not only is it in contradiction to common empirical experience of the community between pleasure and satisfaction, but it is also not clear that this is Mill's intended meaning. It is much more likely that Mill is merely asserting a psychological fact that the higher pleasures are necessary for man.[39] In other words his famous and controversial modification has no sinister, arbitrary or careless motivation, but is a simple matter of empirical observation. It is thus not, in origin, a philosophical problem but a question of awareness. In accepting the difficulties for the sake of the empirical truth Mill is valuing awareness over sectarian consistency.

Now this conclusion is valuable evidence. We have seen that of the three major cruxes in Mill's essay, two – the so called fallacy of composition, and the equation of empirical 'is' with ethical 'ought' – were endemic in the fundamental structure of utilitarianism, and were faced by Bentham also. But the third difficulty is original to Mill, and its source is not philosophical incompetence or political deviousness, but rather extended awareness. Broadly, it is safe to find the roots of this awareness in Mill's early contact with idealism.[40]

Coleridge's ethics is not essentially remote from Mill's. The most recent attempt to summarize his diverse ideas places as the opening and decisive assertion of his ethics the analysis of the word "good" which concludes that, "the meaning of 'good' can be decided only by an appeal to universal usage, for the distinction between 'good' and 'pleasurable' . . . must 'be the consequent of a common consciousness of man as man'."[41] Coleridge is returning ethical decisions to empirical experience, a fundamentally similar aim to Mill's.

Coleridge's mature philosophy believes that moral ideas are the root of all ideas, in as much as all human categorizing of the manifold is done in terms of human needs, and thus of human values. He also

---

[38]Daiches Raphael, *op.cit.*, 352-353.

[39]Seth, *op.cit.*, p.43.

[40]Douglas, *op.cit.*, pp.lxxiii-lxxiv, lxxvi-lxxvii.

[41]Michael Moran, "Coleridge," in *The Encyclopedia of Philosophy*, ed. Paul Edwards, 8 vols. (New York, Macmillan & Co., 1967), II, 137.

believes that ethical concepts such as good, happiness, self, and so on can only be referred to common usage. Similarly Mill's arguments in *Utilitarianism* show that he places ethical experience above dogmatic utilitarianism and, furthermore, is clearly aware that normative statements are not susceptible of proof in the manner of factual statements, and are therefore radically distinct.

Mill and Coleridge have thus a common attitude which is philosophically hybrid because it is, in both, tied firmly to experience and usage. Both equate educated self-development with moral excellence. The doctrine of the equivalence of pure knowledge and pure morality comes, for both, ultimately from Plato. But what for Coleridge became the foundation, for Mill became the inescapable consequence. Both insist on the value of education not as training for production and obedience, but as something morally valuable. Thus Coleridge's *Friend* is pre-eminently a course of education, and Mill's Socrates is the symbol of the cultured man, an enviable status which Mill was determined should be offered to all. Coleridge rejected Kant's notion of duty as inhuman, and Mill rejected the utilitarian notion of imposed patterns of association. Both embraced the ideal of a cultured man, freed by fidelity to his individual ethical experience. The educational implication of Mill's and Coleridge's ethics is a common and distinguishing factor of their outlooks.

I

Almost as much as *Utilitarianism*, Mill's essay on *Liberty* became a *cause célèbre* of Victorian controversy, and the text book of liberalism for a century.[42] Thus *Liberty* represents a measure of Mill's influence, and a detailed comparison between Coleridge's ideas of individual self-development, and Mill's doctrines in *Liberty* is important.

Coleridge's belief in the value and sanctity of the individual stands with, and as part of, his fundamental beliefs in the moral nature of

---

[42]See for instance, *New Letters of Thomas Carlyle*, ed. Alexander Carlyle, 2 vols. (London, John Lane, 1904), II, 196; Edward Lucas, "Mr.Mill upon Liberty of the Press," *Essays on Religion and Literature*, third series, ed. Henry Edward Manning, Archbishop of Westminster (London, Henry S.King & Co., 1874), pp.142-173.

truth, and in the freedom of the human spirit. The organic nature of creativity is an image as central to our experience of Coleridge's ideas as any of his great distinctions. Individuality is a central idea; it is Coleridge's belief in politics that individual reform is the key to social reform. In literature he believes that creativity, the highest expression of the human spirit, is also the highest peak of individuality. In education he believes that teaching can help the mind's self-development, but not form it, and in religion he believes that the centre of the mystery lies in an individual relationship with a highly personal God. The point hardly needs extensive support by citation.

Coleridge developed it into a philosophical concept of 'bicentrality', and a theological doctrine of personality in God. Bicentrality combines universality with individuality in a controlled paradox which runs closely parallel with the other verbal contradictions of Coleridge's dialectic.

> An atom and a finite Universe are both alike Fictions of the Mind, *entia logica*. Nevertheless, not the Imagination alone, but the Reason requires a Centre. It is a necessary Postulate of Science. That therefore which can be found nowhere absolutely and exclusively must be imagined everywhere relatively and partially. Hence the law of Bicentrality, i.e. that every Whole ... must be conceived as a possible centre in itself, and at the same time as having a centre out of itself and common to it with all other parts of the same System.[43]

Both the human mind and external nature are thus variously self-developing and uniform. The concept is parallel to that of the 'Idea', which is both universal and particular.

Coleridge's treatment of personality in God further illustrates his conception of individuality. Limitation, that is separation, cannot be of the essence of personality, because if it were then,

> the wiser a man became, the greater (that is) his power of self-determination, with so much less propriety can he be spoken of as a person; and *vice versa* the more exclusive the limits, and the smaller the sphere enclosed – in fact the less Will he possessed – the more a person; till at length his personality would be at its maximum when he bordered on the animal or the idiot, when, according to all use of language, he ceased to be a person at all.[44]

Coleridge's argument again does two characteristic things. It

---

[43]Quoted by Muirhead, *op.cit.*, p.122, from MS c., p.108.
[44]Quoted by *Ibid.*, p.228, from MS B, *Magnum Opus*.

appeals for its primary sanction to "all uses of language," and in doing so it produces a logical paradox between personality and absoluteness which in another thinker would be evidence of the malfunctioning of the argument and in Coleridge is accepted as its necessary conclusion.

The argument in Mill's *Liberty* is widely familiar, and it is unnecessary to try to summarize his neat and often ironic treatment of the possible alternatives to the tyranny of the majority, both in the conflict of opinion, and the liberty of the individual; the essay itself still makes exciting reading. Mill believes in the need for freedom of speech for the sake of truth through conflict. The main points in the essay are, firstly, his fundamental belief that freedom is a human good of the highest order and that "the only freedom which deserves the name, is that of pursuing our own good in our own way."[45] Mill's belief is that, "human nature is not a machine to be built after a model, and set to do exactly the work prescribed for it, but a tree, which requires to grow and develop itself on all sides, according to the tendency of the inward forces which make it a living thing."[46] It is thus only by cultivating "all that is individual in themselves . . . and calling it forth . . . that human beings become a noble and beautiful object of contemplation."[47]

The second point in Mill's defence of freedom relies on a distinction between self-regarding and other-regarding actions. Mill declares that, "the liberty of the individual must be thus far limited; he must not make himself a nuisance to other people."[48] But, equally, "the sole end for which mankind are warranted, individually or collectively, in interfering with the liberty of action of any of their number, is self-protection . . . Over himself, over his body and mind, the individual is sovereign."[49]

The *London Review* in 1859 declared that it was impossible to distinguish, as Mill had done, between self-regarding and other-regarding actions. "No moral quality is limited in its action to the sphere of the possessor's own history and doings . . . society has an

---

[45]*Liberty*, p.75.

[46]*Ibid.*, p.117.

[47]*Ibid.*, p.120.

[48]*Ibid.*, p.114.

[49]*Ibid.*, pp.72-73.

interest, over and above that of mere self-defence, in the conduct of every one of its members."[50] The argument was most forcibly set out by FitzJames Stephen in his *Liberty, Equality, Fraternity*, which "set the pattern for much of the criticism directed against Mill up to the present time."[51] But the attack has been warded off by pointing out that Mill recognizes the claim of society by limiting it,[52] although the idea of "interests" may be difficult to apply in practice. There are, however, deeper paradoxes in Mill's attitude to the description of liberty. The principles by which he defends his assertion change from place to place in the essay, and are sometimes mutually contradictory. Thus at one stage he claims that liberty is the benefit of "utility in the largest sense, grounded on permanent interests of a man as a progressive being"[53] and that "the peculiar evil of silencing the expression of an opinion is, that it is robbing the human race."[54] Yet, a few sentences before, Mill had made the celebrated statement that,"if all mankind minus one were of one opinion, and only one person were of the contrary opinion, mankind would be no more justified in silencing that one person, than he, if he had the power, would be justified in silencing mankind.[55] Mill's argument that free-speech is justified by the social utility of truth is a paradox.

> In suggesting that the values of freedom are primarily social values, he opens the way for society itself to be the judge of freedom's social unity ... this (ironically enough) is to invite that very tyranny of the majority.[56]

Clearly, utility cannot logically be the criterion for liberty – liberty must be a self-evident ideal if it is to withstand the sort of rationalism which Mill invites. Cowling has demonstrated this quite clearly.

Mill is also charged with varying his criteria, and in practical

---

[50]Quoted by J.C.Rees, "A Re-reading of Mill on Liberty," *Political Studies*, VIII (1960), 116, from *London Review*, XIII (1859), 274. His reference appears to be incorrect.

[51]*Ibid.*

[52]*Liberty*, pp.137-138.

[53]*Ibid.*, p.74.

[54]*Ibid.*, p.79.

[55]*Ibid.*

[56]Albert William Levi, "The Value of Freedom: Mill's Liberty (1859-1959)," *Ethics*, LXX (1959-60), 39.

applications easily overriding the priciple of non-interference when it seems to him to be sensible to do so. This is, of course, especially true in colonial matters, and in educational situations.[57] Equally he views the conflict between self and other sometimes from the position of the self, sometimes from that of the others. His concern for happiness becomes a concern for self-development, and the change from quantity to quality in *Utilitarianism* is echoed.[58]

It is possible to argue for Mill as a consistent utilitarian in response to FitzJames Stephen's type of criticism. His introduction makes it quite clear that his doctrine of protection for individual liberty is a simple extension of the principles, though not of the results, of Benthamism. The situation he believes, having been dramatically awakened by Tocqueville's analysis, has changed since Bentham's days. "protection, therefore, against the tyranny of the magistrate is not enough: there needs protection also against the tyranny of the prevailing opinion and feeling.[59]

Even so, criticism of Mill's methodological foundations makes it clear that liberty stood in Mill's mind as its own sanction, as a self-evident ideal. Mill has substantially changed the Benthamite tradition in *Liberty*, as in *Utilitarianism*.[60] The richness, complexity and nobleness of human nature, attributes measured by quality and promoted by individual liberty, are Mill's end, and not a simple quantitative measure of happiness.[61] What for Bentham was a "psychological datum" has become in Mill an ideal.[62] The complexity of the situation is magnified by Mill's continuing insistence that his philosophy is utilitarian when it had in fact absorbed and allowed for a far greater awareness than it could subsume.[63]

[57]H.J.McCloskey, "Mill's Liberalism," *Philosophical Quarterly*, XIII (1963), 155.

[58]Richard Lichtman, "The Surface and Substance of Mill's Defence of Freedom," *Social Research*, XXX (1963), 478.

[59]*Liberty*, p.68.

[60]Sir Isiah Berlin, *John Stuart Mill and the Ends of Life*, (London, Council of Christians and Jews, 1959), p.6.

[61]R.S.Downie, "Mill on Pleasure and self-development," *Philosophical Quarterly*, XVI (1966), 70.

[62]Berlin, *op.cit.*, p.8.

[63]Letwin, *op.cit.*, p.297.

Mill's position is an uneasy compromise. He tried to avoid the despotic majority rule Bentham's system provided for, and also the unguarded rule of the few which his inherited experience of the eighteenth century situation made unthinkable.[64] The result was more conservative in implication, if not in fact, than Mill realized. The limits of interference by others in self-regarding actions are apparently determined by custom, that is by existing agreements of society as to which actions are purely self-regarding. This principle would enshrine the *status quo* in an essentially conservative manner.[65] Thus, although the genesis of *Liberty* is, as in *Utilitarianism*, an extension of Mill's original principles,"[66] the extension has lead him into difficulties. However seriously, or lightly, the accumulated critiques of the essay are taken, we must conclude that liberty, like qualities of pleasure, is not a strictly utilitarian principle. It relies for its conviction on a new ideal, derived from a broader experience of human life, and not a refined inference from Bentham's principles.

The source of this ideal must remain, in all but outline, obscure. Not only is it latent in a great deal of Western culture from Plato onwards, it was in Mill's age going through a general rejuvenation from which it was to emerge as one of the major shaping ideals of the century. While it is true that Mill's argument, despite the idealistic undertone, still rests explicitly on the social utility of freedom, rather than its absolute value,[67] it is also true that Benthamism was an offspring of the protestant tradition. Mill's ideal of liberty was thus partly inherited.[68]

But the more immediate and personal sources of the ideal are a different branch of the same English tradition. Mill's ideal is, on analysis, "neither Greek, nor Goethian – nor Arnoldian: it is

[64]Richard B.Friedman, "A New Exploration of Mill's Essay *On Liberty*," *Political Science*, XIV (1966), 303.

[65]Ted Honderich, "Mill on Liberty," *Inquiry*, X (1967), 293.

[66]Clark W.Bouton, "John Stuart Mill: On Liberty and History," *Western Political Quarterly*, XVIII (1965), 573-574.

[67]Lichtman, *op.cit.*, 477.

[68]Vernon F.Storr, *The Development of English Theology in the Nineteenth Century, 1800-1860* (London, Longmans, Green, and Co., 1913), p.396.

Romantic."[69] The limiting expression of the ideal is the individual alone with nature, cultivating the unique creative power of his own experience. It is Coleridge and Wordsworth's Romanticism, which centres around the unique and solitary experience of spontaneous individual moral development[70] – the experience which went to make the *Prelude* and the *Ancient Mariner* – and not Shelley's and Byron's Romanticism,[71] not Arnold's proud and dominating Greek independence, that is the image Mill's essay provokes.

Growth is an important corollary of Coleridge's imagery of organism. His "Ideas" are differentiated from simple principles mainly by their capacity for flexible and organic growth, for inner self-development. Growth is often the basis of Coleridge's thoughts, "the *rules* of the Imagination are themselves the very powers of growth and production."[72] Mill's ideas of growth seem to be closer to the germinal "Ideas" of Coleridge than to anything. Mill believes in the self-development of the individual,[73] and although the logical form of Coleridge's moral idea did not appeal to him, the self-directing and self-justifying individualism that results is similar.

II

Mill and Coleridge are close in their educational ideals and their belief in free-will. The concept of liberty must necessarily be based on a belief in free-will. Similarly the concept of self-development involves a belief in education as aiding and not imposing on the mind. Indeed, Coleridge's arguments in *The Friend* that the teacher can only encourage, not inculcate, are echoed by Mill's assertion in *Liberty* that

[69]Walter E.Houghton, *The Victorian Frame of Mind, 1830-1870* (Yale University Press, 1957), p.290.

[70]Charles Larabee Street, *Individualism and Individuality in the Philosophy of John Stuart Mill* (Milwaukee, Morehouse Publishing Co., 1926), p.55.

[71]F.L.Lucas, *The Decline and Fall of the Romantic Ideal* (Cambridge University Press, 1937), p.39.

[72]S.T.Coleridge, *Biographia Literaria*, ed. J.Shawcross, 2 vols. (Oxford, Clarendon, 1907), II, 65.

[73]Abram L.Harris, "John Stuart Mill's Theory of Progress," *Ethics*, LXVI (1955-1956), 162.

each man must be free to develop his own mind as he thinks best. And Coleridge's paternalism in the *Lay Sermons*, where he argues for a carefully directed moral education, is equally echoed by Mill in his attitude to infants and aliens in *Liberty* where paternalistic manipulation of acquired association is envisaged as an appropriate prelude to adult liberties.[74] Mill and Coleridge belong to the same movement of liberal education which through Matthew Arnold was to have a profound effect on the educational system of the country.[75]

Coleridge's belief in free-will is a fundamental part of his reaction to mechanism. He was "convinced, that there is more in man than can be rationally referred to the life of Nature and the mechanism of Organization; that he has a will not included in this mechanism; and that the Will is in an especial and pre-eminent sense the spiritual part of our Humanity."[76] The will stands as the symbol of the active part of our minds – the self-moving. This is the heritage of idealism. Coleridge has followed the traditional opposition to necessitarianism, an opposition which is one of the generating points of his idealism.

Mill, by contrast, avoids necessitarianism only by a sleight of hand which is unsatisfactory because it generates the will in a verbal quibble and does not, like Coleridge, make it a central part of experience. Mill's major achievement is an application of a sophisticated analysis of the laws of casuality. In dealing with human actions, however, volition is a conflicting consideration. Mill distinguishes volition from cause by claiming that, "to my apprehension, a volition is not an efficient, but simply a physical cause."[77] He goes on to preserve free-will in an ingenious argument which makes it a cause of its own decisions with adroitly concealed circularity.[78]

Mill's concern for freedom shows the power of the idealism latent in his orientation, and the free-will bought at such cost to his logical coherence kept him firmly in the English tradition that Coleridge also

[74]E.G.West, "Liberty and Education: John Stuart Mill's Dilemma," *Philosophy*, XL (1965), 138, 142.

[75]J.MacCunn, *Six Radical Thinkers* (London, Edward Arnold, 1910), pp.68-69.

[76]S.T.Coleridge, *Aids to Reflection* (London, G.Bell and Sons, 1884), p.80. Subsequently referred to as *Aids to Reflection*.

[77]*Logic*, I, 410.

[78]Letwin, *Op.cit.*, pp.266-267.

shared. Based on an epistemology whose relativism allowed
considerable latitude, and on a defensive criticism of the opposing
party which was politically, but not philosophically exclusive, both
systems thus set the evidence of experience sufficiently above that of
reason to enable the qualities of a broad awareness of complexities and
a fidelity to the humane aspects of their national tradition to lead
them to similar conclusions in many important applications of their
ideas.

III

The parallels between Mill's and Coleridge's religious ideas are
interesting because the relationship between them is the reverse of the
relationship between their political methodologies. Mill was a
professional sociologist, but in religious matters he is an amateur,
where Coleridge is the experienced professional, well rooted in
knowledge of past, and participation in present, controversy. The
relationship is also reversed. In politics Coleridge was only one facet of
Mill's total background experience, in religion he was much more. For
such theology as Mill possessed did not come from his father, or
Bentham, or Goethe, or even Carlyle, who was little interested in the
logic of religion. It came, rather, from Sterling, the only other friend he
opened his soul to, and from Coleridge, the only religious writer Mill
had read closely enough who was of sufficient power to interest him.
Mill is the only member of his school to take religion at all seriously.[79]
In Mill's agnostic experience of religion the guiding example is
Coleridge, and not Bentham.

Mill's writings on religion belong to a late period of his life, when
reading Coleridge was an experience of the past. But they have the
character of a reversion to an earlier state of mind, rather than of an
extension of the central achievements of *Logic* and *Political Economy*.
The ideas of the *Three Essays on Religion* are a curious mixture of
Coleridge's speculations, and eighteenth century deism of a limited sort
from his parental background.

---

[79]A.W.Benn, *The History of English Rationalism in the Nineteenth Century*, 2
vols. (London, Longmans, Green, and Co., 1906), I, 305-306.

evidences for God inadequate. Mill carefully recognizes however that no proof is not equivalent to disproof. But, reversing the method of science, he does not say that the hypothesis must lapse unless proved; Occam's razor is strangely laid aside. Mill's unwillingness has puzzled many,[84] and in reality it is difficult to explain it on other than irrational grounds. Certainly Mill was habitually fair, but equally he was, during his mature writing, a party to the opposite sect. The conciliatory tone of these *Three Essays on Religion* is perhaps an indication of how far, when considerations of party could be forgotten, Mill's real thought was a patchwork of acquiesced-in compromises.

Mill says that God is on logical grounds only possible, and not probable. Then what would constitute evidence for God's existence? Here his early reading of Coleridge tells, for the only proof Mill really envisages as having any suasive power is the felt *need* of God. Coleridge's outburst, "*Evidences* of Christianity, I am weary of the word; make a man feel the *want* of it . . . "[85] has registered in Mill's realization that "the reason why I think I shall never alter on this matter is, that . . . there is wanting something positive in me."[86] The experienced need is, Mill believes, the only real evidence which will infect the balance of probability with certainty. Coleridge's lesson has been more thoroughly absorbed by the utilitarian than by the theists to whom it was directed.[87] Thus Mill, knowing he had no feeling for God, declared to Carlyle that belief in God was, for him, impossible.

And here Mill was wrong, not in logic but in fact. He had, in any case, contradicted himself in this letter, and his own need was real enough at times. He wrote to Sterling, "I can understand your need of something beyond it & deeper than it, & I have often bad moods in which I would most gladly postulate like Kant a different ultimate foundation 'Subjectiver bedürfnisses willen' if I could."[88] After Harriet died the need became even more pressing.[89] But the contradiction

[84]Benn, *op.cit.*, II, 327; see also Robert Carr, "The Religious Thought of J.S.Mill," *J.H.I.*, XXIII (1962), 485.

[85]*Aids to Reflection*, p.272.

[86]*Works*, XII, 206.

[87]Carr, *op.cit.*, 478.

[88]*Works*, XIII, 406-407.

[89]Wilfrid Ward, "John Stuart Mill," *Quarterly Review*, CCXIII (1910), 274.

between these needs and the denial of the possibility of experiencing them is not a real one. The letter to Carlyle is concerned to re-assert Mill's philosophical radicalism, and this explains some of the exaggerations. But the truth was that although Mill felt and recognized the need for some certainty, he did not feel what reading Coleridge had taught him to recognize as a true religious feeling; namely the intense need for a personal God.

Coleridge's personal need for God expressed itself in his theology in many ways. It was the reason for his rejection of both Spinoza and Schelling.[90] Similarly, he defined prayer as the attempt to mitigate the misery of not being in God, rather than by willing not to be in God. He also argued for the personality of God by destroying the notion that personality implies limitation, though he did insist that personality in God is not the same as personality in man. This personal need for a relationship Mill knew he did not understand in Coleridge's sense of inner knowledge. Although he had insisted against Coleridge and intuitionism that belief is not equivalent to proof as evidence in religious matters,[91] Mill did add that "there is no appeal from the human faculties generally, but there is an appeal from one human faculty to another."[92] His sensitivity to human needs, above the contradictions of human logic, finally led him to accept Coleridge's arguments for the human need of religion sufficiently to write a series of essays on religion.

What, on the other hand, might Mill consider as evidence *against* the existence of God? Here he fell into as unsatisfactory a piece of argument as any in his works. Mill said in the letter to Carlyle that "ordinary difficulties" such as the origin of evil were no difficulty to him. This is contradicted by his later essays on religion, for the problem of evil is at the heart of these essays. But yet, at a profounder level he was right, for Mill never fathomed the depths of the problem. For Coleridge it had, indeed, been a focus of a great struggle. Yet far from being a disproof of God, it is the ground of his necessity. Evil,

---

[90]*Collected Letters of Samuel Taylor Coleridge*, ed. E.L.Griggs, 4 vols. (Oxford, Clarendon, 1956-59), IV, 883. Subsequently referred to as *Letters*.

[91]*Logic*, II, 96-97.

[92]*Ibid.*, 97.

Coleridge defines as the Will (which must be free, potentially) willing to be separated from God. Since only God is being, to be separated from God is not to be, "a strange and appropriate contradiction."[93] In adopting a form of Manicheism Mill was following his father's lead, for James Mill seemed to think it the most tenable of religious doctrines and is said to have been surprised that it did not have a larger contemporary following.[94]

The *Three Essays of Religion* end with a tentative faith[95] because two factors also constitute positive evidence of the existence of God for Mill. The first is the ethical value of religion, the second the hope of immortality. Mill saw, in faith in goodness, a profound and valuable ethical force. The ethical criterion is probably more basic than any other in Mill's religious ideas. It is the reason for his Manicheism, and the proud and famous outburst in the essay on Hamilton.[96] Mill had always been attracted by the morality of religion.[97] And once again the intensity of his moral ideals held him to positions which his logic would not easily explain.[98] The moral value of religion remains for him, as for Coleridge, one of its best recommendations, despite its irrelevance to utilitarian priciples.

The second of the factors that seems to predispose Mill to the possibility of belief is the strength of his hope for immortality. Mill is careful to distinguish between hope and belief, and yet he accepts the hope of immortality, the most powerful of religious impulses, as innocuous and consoling, even in the absence of belief. Immortality had always been a central question for Mill. In the letter to Carlyle which has been taken as a measure of his earlier beliefs, he wrote,

> with respect to the immortality of the soul I see no reason to believe

---

[93]*Opus Maximum*, transcribed by Muirhead, *op.cit.*, p.241.

[94]Letwin, *op.cit.*, p.195.

[95]J.S.Mill, *Three Essays on Religion* (London, Longmans, Green, and Co., 1885), pp.255-257.

[96]J.S.Mill, *An Examination of Sir William Hamilton's Philosophy*, 5th ed. (London, Longmans, Green, Reader, and Dyer, 1878), p.129.

[97]Ward, *op.cit.*, 277; R.V.Sampson, "J.S.Mill: An Interpretation," *Cambridge Journal*, III (1950), 234.

[98]Albert L.Hammond, "Euthyphro, Mill and Mr. Lewis," *The Journal of Philosophy*, XLIX (1952), 377.

that it perishes; not sufficient ground for complete assurance that it survives; but if it does, there is every reason to think that it continues in another state such as it has made itself here, and no further affected by the change than it would be by any equally great event during its sojourn on earth, were such possible. Consequently in all we do here we are working for our 'hereafter' as well as our 'now.'[99]

After Harriet's death, this 'hope' became much stronger and stands out in the *Three Essays on Religion* as the cause of some special pleading.

The hope is perhaps a basic religious instinct in man, and yet it is supported by little evidence. Mill might have rejected it as wishful thinking as sternly as his father did, had he not Coleridge's example to tell him that the deeply felt needs of the true self were to be respected as real evidence; and Coleridge's assertion that,

I have so deep an intuition that *to cease to be* are sounds without meaning, that though I wish to live, yet the Thought of Death is never for a moment accompanied by Gloom, much less terror, in my feelings or imagination.[100]

Not surprisingly, Mill's essays caused some unease when they were published – his delay of a decade or so in publishing them shows that he had expected such a reaction. The religious press was "jubilant" and the utilitarians dismayed.[101] The essays were used as triumphant evidence against Mill and his doctrines by many incautious commentators, and for many more serious attempts to do justice to Mill they remained a source of "perplexity."[102] Yet the interest in them seemed to be a passing one for the general public, perhaps because interest in Schopenhauer's pessimism soon displaced them.[103] They were taken as a "biographical curiosity,"[104] but the disturbing lack of the penetrating insight that informs *Liberty* caused them to become one of Mill's least read works. But much of the reaction was based on a misunderstanding. The essays are not confessions of faith, but

[99]*Works*, XII, 207.
[100]*Letters*, II, 719.
[101]Ward, *op.cit.*, 289.
[102]W.S.Jevons, "John Stuart Mill's Philosophy Tested," in *Pure Logic and Other Minor Works* (London, Macmillan & Co., 1890), p.200.
[103]Benn, *op.cit.*, II, 323.
[104]*Ibid*, 327.

confessions of the impact of ideals which had been patent throughout his mature work.

Despite an apparent concern with the argument from design, the main tenor of Mill's ideas is different from the typical discussions of the eighteenth century, of Bentham and James Mill. It is first and foremost human needs and human hopes which he takes as the valid evidence for a discussion of religion, and in a framework of relativism, the ontological arguments are insignificant in the face of the ethical. It is here that Mill has learnt from Coleridge, for these arguments were not taken from Mill's inheritance. Indeed, the methodology of the essays springs from a familiar combination of the methods of Bentham and Coleridge, in the attempt to understand the reason for religion's continued existence, and to make an impartial assessment of its social value.[105]

IV

All Englishmen are liberals; the Conservatives are liberals on the right, and the Labourites, liberals on the left. That is the plain truth. Politics which divides these parties is far less important than the ideal of liberalism which unites them.[106]

Mill and Coleridge are both transitional figures. This is especially true in the way their ideas comprise revolutions of thought. Each had lived within the opposed systems, each had experienced the gamut of opinions available in a turbulent age when religion was undergoing dramatic changes and materialism undergoing fundamental modifications.[107] Mill, in particular, is a transitional figure between "sensationalism" and "scientific empiricism," and in the confusion is, by absolute standards, "doubly wrong."[108] He is the "fascinating" locus

---

[105]Carr, *op.cit.*, 491.

[106]J.Selwyn Shapiro, "John Stuart Mill, Pioneer of Democratic Liberalism in England," *J.H.I.*, IV (1943), 127.

[107]Ward, *op.cit.*, 281.

[108]William Leonard Courtney, *The Metaphysics of John Stuart Mill* (London, C.Kegan Paul and Co., 1879), p.150.

of "every crux and conflict" of his age.[109] His personal philosophy "falls between the two" ages, and results in his "unstable eclecticism."[110] Yet, in this unfortunate[111] and confusing position his contributions in modifying Benthamism have always been judged to be significant.[112] Coleridge, too, straddles the transition between the unitarian echoes of deism and Hartley's quasi-Christian materialism typical of the eighteenth century, and the liberal theology of the nineteenth century. *Confessions of an Inquiring Spirit* is one of the documents of this change, as *Biographia Literaria* is of the major change in aesthetics of the time.

Some commentators believe that T.H. Green said what Mill would have said, had he lived in a later age.[113] Yet Green's inheritance comes mainly from Coleridge. Again the cross-links of the relationship become so complex as to knit together the ideas of Mill and Coleridge in a way that suggests more community than has previously been allowed them. The common English national background is another explanation of their similarities. To a remarkable extent their reaction to continental political theories, whether idealist or revolutionary, was the reaction of the liberal English tradition. Coleridge warned against the "political fanatics of both sides with the suspicion always characteristic of the predominant strain in English political thought."[114] And the outstanding feature of Mill's relation to Comte was his rejection of Comte's dogmatic authoritarianism in favour of English liberalism. Comte, Street remarks, "had the Catholic Church for his background,"[115] and Mill had tolerant English protestantism for his.

Coleridge's politics retained a clear distinction between state and

---

[109] A.O.J.Cockshut, *The Unbelievers, English Agnostic Thought, 1840-1890* (London, Collins, 1964), p.19.

[110] Jevons, *op.cit.*; J.C.Rees, "A Phase in the Development of Mill's Ideas on Liberty," *Political Studies*, VI (1958), 33.

[111] Bertrand Russell, "Lecture on a Master Mind; John Stuart Mill," *Proceedings of the British Academy*, XLI (1955), 43.

[112] MacCunn, *op.cit.*, 86.

[113] Adam B.Ulam, *Philosophical Foundations of English Socialism* (Cambridge, Harvard University Press, 1951), p.28.

[114] John Bowle, *Politics and Opinion in the Nineteenth Century* (London, Jonathan Cape, 1954), p.94.

[115] Street, *Op.cit.*, p.30.

individual rights, not different in practical effect to Mill's distinction in
Liberty.[116] In Mill's and Coleridge's historiography, too, a common
English flavour can be detected. They, and their disciples, both
retained "the habitual suspicion with which English thinkers have
regarded deterministic theories," one of the "archetypal traits of the
English mind of the period," according to Preyer.[117]

Mill and Coleridge agreed in their opposition to Marxian and
Comtian socialism. They both believe "to put the point in pregnant
words of his own drawn from Coleridge, that 'revolutions are sudden to
the unthinking only'."[118] Although they had different views on the
pace appropriate to social change, they both agreed as to the agent of
this change – the gradual moral maturing of the individuals in the
society. Mill did not even insist on the maturity of the majority, but
followed Coleridge in believing that the leavening of a privileged,
educated minority would direct society on the right lines. Both also
display a fundamental empiricism which is typical of the English
tradition. They adhere to experience in preference to inference, the
only separation between them being in what was admitted as
experience, and what was discarded as illusion.

Mill belonged with Coleridge to the century which could not
envisage liberty, once gained, being voluntarily surrendered in favour of
efficient authoritarianism.[119] Neither did Mill, like Coleridge, face the
need to distinguish between liberty and socialism. An attempt to read
the problem into his thought leads to a "perplexing inconsistency."[120]
Mill was the great liberal, "in Mill, one 'sees an age, and one sees a
man'; and, it might be added, one sees a nation, – liberal England."[121]
and one of the important members of the same liberal tradition is
Coleridge.

---

[116]See Laure J.Wylie, *Studies in the Evolution of English Criticism* (Boston, Ginn
& Co., 1903), pp.181-182; also R.O.Preyer, *Bentham, Coleridge, and the Science of
History*, Leipziger Beitrage zur Englischen Philologie, 41 Heft (Bochum-Langendreer,
Verlag Poppinghaus, 1958), p.25.

[117]*Ibid.*, p.81.

[118]MacCunn, *op.cit.*, p.51.

[119]Schapiro, *op.cit.*, 158.

[120]Street, *op.cit.*, p.4.

[121]Schapiro, *op.cit.*, 127.

Perhaps the final explanation of their similarities lies in their common teachers. William Godwin, Coleridge's close friend and one time teacher was a friend of James Mill and a "frequent visitor."[122] Many of the intellectuals of the time remained in touch with both movements. Peacock, for instance, knew both Coleridge and Mill. The intellectual background on which they were fed was the same. Locke gave both Mill and Coleridge a common sense of relativism profoundly typical of the tenor of English philosophy. Locke's advice to,

> the busy mind of man to be more cautious in meddling with things exceeding its comprehension . . . and to sit down in a quiet ignorance of those things which, upon examination, are found to be beyond the reach of our capacities,[123]

had evidently a seminal effect on the temper of mind of the two exponents of the opposite branches of the English tradition in the nineteenth century. Both of them worked in the tradition whose major task for over a century was to attempt to clarify the difficulties of Locke's assumptions and terminology. Among Locke's intellectual heirs there remained, whatever their differences, a sense of community.

[122]West, *op.cit.*, 130.

[123]John Locke, *An Essay Concerning Human Understanding*, ed. A.S.Pringle-Pattison (Oxford, Clarendon, 1924), p.12.

7 The uncertain allies: church and clerisy

We honour Coleridge for having rescued from the discredit in which the corruptions of the English Church had involved everything connected with it, and for having vindicated against Bentham and Adam Smith and the whole eighteenth century, the principle of an endowed class, for the cultivation of learning, and for diffusing its results among the community. – John Stuart Mill[1]

The parallels discussed in the last chapters between two great but opposed thinkers are, at best, fitful. This is not to be disloyal to the argument which has just been made; it is to say that care is needed to make a correct estimate of the similarities in the true perspective of the differences. That there are similarities is highly illuminating, but none of the parallels dealt with so far are anything but minor. Individually they mean little; as much community could be claimed between many writers by mere virtue of the complexities whereby ideas are propagated.

In the next three chapters, however, three strong parallels are dealt with; in several instances they are clearly borrowings, often extensively acknowledged. These are parallels in the idea of an endowed "clerisy" for national cultivation, in the theory of poetry, and in the important apologia for eclecticism, the "half-truth" theory. It is important, however, to keep the evidence of the opposed philosophies of Mill and

[1]*Mill on Bentham and Coleridge*, with an introduction by F.R.Leavis (London, Chatto and Windus, 1962), p.148; subsequently referred to as *Bentham and Coleridge*.

Coleridge carefully in mind. In dealing with the parallels the major opposition may be blurred and unless the balance between them is carefully kept the sharpness of the argument is lost. Only in the context of opposition are the parallels so interesting.

I

Of the three major parallels the first, and most important, is Mill's use of Coleridge's idea of the "clerisy". From his first reading of *Church and State* Mill was excited by the idea of the "clerisy". "Did you ever read [Coleridge's] little work on Church and State? If not, read it; if you have, tell me whether you agree with it in the main (I mean the Church part of it) as I do." He immediately goes on to avow that, "few persons have exercised more influence over my thoughts and character."[2] The close conjunction of the two comments suggests that it was perhaps admiration for this work more than for any other which prompted Mill's gratitude.

Undoubtedly *Church and State* was the most important of Coleridge's works for Mill. He read it, and re-read it,[3] even though it was not published until after that change of opinions which put him in his closest contact with Coleridge. In the "Coleridge" essay he devoted most of his attention to the clerisy, as well as using the ideas, with explicit acknowledgement, in the earlier essay on "Corporation and Church Property" (1833),[4] and in a review of Tocqueville's *Democracy in America*.[5] Whatever his reservations, he never retracted his admiration for its principles,[6] and accorded it praise even in the works

[2]*The Collected Works of John Stuart Mill*, ed. F.E.L.Priestley, Vols.XII and XIII, "The Earlier Letters, 1812-1848," ed. F.E.Mineka (University of Toronto Press, 1963), XII, 221. Subsequently referred to as *Works*, XII or XIII.

[3]*Ibid.*, XIII, 408.

[4]J.S.Mill, "Corporation and Church Property," *Jurist*, IV (February, 1833), 1-26; reprinted in *Dissertations and Discussions*, 4 vols. (London, Longmans, Green, Reader, and Dyer, 1867-75), I, 1-41. Subsequently referred to as *Dissertations and Discussions*.

[5]"Democracy in America," *Edinburgh Review*, LXXII (October, 1840), 1-47. Reprinted in *Dissertations and Discussions*, II, 1-83.

[6]J.H.Burns, "J.S.Mill and Democracy, 1829-61," *Political Studies*, V (1957), 175.

of his maturity, such as the *Logic* and the *Political Economy*.[7]

Although Coleridge's *Church and State*, where the idea of the clerisy is set out is, in origin, a distinctively conservative book it represented for Mill new and important political truths which complemented some of the deficiencies of Bentham's system. It was Coleridge's last publication during his lifetime, and contained the results of his latest political speculation. It was undoubtedly, also, an influential work. Both the Broad Church movement, through F.D. Maurice,[8] and the High Church movement, through Keble and Newman,[9] were profoundly affected by it. Through Mill and the Arnolds,[10] Coleridge's idea of culture and its guardians became widely current in the nineteenth century and it is probably on this book that his claim to importance among his own contemporaries and immediate successors must largely rest. Its popularity in the nineteenth century was due both to the fact that it is by far the most systematic and coherent of all Coleridge's productions, and to its contemporary relevance to the problem of the function of an established church within a progressive society. Conversely, as that problem waned with the decreasing political importance of religious questions in the twentieth century, so Coleridge's book was forgotten. It is, indeed, of largely historical interest, and of little relevance today; it does, however, represent the peak of Coleridge's achievement as an influential and coherent political writer.

Coleridge analyses the English constitution into two constituent orders, the Landed and the Mercantile. These "two antagonist powers or opposite interests of the state, under which all other state interests are comprised, are those of *permanence* and of *progression*."[11] He distinguishes the "Proprietry" from a different group of property-

---

[7] J.S.Mill, *Principles of Political Economy* (London, Longmans, Green, and Co., 1900), p.589.

[8] See F.D.Maurice, *The Kingdom of Christ*, ed.A.R.Vidler, 2 vols. (London, S.C.M.Press, 1958), II, 352-364.

[9] See W.R.Castle, "Newman and Coleridge," *Sewanee Review*, XVII (1909), 152.

[10] Leon Gottfried, *Matthew Arnold and the Romantics* (London, Routledge and Kegan Paul, 1963), pp.164-176.

[11] S.T.Coleridge, *On the Constitution of Church and State* (London, Hurst, Chance, & Co., 1830), p.18. Subsequently referred to as *Church and State*.

holdings, called the "Nationality." The "proprietry" is the private property of individuals, yet their title is not absolute, but conditional since it is,

> declared, by the spirit and history of our laws, that the possession of a property, not connected with especial duties, a property not fiduciary or official, but arbitrary and unconditional, was in the light of our forefathers the brand of a Jew and an alien; not the distinction, nor the right, or honour, of an English baron and gentleman.[12]

This doctrine was radical enough in spirit, if not in application, to attract the Liberals, and to disturb the Tories.

The "Nationality," however, is even more specifically linked with the performance of a duty. It is reserved for the endowment of the National Church, "the third remaining estate of the realm," whose function is "to secure and improve that civilization, without which the nation could be neither permanent nor progressive."[13] The functionaries of the National Church are the clerisy, and their duty is to preserve the civilization and thereby the identity, as well as the moral and physical strength of the nation. Coleridge draws a distinction between civilization and cultivation which echoed throughout the nineteenth century.[14] It is the duty of the clerisy to keep this distinction clear. Without them, he told his hearers at Highgate, "there could be no order, no harmony of the whole."[15]

The clergy have a number of valuable functions in the state, corollaries of their status as cultivators. Firstly they provide hope for advancement for all, because, while the "Proprietry" is essentially inherited, the "Nationality" is "circulative," and its benefits are open to anyone capable of proving himself worthy of it. Secondly, the clerisy "develop, in every native of the country, those faculties, and provide for every native that knowledge and those attainments, which are necessary to qualify him for a member of the state."[16] It also gives

---

[12]*Ibid.*, p.42.

[13]*Ibid.*, pp.44-45.

[14]See Raymond Williams, *Culture and Society, 1780-1950* (London, Chatto and Windus, 1958), p.254; see also *Church and State*, p.43.

[15]S.T.Coleridge, *The Table Talk and Omniana*, ed. T. Ashe (London, G.Bell and sons, 1923), p.158.

[16]*Church and State*, p.77.

individual care to all, in contrast to the impartial anonymity of the state. It is, indeed, one of the glories of the English clergy that they are able to give this classless and individual attention to the people by virtue of living among them as family men.[17]

The function of the National Church, then, is to protect and foster the cultivation and individual self-fulfillment of the people. Coleridge sees four ways in which the endowments of the National Church should be distributed to achieve this end.

> 1st. To the maintenance of the Universities and the great liberal schools. 2ndly. To the maintenance of a pastor and a schoolmaster in every parish. 3rdly. To the raising and keeping in repair of the churches, schools, &c., and, Lastly: To the maintenance of the proper, that is, the infirm, poor whether from age or sickness.[18]

The main part of this distribution, and that which concerns Coleridge most closely, is the maintenance of the clergy of whom

> a certain smaller number were to remain at the fountain heads of the humanities, in cultivating and enlarging the knowledge already possessed . . . being, likewise, the instructors of such as constituted . . . the remaining more numerous classes of the order [which] were to be distributed throughout the country, so as not to leave even the smallest integral part or division without a resident guide, guardian, and instructor.[19]

In each parish Coleridge envisages a schoolmaster and a pastor, carrying out as colleagues their function as guardians of humane culture.[20]

Coleridge now goes on to discuss, in some detail, the nature of the connection between the National Church, and the established Christian Churches, the historical and accidental connection between them he would see as evidence for the absolute necessity of their continued unity. Coleridge points out that the link between culture and religion is valid, not only for the Middle Ages, when the church was the only preserver of human learning, but for all times because, "to divinity belong those fundamental truths, which are the common ground-work of our civil and religious duties (Not without celestial observations can

[17]*Ibid.*, pp.79-80.
[18]*Ibid.*, p.72.
[19]*Ibid.*, pp.43-44.
[20]*Ibid.*, pp.55-56.

even terrestrial charts be accurately constructed)."[21] Religion is therefore seen as essential to the proper function of the clerisy. Coleridge concludes, in one of many passages of fine invective, by insisting again that,

> a national clerisy or church, is an essential element of a rightly constituted nation, without which it wants the best security alike for its permanence and its progression; and for which neither tract societies, nor conventicles, nor Lancastrian schools, nor mechanics' institutions, nor lecture-bazaars under the absurd name of universities, nor all these collectively, can be a substitute.[22]

II

Mill's understanding of the importance of "culture" made him conscious that there was much truth in Coleridge's arguments. Indeed, at first he was apparently prepared to accept Coleridge's ideas in their entirety, writing to Sterling in 1831, "I certainly think it desirable that there should be a national clergy or clerisy, like that of which Coleridge traces the outline, in his work on Church & State."[23] Three years later Mill still agreed "with it in the main,"[24] and when he came to write the "Coleridge" essay in 1840 he felt that, "his 'Church & State' must of course be very prominent in any such view of him as I should take I think the Church & State the best of Coleridge's writings yet known to me."[25] He was so impressed by Coleridge's idea of the "clerisy" that he incorporated it as a permanent part of his political ideology, and refers to it in many of his writings.

There is little doubt that Mill was greatly impressed by the idea of a "clerisy". But his acceptance of Coleridge's idea needs some explanation. *Church and State* was primarily intended to support the establishment, and was often used by Coleridgeans to justify the Church in its existing form. If it is in some ways a doubtful support Coleridge had not intended it to be. Mill, in direct contrast, was firmly

---

[21]*Ibid.*, p.50.
[22]*Ibid.*, p.70.
[23]*Works*, XII, 75.
[24]*Ibid.*, 221.
[25]a*Ibid.*, XIII, 408-409.

in favour of disestablishment. How did he reconcile this with his admiration for *Church and State*?

Perhaps Mill was attracted by the superficial similarity between Utilitarian theories of self-interest as the basic datum of political life, and Coleridge's division of the constitution into three "estates" according to the balance between various conflicting self-interests.[26] But the problem remains that Mill was using the same theory as part of a radical political platform that Maurice was able to use to support his adherence to the thirty-nine articles. The answer is probably that Mill is not as entirely in agreement with Coleridge as he claims. While justly stressing radical elements in Coleridge's thought (which some of the Coleridgeans ignored) he is, on the other hand, omitting much of Coleridge that embodies the spirit of a very real desire to conserve.

Neither Mill nor the Coleridgeans preserved the fine balance of Coleridge's analysis which sought to transform the spirit of the Church while maintaining the sanctity of its outward form. And as much as some Coleridgeans over-emphasized Coleridge's conservatism, Mill over-stresses the radical element. He soon recognized his divergences from Coleridge, for when he first discussed *Church and State* in detail, writing to Sterling, he qualifies his approval in an important way.

> If therefore I thought that the present Peerage & Clergy would ever consent to become the peerage of a government constituted on anti-jobbing principles, & the clergy of a non-sectarian Church, I should pray for their continuance. But they never will . . . the clergy . . . are mainly divisible into two great categories, the worldly-minded, & the sectarians. I know that you will not agree with me, but I think that Coleridge would, in thinking that a national clergy ought to be so constituted as to include all who are capable of producing a beneficial effect on their age & country as teachers of the knowledge which fits people to perform their duties & exercise their rights . . . now I contend that such persons are to be found among all denominations of Christians, nay even among those who are not Christians at all: provided . . . they abstain from . . . directly attacking . . . Christianity.[27]

The passage, especially Mill's belief that Coleridge would side with him against the Coleridgean Sterling, is first hand evidence of how thoroughly Mill absorbed the spirit of *Church and State*. As well as

---

[26] J.H.Burns, *op.cit.*, 175.
[27] *Works*, XII, 75-76.

accepting Coleridge's ideal of the clerisy he has accepted the need for them to be at least not anti-Christian. But while approving of the connection between the National and Christian Churches on grounds of present expediency, which are partly the grounds on which Coleridge accepted it, he has not accepted Coleridge's political arguments for their identity on the grounds of security. Neither has he accepted Coleridge's insistence that religion is essential to the proper function of the clerisy in absolute terms. This, Mill is right in suggesting, was part of Coleridge's argument in *Church and State*, but it was not the whole of it. Mill's concept of expediency is different from Coleridge's and this difference is the source of Mill's divergence from Coleridge's original position.

Mill's expediency is the preservation of order, and it is proposed as a temporary measure. Coleridge's conception of expediency is basic to his conservatism. His argument in *Church and State* can be expressed as a distinction between four categories of justification for the existence of institutions. These categories are: necessity in principle, contingency in principle, historical necessity, and historical contingency. The first category comprises what could not be otherwise because of basic human social nature; the second what could, in principle, have been differently instituted; the third what has, in historical fact, become so established that it could not be otherwise; and the fourth what is by chance in one form but may be transformed into another form without difficulty.

Coleridge is at great pains to make the distinction between the second and third category quite clear and at the same time to insist that they are, in practice, to be equated. In specific terms, he points out that the connection between the National Christian Churches is only contingent in principle. They serve distinct purposes in the community. The National Church attends to "culture", its aim is temporal, while the Christian Church worships God, and its aim is supernatural. There is no necessary connection between these functions and it is quite possible to fulfill them independently. Indeed, Coleridge suggests, there is some conflict between these aims. The worship of the eternal demands some sacrifice of the temporal interests of man, and the institutionalization needed for the propagation of culture interferes with the spirituality of religion.[28] However, moving from the realm of

[28]*Church and State*, pp.59-61.

principle to that of historical fact, he argues that these two functions have grown up together round the same institution and body of men, the "clergy." Thus the historical fact is so established as to have the same effect as a necessary condition in principle. The Churches are in Coleridge's view totally inseparable.

It is undoubtedly a measure of Coleridge's conservatism that he should argue that what is no more than contingent in principle is necessary historically in view of its actual existence. Or, rather, to say that he equates these two things is to define what is meant by conservatism in philosophical terms. It is equally, of course, a measure of Mill's radicalism that he does not accept this equation between the contingent in principle and the historically necessary. The category of the historically necessary does not exist for him. Although he understood Coleridge, and was aware that the link between religion and culture "is the natural result of his system of metaphysics," he feels that Coleridge "runs riot"[29] with the idea. Thus he not only ignores Coleridge's fine distinction between various relations of the contingent and the necessary, he even claims Coleridge's sanction for doing so. In this way he is able to use Coleridge's arguments to support conclusions quite different from Coleridge's.

III

Mill's essay on "Corporation and Church Property" is a radical discussion of the whole question of endowments. He argues that no founder can know the best use his money might be put to several centuries after his death. After the period of time during which he might be judged to be able to exercise reasonable foresight, the State has a right, if not an obligation, to divert the legacy into channels more likely to fulfill the spirit of the bequest. The argument is, however, prefaced and concluded by considerations which derive, essentially and explicitly, from Coleridge's "idea" of endowed institutions in *Church and State*.

Mill starts by pointing out that the problem of endowments, like all political problems, is a twofold one, "a question of expediency, and

[29]*Works*, XIII, 408.

a question of morality: the former complex, and depending upon temporary circumstances, the latter simple, and unchangeable."[30] Mill follows Coleridge's premises when he defines two sorts of property. The first is "Corporation property," the second "Church property," which "is held in trust, for the spiritual culture of the people of England."[31] After he has presented his main arguments he repeats Coleridge's ideas closely while discussing the resultant problems. He asserts that man needs more from government than protection from interference. For, "the primary and perennial sources of all social evil, are ignorance and want of culture. These are not reached by the best contrived system of political checks, necessary as such checks are for other purposes."[32]Mill is here foreshadowing his criticisms of Bentham in 1838. What he affirms is true, but only half the truth; men need protection from government but they also need "culture," and the word on Mill's lips comes straight from Coleridge.[33] This is the other half of the truth which he added to his Utilitarianism.

Mill argues that the best remedy for this "want of culture" is "the unremitting exertions of the more instructed and cultivated,"[34] which is in essence the clerisy working he suggests, following Coleridge, from the Universities and Colleges as well as by preaching and writing. And it is this work which, above all, provides "a wide field of usefulness open for foundations."[35]

He concludes that,

> the endowments of an established church should continue to bear that character, as long as it is deemed advisable that the clergy of a sect or sects should be supported by a public provision of that amount: and under any circumstances, as much of these endowments as is required should be sacredly preserved for the purposes of spiritual culture; using that expression in its primitive meaning, to denote the culture of the inward man – his moral and intellectual well-being, as distinguished from the mere supply of his bodily

[30]*Dissertations and Discussions*, I, 2.
[31]*Ibid.*, 12.
[32]*Ibid.*, 28.
[33]See *Early Essays by J.S.Mill*, ed. J.W.M.Gibbs (London, G.Bell & Sons, 1897), p.233.
[34]*Dissertations and Discussions*, I, 28.
[35]*Ibid.*

wants.[36]

The Nationality, he is arguing, is given to the Christian clergy only as far as it is expedient, not by any essential necessity. But, he adds, "culture" is "sacred," and the real goal of endowments should be its preservation. Mill has used Coleridge's ideas extensively in this essay, and his debt is quite explicit.

> Such, as has been forcibly maintained by Mr. Coleridge, was the only just conception of a national clergy, from their first establishment. To the minds of our ancestors they presented themselves, not solely as ministers for going through the ceremonials of religion, nor even solely as religious teachers in the narrow sense, but as the *lettered* class, the *clerici* or clerks; who were appointed generally to prosecute all those studies, and diffuse all those impressions, which constituted mental culture, as then understood; which fitted the mind of man for his condition, destiny, and duty, as a human being. In proportion as this enlarged conception of the object of a national church establishment has been departed from, so far, in the opinion of the first living defender of our own establishment, it has been perverted both in idea and in fact from its true nature and ends.[37]

The way in which Mill is merely repeating Coleridge's arguments from *Church and State* with approval hardly needs comment. But, although Mill is doing nothing to undermine the position of the Christian Church as the trustees of this function, neither is he concerned, as Coleridge was, to stress any necessary connection between them. Rather, he stresses the possibility of their disjunction; and he lends Coleridge's authority to this possibility.

> The perfect lawfulness of such an alienation as this is explicitly laid down by the eminent writer to whom we have just referred. It is part of his doctrine, that the State is at liberty to withdraw the endowment from its existing possessors, whenever any body of persons can be found, whether ministers of religion or not, by whom the ends of the establishment, as he understands them, are likely to be more perfectly fulfilled.[38]

This is an exaggeration, for Coleridge meant theoretical liberty, and insisted that there was no practical liberty, but Mill chose to ignore the distinction. He has thus used Coleridge's authority improperly. Unable to see the value of Christianity and doubtful of the

---

[36] *Ibid.*, 37.
[37] *Ibid.*, 37-38.
[38] Ibid., 38.

Church's capacity for reform, he prefers to see it as only in temporary connection with the National Church.

IV

Mill deals with Coleridge's concept of the clerisy in a similar way in the 1840 essay on Coleridge, although he is now at odds with Coleridge's intention in a more calculated way. He allows Coleridge to explain his doctrine in his own words; four pages of the essay[39] comprise extended quotation and summary of chapters five and six of *Church and State*, a significant number since Mill was not in the habit of quoting at length from the authors he reviewed except where he agreed with their opinions. In particular, Mill quotes the passages where Coleridge expounds the idea of the "clerisy" very fully, but he omits, in each case, passages where Coleridge stresses the connection of the National and Christian Churches. He quotes, for instance, the statement that Christianity is "no essential part of the being of the national Church, however conducive or even indispensable it may be to its well-being."[40] At this point Mill stops. But in *Church and State* Coleridge goes on to "earnestly entreat" that the two conditions of his statement be remembered, that it is only a theoretical ideal, not a practical fact, and that the two churches do not require two distinct staffs.[41]

Thus Mill uses Coleridge's apparent authority, as he did in the earlier essay, to stress the possible disjunction between the two Churches. Again, it is a distortion of Coleridge's original intention, but it is now for a slightly different purpose. In "Corporation and Church Property" Mill was attempting to convince the present supporters of the Established Church that their principle defender was himself prepared to countenance the diversion of their endowments. In the 1840 essay, he is demonstrating his own catholicity of mind by showing the Utilitarians the extent to which he is able to sympathize with Coleridge's apparently alien positions. But he is also trying to

[39]*Bentham and Coleridge*, pp.142-145.
[40]*Ibid.*, p.145.
[41]*Church and State*, p.61.

demonstrate Coleridge's liberality of thought. He is addressing the
Benthamites when he turns to consider Coleridge's doctrine of the
clerisy. "We would assist them to determine," he writes, "whether they
would have to do with Conservative philosophers or with Conservative
dunces; and whether, since there are Tories, it be better that they
should learn their Toryism from Lord Eldon, or even Sir Robert Peel,
or from Coleridge."[42] Mill then concludes his discussion of the clerisy
triumphantly, with the exclamation, "what would Sir Robert Inglis, or
Sir Robert Peel, or Mr. Spooner say to such a doctrine as this? Will
they thank Coleridge for his advocacy of Toryism?"[43]

It is tempting to wonder what Coleridge himself would have
thought of Mill's use of his doctrines. Although Mill is prepared to
admit that, "in any person fit to be a teacher the view he takes of
religion will be intimately connected with the view he will take of all
the greatest things which he has to teach," he insists that "the most
unfit body for the exclusive charge of [education] that could be found
among persons of any intellectual attainments [is] . . . among the
established clergy as at present trained and composed."[44] He then
repeats his argument that Coleridge himself had claimed that the State
is at perfect liberty to transfer the Nationality in order to "establish
any other sect, or all sects, or no sect at all."[45]

Mill has used Coleridge to make a point which is alien to
everything Coleridge stood for. The bare theoretical bones of
Coleridge's thought, stripped of its conservative elements, are
endorsing a radical conclusion. And so Mill is able to claim that it is
the radicals, and not the conservatives, who find in Coleridge their
most useful ally. What he did with *Church and State* is, of course,
characteristic of his method. He took from it what was useful and
ignored the remainder. This is the practical reality of his belief in
combining the 'half-truths' of opposed schools. It is only half of
Coleridge's ideas which he uses to add to Bentham's half; the rest he
ignored. In the end, though, it is probably to Mill's credit that he so

---

[42]*Bentham and Coleridge*, p.141.
[43]*Ibid.*, p.146.
[44]*Ibid.*, pp.146-147.
[45]*Ibid.*, p.146.

openly adopted and utilized what he could from another thinker, even if he did do violence to the other system in the process. And it is undoubtedly to Coleridge's credit that his political philosophy was so firmly based on principles and not on party prejudices that Mill was able to use it, albeit in an altered form. It is thus the radicals as well as the conservatives who were Coleridge's heirs.

V

Mill's acceptance of Coleridge's idea of the clerisy is based on important modifications of its principles. The results of this acceptance are that, for the first time, Mill had a rational and benevolent basis for urging the domination of the educated few. James Mill wished the middle class to become the controlling class,[46] but it was left to his son to provide a complete framework for this victory.[47] John Mill showed his valuation of the rights of the educated not only in *Liberty* and in his championship of the proportional voting system, but also in his belief in the importance and power of the "few."[48] These were the same as Coleridge's "few that really govern the machine of society."[49] "What is Mankind," Coleridge declared, "but *the Few* in all ages?"[50] The few were to be scattered as the leaven of the land, the clerisy. J.S. Mill even wished to see a 'few', a "lettered class" in India to bring culture to the mass, and they would necessarily be endowed.[51] The closeness of Coleridge's ideas to Mill's is best seen, however, in the role they play in Mill's contact with the superficially similar idea of the "pouvoir spirituel" of the Saint-Simonians. Coleridge's concepts,

---

[46]Joseph Hamburgher, "James Mill on Universal Suffrage and the Middle Class," *Journal of Politics*, XXIV (1962), 168.

[47]See George Cornwall Lewis, *Letters*, ed. G.F.Lewis (London, Longmans, Green, and Co., 1870), p.49.

[48]*Dissertations and Discussions*, I, 469.

[49]S.T.Coleridge, "The Statesman's Manual," in *Political Tracts of Wordsworth, Coleridge, and Shelley*, ed. R.J.White (Cambridge University Press, 1953), p.16.

[50]*Collected Letters of Samuel Taylor Coleridge*, ed. E.L.Griggs, 4 vols. (Oxford, Clarendon, 1956-59), IV, 714.

[51]Abram L.Harris, "John Stuart Mill: Servant of the East India Company," *Canadian Journal of Economics and Political Science*, XXX (1964), 197.

particularly that of the clerisy, prepared Mill to understand the doctrines of the Positivist school. His initial acceptance of Comte's historical analysis, for instance, may have been due to the fact that, in his own words, the same "tendency first showed itself [in England] in some of the minds which had received their earliest impulse from Mr. Coleridge they have, after their own fashion, a philosophy of history."[52]

Mill's absorption of the idea of the 'Pouvoir Spirituel' was equally rapid, undoubtedly for the same reason. In the 1831 essays on the "Spirit of the Age," which showed a great deal of Positivist influence, Mill argues that "most men must, in the last resort, fall back upon the authority of still more cultivated minds, as the ultimate sanction of the convictions of their reason itself."[53] Here is the doctrine of the 'Pouvoir Spirituel' reproduced in Mill's own words, and Mrs. Mueller argues that his acceptance of this doctrine was at this stage at its height.[54] But such an abdication to Saint-Simonism is against the more permanent tenor of Mill's opinions, and in fact in this essay he has accepted explicitly no more than the need for an informed body to lead the masses. This body is evidently the same as the clerisy. At first, however, he ignored the difference between Coleridge's liberal clerisy, working by education, not by instruction, and Comte's 'Pouvoir Spirituel', which imposed the superior conclusions of the new social science. When the difference did become a matter of concern, partly as a result of reading Tocqueville, Mill remained closer to Coleridge than to Comte. He preferred the guardians of culture to the hierarchy of moral authority.

In *Comte and Positivism*, (1867) Mill is still "without doubt" that it is "the necessary condition of mankind to receive most of their opinions on the authority of those who have specially studied the matters to which they relate,"[55] but, he now adds, "in order that this

---

[52]*Dissertations and Discussions*, II, 222.

[53]J.S.Mill, "The Spirit of the Age," *Examiner*, January 23rd., 1831, p.52.

[54]Iris Mueller, *John Stuart Mill and French Thought* (Urbana, University of Illinois Press, 1956), p.55.

[55]*The Collected Works of John Stuart Mill*, ed. F.E.L.Priestley, Vol.X, "Essays on Ethics, Religion, and Society," ed. J.M.Robson (University of Toronto Press, 1969), 313.

salutary ascendancy over opinion should be exercised by the most eminent thinkers, it is not necessary that they should be associated and organized."[56] He does not consider how authority that is not unanimous can be effective, nor how any authority which is not organized can be unanimous. He is assuming that the presentation of truth will elicit a natural response – assuming, that is, the presence of something akin to Coleridgean 'Reason' in men.

Here, in the rejection of organization as unnecessary and dangerous, Mill follows Coleridge's concept of the function of a clerisy who encourage the growth of inner culture more closely than the Positivist ideal of a doctrinaire moral and religious authority with a hierarchical structure.

VI

Mill also used the idea of the clerisy to defend his own beliefs against Tocqueville's criticism of democracy. Mill admired Tocqueville's work, but he did not accept his pessimistic view of the results of democracy. Tocqueville was afraid that democracy would result in "tyranny over opinions, not over persons," and his "fears are for the moral dignity and progressiveness of the race."[57] Mill was aware that this would be a very real criticism of democracy if it were true, but he believed that these fears were, at least in the case of Europe, exaggerated. He based his confidence on the existence of a body which is akin to Coleridge's clerisy.

> In countries where there exist endowed institutions for education, and a numerous class possessed of hereditary leisure there is a security, far greater than has ever existed in America, against the tyranny of public opinion over the individual mind. . . . A leisured class would always possess power sufficient not only to protect themselves, but to encourage in others the enjoyment of individuality of thought. . . . In the existence of a leisured class we see the great and salutary corrective of all the inconveniences to which democracy is liable.[58]

Endowed leisure for the cultivation of the people is the basic

---

[56] *Ibid.*, 314.

[57] "De Tocqueville on Democracy in America," *London and Westminster Review*, XXX (1835), 121.

[58] *Ibid.*, 125-126.

concept of the clerisy and, although Coleridge did not intend his clerisy to work as specifically for the preservation of individuality as does Mill, his ideas are not radically different. For the clerisy is to be a third, independent estate, and to provide one of the checks and balances which Coleridge, like Mill, saw as an essential part of any free constitution. Thus Mill was able to conclude his first (1835) review of Tocqueville with the confidence that, "we see nothing in any of these tendencies from which any serious evil need be apprehended."[59]

But it was in Mill's review in 1840 of the second book of Tocqueville's *Democracy in America* that he turned most clearly to Coleridgean ideas to answer Tocqueville's more insistent criticism of democracy. Between writing the first and second parts of his work, Tocqueville's fears that the tyranny of the majority was the ultimate danger in society had been considerably strengthened, and in 1840 Mill understood more thoroughly what it was that concerned Tocqueville. But Mill again turned to the idea of a clerisy as the natural guardians of liberty of thought.

> What is requisite in politics is not that public opinion should not be, what it is and must be, the ruling power; but that, in order to the formulation of the best public opinion, there should exist somewhere a great social support for opinions and sentiments different from those of the mass. . . . there can be no doubt about the elements which compose it: they are, an agricultural class, a leisured class, and a learned class. The natural tendencies of an agricultural class are in many respects the reverse of those of a manufacturing and commercial.[60]

The argument uses Coleridge's idea of the two balancing forces needed in a constitution, those of progression which he identified with the commercial interest and those of permanence which he identified with the landed interest. The leisured and learned classes provide a cultural individualism protected by the balanced opposition of the two great interests. Mill thus took Coleridge's analysis of the English constitution as the centre of his answer to Tocqueville's criticism of democracy.

Coleridge's idea of the clerisy played an important role in Mill's thinking. Although Mill chose to ignore his insistence that the rights of

[59] *Ibid.*, 126.
[60] *Dissertations and Discussions*, II, 73-74.

the Nationality belonged inalienably to their present possessors, the part of the doctrine Mill did accept was the most important part in practical political terms. The importance of this is that Mill's essays, which had, and still have, a vastly wider circulation than *Church and State*, must have been most effective in propagating Coleridge's ideas to a wider audience. In this way Coleridge influenced the developing recognition amongst the inheritors of the radical tradition of the place of culture in society.[61]

[61]See R.J.White, "John Stuart Mill," *Cambridge Journal*, V (1951), 89.

8 Mill on poetry

Between *Biographia Literaria*, and "The Function of Criticism at the Present Time,"[1] to take two peaks from the range of criticism that links the Romantics to the Victorians, attitudes to the function of poetry in society changed in important ways. If the change is not as dramatic as that in the previous fifty years, between say Johnson and Coleridge, it is still a major change. The broad outlines of Arnold's critical theories had already been laid down by Coleridge; what changed was the often unspoken assumptions that regulated the intuitive sympathies of the critics. For all the mysteries of the "Imagination" Coleridge believed in the importance of "good sense" in criticism,[2] and in poetry's real social function. Arnold, however, convinced of the "high" calling of poetry,[3] struggled with a janus-faced belief that poetry was withdrawn from this world, sometimes believing the poet was a purifier, and sometimes fearing he was a deserter.[4]

There are, of course, transitional stages between Coleridge and Arnold, as there are between Johnson and Coleridge, and Mill's writings on art form one of these stages. They are not usually given

---

[1]Matthew Arnold, *Lectures and Essays in Criticism*, ed. R.H.Super, *The Complete Prose Works of Matthew Arnold*, III (Ann Arbor, University of Michigan Press, 1962), pp.258-285.

[2]S.T.Coleridge, *Biographia Literaria*, ed. J.Shawcross, 2 vols. (Oxford, Clarendon, 1907), II, 13. Subsequently referred to as *Biographia Literaria*.

[3]S.T.Coleridge, *Biographia Literaria*, ed. J.Shawcross, 2 vols. (Oxford, Clarendon, 1907), II, 13. Subsequently referred to as *Biographia Literaria*.

[4]*The Letters of Matthew Arnold to Arthur Hugh Clough*, ed. H.F.Lowry (London, Oxford University Press, 1932), P.146.

much historical importance,[5] and undoubtedly they are an early, and marginal part of Mill's output. But, obviously derivative, they are also prophetic, and this paradox is of special interest in the context of a study of Mill and Coleridge. In his writings on art Mill was greatly influenced by both Coleridge's and Wordsworth's ideas on aesthetics, but he also modified them in very important ways, which enable us to see the beginnings of characteristically "Victorian" critical theories.[6]

Mill was in an unusual situation. He had the normal educated man's acquaintance with Augustan poetry, but he had learnt nothing about the theories of poetry that went with it. Consequently, when he became sufficiently interested to theorize about poetry in his early twenties, he had no foundation of previous conceptualizations to work from. The elements of "good sense" and decorum, which play their part in Wordsworth and Coleridge alongside Romanticism, were lost on Mill. He thus acquired the sort of theoretic attitude to poetry which was to be common only in Victorian times; a Romanticism more disparate from Augustan theory than Coleridge's or Wordsworth's could ever have been. Thus poetry for Mill was a private experience, damaged by contact with the "vulgar"[7] world of the everyday. He is recognizably Victorian in the way in which, once having relegated poetry to a private world, he began to stress the prior claims of public life. Coleridge and Wordsworth also gave him useful insight into the essential role of thought in poetry, but Mill inverted the relation between the intellectual and the poetic and claimed that theoretical "truth" must come first, poetry's function merely being to clothe it. In the end he was led to argue that work on poetry should be postponed until the political battles of the time were over.

Mill's poetic theory also offers an interesting sidelight on the modifications Utilitarianism underwent in his hands. In accepting

[5]René Wellek, "The Age of Transition," in *A History of Modern Criticism, 1750-1950*, 5 vols. (London, Jonathan Cape, 1955), III, 135.

[6]F.R.Leavis, *New Bearings in English Poetry* (London, Chatto and Windus, 1932), pp.9-15.

[7]*Early Essays by J.S.Mill*, ed. J.W.M.Gibbs (London, G.Bell and Sons, 1897), p.233n; reprinted in *Dissertations and Discussions*, 4 vols. (London, Longmans, Green, Reader, and Dyer, 1867-75), I, 91n. These two works are subsequently referred to as *Early essays*, and *Dissertations and Discussions*..

Romantic poetic theories in the early eighteen-thirties Mill adopted the model of the mind as an active participant in perception, rather than the passive "tabula rasa" of Hartley and James Mill. Although he rejected the intuitionism which was the ground of this theory, the extent to which he was able to understand it is significant, and is possibly one source of his modifications of the Benthamite tradition.

I

Despite the myth, for which he was himself pre-eminently responsible, the adolescent Mill was never entirely indifferent to poetry. He was "theoretically indifferent" indeed, but in practice he had read and appreciated a great deal of poetry as a normal part of his education.[8] What he lacked was not appreciation, but the habit of attaching importance to this appreciation.

This changed around the time of the "crisis" in 1826, after which Mill did take an active interest in poetry and music, and wrote a number of essays and articles on it.[9] He would probably have read Wordsworth and Coleridge as a normal part of his self-education, but doing so coincided with a new need, and their theories, which explained this need, rapidly became Mill's own. The orientation of his ideas probably never altered more than superficially, but his intellectual passivity towards poetic culture was radically changed during the crisis. Art, Mill had discovered, could provide happiness. He had "learned from W. that it is possible by dwelling on certain ideas and proper regulation of the associations to keep up a constant freshness in the emotions."[10] He had found in poetry an antidote to cynicism and world-weariness, an antidote to the "accidie"[11] of his crisis.

The result was an active incursion into the field of criticism. This

---

[8]Shirley R.Letwin, *The Pursuit of Certainty* (Cambridge University Press, 1965), pp.195, 203; see also J.S.Mill, *Autobiography*, 3rd ed. (London, Longmans, Green, Reader, and Dyer, 1874), pp.10, 71, 112. Subsequently referred to as *Autobiography*.

[9]John R.Hainds, "Mill's Examiner Articles on Art," *J.H.I.*, XI (1959), 215-234.

[10]Karl Britton, "J.S.Mill: A Debating Speech on Wordsworth, 1829," *Cambridge Review*, LXXIX (1958), 420.

[11]Aldous Huxley, "Accidie," in *On the Margin, Notes and Essays* (London, Chatto and Windus, 1923), pp.18-25.

took its first form in the advocacy of Wordsworth in 1828 at the Debating Society,[12] which brought about a closer acquaintance with the Coleridgeans, and its final form, some years later, in a number of articles on art. Little more than an evident determination to be involved with art and propagate its appreciation can be deduced from the first reviews Mill wrote for the *Examiner*. But these were soon followed by the reviews of the music of Eliza Flower, which show a very considerable sensibility becoming explicit, although there is evidently a personal motive behind the extravagant praise Mill lavishes on her compositions.[13]

Mill's writings on art culminated in a series of articles in W.J. Fox's *Monthly Repository*,[14] and in the reviews of Tennyson, Carlyle, de Vigny and Milnes.[15] After the second of the two *Repository* articles had been published, he still felt "that it is far from going to the bottom of the subject, or even very deep into it: I think I see somewhat further

[12]*Autobiography*, pp,149-150; see also Britton, *op.cit.*.

[13]Hainds, *op.cit.*, 219n-220n.

[14]W.J.Fox (1786-1864) edited the *Monthly Repository* with Robert Aspland, and owned it between 1831 and 1836. Mill wrote for it between 1832 and 1835, see F.E.Mineka, *The Dissidence of Dissent: The Monthly Repository, 1806-1838* (Chapel Hill, University of North Carolina Press, 1944), p.275. Mill contributed a number of reviews (see Hainds, *op.cit.*), a long letter "On Genius," VI (1832), 649-659; "What is Poetry?" VII (January, 1833), 60-70; "The Two Kinds of Poetry," VII (November, 1833), 714-724; "On the Application of the Terms Poetry, Science and Philosophy," VIII (1834), 323-331. All except the last one are signed "Antiquus." The last one is signed "Philo-mousos," and is not mentioned in Mill's own list of his works, see J.R.Hains, Ney MacMinn and James McCrimmon, *Bibliography of J.S.Mill*, Northwestern University Studies, 12 (Northwestern University Press, 1945). The article is identified as by Mill in the Ms *Index* to *Monthly Repository*, Vols. IV to X in the British Museum.

[15]"Tennyson's Early Poems," *Westminster Review*, XXX (July, 1835), 402-424, reprinted in Early essays, pp. 239-267; "The French Revolution," *Westminster Review*, XXVII (July, 1837), 17-53, reprinted in *Early Essays*, pp.271-323; "poems and Romances of Alfred de Vigny," *Westminster Review*, XXXI (April, 1838), 1-44, reprinted in *Dissertations and Discussions*, I, 312-354; "Tennyson," *Quarterly Review*, LXX (September, 1842), 385-416; "Milnes' Poems of Many Years," *Westminster Review*, XXIX (April, 1838), 308-320.

into it now, and shall perhaps understand it in time."[16] He even
proposed, some months later, to take over the literary department of
the *Examiner* himself, leaving Fonblanque to be the political editor.[17]
When James Mill died it finally gave Mill the opportunity to expand
the horizons of the Utilitarian review, the *London and Westminster*,[18]
and to present "a utilitarianism which takes into account the whole of
human nature not the ratiocinative faculty only ... which holds
Feeling at least as valuable as Thought."[19] Mill's interest in art,
however, seems to have declined sharply after 1834 as other concerns
became more pressing.

Carlyle said of Mill that if he ever got into heaven he would not be
happy until he had made out how it all was; Mill's new love of art was
therefore not without a theory. The sources of this theory are obvious,
since to a very large extent Mill reproduces the critical theories of
Wordsworth and Coleridge. He had spent some time in Wordsworth's
company on a visit to the Lakes in 1831,[20] and discovered that "when
you get Wordsworth on the subjects which are peculiarly his, such as
the theory of his own art ... no one can converse with him without
feeling that he has advanced that great subject beyond any other
man."[21] "The science of criticism," he felt, "can almost be said to have
commenced in this country with Wordsworth's Prefaces."[22] And

---

[16]*The Collected Works of John Stuart Mill*, ed. F.E.L.Priestley, Vols. XII and XIII,
"The Earlier Letters, 1812-1848," ed. F.E.Mineka (University of Toronto Press, 1963),
XII; 162. Subsequently referred to as *Works*, XII and XIII.

[17]*Ibid.*, 198.

[18]The *London and Westminster Review* was formed in 1836 by merging the
Westminster Review, edited by Sir John Bowring, and subsequently by J.S.Mill
between 1824 and 1836, with the *London Review*, started in 1835. The *London and
Westminster* ran as a Utilitarian review until it was sold to W.E.Hickson, with the
condition that it resumed the title of *Westminster Review*, in 1840. It changed hands
several times and finally ceased publication in 1914.

[19]*Works*, XII, 312.

[20]Anna J.Mill, "John Stuart Mill's Visit to Wordsworth, 1831," *Modern Language
Review*, XLIV (1949), 341-350.

[21]*Works*, XII, 81.

[22]Britton, *op.cit.*, 418.

Wordsworth led Mill to Coleridge.[23]

It is not, of course, always feasible to distinguish between the influences of Wordsworth and Coleridge, but it is occasionally clear that Coleridge's ideas alone are influencing Mill. Mill undoubtedly derived most of the ideas in his essays on art from one or the other. He inherited, for instance, the distinction between Imagination and Fancy, which is the most characteristic Romantic doctrine,[24] and he follows the trail of Imagination to the very threshold of Idealism. But perhaps most valuable was a new awareness of the need to interpret a work of art before judging it, although the result was that he relied heavily on his inner feelings without the unspoken, but very real, awareness of decorum which is to be found in Coleridge and Wordsworth. Mill took over unaltered attitudes common in Romantic criticism, such as the depreciation of the epic in favour of the lyric.[25] He also entered the fundamental argument about the nature of the true distinction between poetry and prose. But he developed a test of the poetic which is wholly his own, and it is really this that is the key to the characteristically Victorian element in his criticism. Mill ultimately distinguished poetry (which, as in Shelley, means not verse but any work of the imagination)[26] not from prose, or even as in Wordsworth from science, but from eloquence. Eloquence is public and suasive, poetry is private and withdrawn. Mill's own ideas were here at war with the basic perception of Wordsworth and Coleridge that poetry communicates truth, and this is the point at which Mill's thought

---

[23]*Memories of Old Friends: Being Extracts from the Letters and Journals of Caroline Fox, from 1835 to 1870*, ed. H.N.Pym, 2 vols. (London, Smith, Elder, & Co., 1882), I, 147.

[24]*Biographia Literaria*, II, 12; *Poetry and Prose of William Blake*, ed. Geoffrey Keynes (London, Nonesuch Press, 1943), p.835; *The Letters of John Keats, 1814-1821*, ed. Hyder Rollins, 2 vols. (Cambridge University Press, 1958), I, 170; *The Complete Works of William Hazlitt*, ed. P.P.Howe, 21 vols. (London, J.M.Dent & sons, 1930-1934), V, 4.

[25]*Shelley's Prose*, ed. David Lee Clarke (Albuquerque, University of New Mexico Press, 1954), p.281; Alexander Smith, "The Philosophy of Poetry," *Blackwoods*, XXXVIII (December, 1835), 836; Edgar Allen Poe, "The Poetic Principle," in *The Complete Poetical Works with Three Essays on Poetry*, ed. R.Brimley Johnson (London, Oxford University Press, 1909), p.213.

[26]Shelley, *op.cit.*, p.279.

moves from the derivative to the prophetic.

II

The most important idea Mill inherited from the Romantics was the distinction between Imagination and Fancy which was the centre of Coleridge's poetic theory. Mill often uses the terms "Imagination" and "Fancy" without any rigour. Shelley, for instance, is praised for his "teeming fancy."[27] But this does not preclude Mill from understanding Coleridge's more exact desynonymization, and where he uses the words "Fancy" and "Imagination" together it is clear that they possess definite and distinct connotations. Thus Mill writes that, "the wholes which Imagination constructs out of the materials supplied by the Fancy, will be indebted to some dominant *feeling.*"[28]

If Mill's usage is sometimes casual, he has grasped what is in practical terms the essential part of Coleridge's distinction, that of the unity of a work of Imagination. Reviewing two of Tennyson's early poems he writes, "in both there is what is commonly called imagination – namely, fancy: the imagery and the melody actually haunt us; but there is no harmonizing principle in either; – no appropriateness to the spiritual elements of the scene."[29] Mill contrasts "real feelings" with the "mere play of fancy,"[30] in terms close to Coleridge's. There are, Mill writes,

> two essential elements of the poetic character – creative imagination, which, from a chaos of scattered hints and confused testimonies, can summon up the Thing to appear before it as a completed whole: and that depth and breadth of feeling which makes all the images that are called up appear arrayed in whatever, of all that belongs to them, is naturally most affecting and impressive to the human soul.[31]

There are close parallels between this and Coleridge's description

---

[27] *Early Essays*, p.230.

[28] *Ibid.*, p.225.

[29] *Ibid.*, p.225.

[30] *Dissertations and Discussions*, I, 296-297; see also M.H.Abrahams, *The Mirror and the Lamp* (New York, Oxford University Press, 1953), p.178.

[31] *Early Essays*, p.279.

of the poet who "diffuses a tone and spirit of unity."[32]

Mill apparently equates genius in poetry with the exercise of the Imagination.

> The property which distinguishes every work of genius in poetry and art from incoherency and vain caprice is, that it is *one, harmonious,* and a *whole*: that its parts are connected together as standing in a common relation to some leading and central idea or purpose. This idea or purpose it is not possible to extract from the work by any mechanical rules.[33]

Of course, Wordsworth, as well as Coleridge, is behind this, and it would be difficult to distinguish the influences. But the idea of the Imagination, whatever the source, has evidently become part of Mill's critical equipment. "A great actor," he writes, "must possess imagination, in the higher and more extensive meaning of the word . . . And this is what is meant by the universality of genius."[34] Mill is equating genius and imagination. He argues that,

> in acting, as in everything else, genius does not consist in being a copyist; even from nature . . . the actor of genius is not he who observes and imitates what men . . . in particular situations, *do*, but he who can, by an act of the imagination, actually *be* what they are,[35]

He writes elsewhere that, "the faculty of thus bringing home to us a coherent conception of beings unknown to our experience . . . is what is meant, when anything is meant, by the words creative imagination."[36] At times, the idea of genius, like that of imagination, becomes really a rather trite tool of criticism, and the muddles illustrate how lamely Mill was able to "hobble after" the poet.[37] But the point emerges that Mill links genius with originality, and with unity of conception, and uses it, both deliberately and casually, as an equivalent of the word "Imagination."[38]

It is thus the letter "On Genius" which Mill wrote for the *Monthly*

---

[32]*Biographia Literaria*. II, 12.
[33]"On Genius," *op.cit.*, 653.
[34]Hainds, *op.cit.*, 218.
[35]*Ibid.*, 226.
[36]*Early Essays*, p.263n.
[37]*Autobiography*, p.176.
[38]"On Genius," *op.cit.*, 653.

Repository, in the same year as the articles on art, that shows how thoroughly Mill absorbed the concept of the Imagination. In reply to a previous article which suggested that genius was the faculty of inventing an historically original idea, Mill asks,

> is genius any distinct faculty? Is it not rather the very faculty of thought itself? And is not the act of *knowing* anything not directly within the cognizance of our senses . . . truly an exertion of genius . . . To *know* these truths is always to *discover* them . . . Knowledge comes only from within; all that comes from without is but *questioning*, or else it is mere *authority*.[39]

Here Mill's conception of genius as "the very faculty of thought itself" is a mixture of Coleridge's primary Imagination which is "the living Power and prime Agent of all human Perception," and his distinction between substantial and superficial knowledge.[40] Genius is seen as the realizing factor in the process of perception, comparable to the creative Imagination. But if genius is equivalent to originality of thought, Mill insists, following Coleridge, that originality consists not in lack of historical precedents, but in the freshness of the act of perception. "To *know* these truths is always to *discover* them." Mill values the act of knowledge only in so far as it involves active perception, rather than passive imitation. In this way Coleridge's idea of the creative imagination can be seen helping Mill to a new valuation of the creative role of the mind.

Coleridge had said that to describe poetry one must first describe the poet,[41] and Mill follows him in "The Two Kinds of Poetry" when he turns his discussion of the nature of poetry into one of the nature of the poetic mind.

> The word poet is the name also of a variety of *man*, not solely of the author of a particular variety of *book* . . . Whom, then, shall we call poets? Those who are so constituted, that emotions are the links of association.[42]

In poets, "feeling, when excited . . . seizes the helm of their thoughts, and the succession of ideas and images becomes the mere utterance of an emotion. . . . what constitutes the poet is . . . the law

---

[39] *Ibid.*, 650-652.
[40] *Biographia Literaria*, I, 202.
[41] *Ibid.*, II, 12.
[42] *Early Essays*, p.223.

according to which [his images] are called up."[43] He distinguishes two different kinds of association, that ruled by thought and that ruled by emotion.

This distinction originally came from a paper by James Martineau,[44]

> the last two pages of [which] . . . made an impression on me which will never be effaced. In a subsequent paper of my own in the 'Repository' headed 'The Two Kinds of Poetry' (October, 1833) I attempted to carry out your speculation into some of those ulterior consequences which you had rather indicated than stated.[45]

Mill saw the possibility of evolving two separate kinds of association to solve the problem of poetic creativity which was a thorn in the side of classic associational theory. But the direction which these speculations took after Martineau's hints was due to Coleridge. Martineau's two kinds of association were succession and simultaneousness, that is thought and feeling. Coleridge's distinction is between the aggregative Fancy and the unifying Imagination, which is qualitatively different from the Fancy, and is not a form of association at all, but a transcendent principle. Coleridge's Fancy is indeed, like Mill's, a principle of association by thought, a mechanical principle. As so often, one half of Coleridge's new desynonymization incorporates the ideas of the eighteenth century, and Mill must have easily recognized the concepts of the Fancy. But Mill's association by emotion is in origin also a mechanical principle, part that is of the "mechanico-corpuscular" philosophy which Coleridge's Imagination was designed to replace. But the implications of association by emotion are radically different. For the principle of organization is no longer an external one, but an internal, dynamic one. Emotion now "seizes the helm" and selects from the objective world only what is required for the expression of its inner state. Essentially, the latent image of the mind in this operation is that of the lamp, and not of the mirror.[46]

---

[43]*Ibid.*, pp.231-232.

[44]James Martineau, "Joseph Priestley; Life and Works," *Monthly Repository*, VII (1833), 19-30; reprinted in his *Essays, Reviews, and Addresses*, 4 vols. (London, Longmans, Green, and Co., 1890-1891), I, 1-42.

[45]*Works*, XII. 247.

[46]Abrahams, *op.cit.*, p.26.

Obviously, Mill was unable to accept the full implications of Coleridge's theory of the Imagination which, without the intuitionism and religious mysticism on which it is based, must be ultimately unintelligible, but he incorporated this "half" of the truth into his own theory. Feeling himself unable to deny the existence of a quality in the poetic mind which could not be accounted for by the traditional theories of association, Mill devised a new principle of association by emotion which in certain ways denies what was fundamental in that tradition.

At this stage Mill told Carlyle that he thought "most of the highest truths, are, to persons endowed by nature in certain ways which I think I could state, intuitive,"[47] and he came to regard logic, not as dispelling the illusions of intuitionism, but as the humble interpreter of intuitionism. It was only for a short time in the early eighteen-thirties that he went as far as this, and he very soon retracted these suggestions and hints – it would be wrong to imagine they were ever any more that this – and he never stated them in published writings. But he clearly accepted at this date the dominance of feeling over logic. Far from being antagonistic to logic, he then believed that the "capacity of strong feeling, which is supposed necessarily to disturb the judgement, is also the material out of which all *motives* are made ... for energy of character is always the offspring of strong feeling."[48] One of his explanations of his crisis was that analysis had worn away his feelings, and thus left him without motives. He turned to Romantic poetry to provide him with those feelings. In doing so Mill had also absorbed some elements of the Romantic theory of the mind. The idea of the creative Imagination had profound repercussions on Mill's epistemology, although the majority of the critical ideas he learnt from Coleridge cast only a dim and borrowed light on Mill's main ideas.

III

Despite his early reading of the Augustans under his father, his approach to the criticism of poetry was that of the Romantics, not the

---

[47]*Works*, XII, 163.
[48]*Early essays*, p.234.

Augustans. Wordsworth and Coleridge insisted that the critic should be sympathetic and interpretative in his approach to a work of art, not as so much neo-classical criticism was, legalistic. "I have one request to make of my Reader," Wordsworth writes in his Preface, "which is, that in judging these Poems he should decide by his own feelings genuinely."[49] He realizes that, "every Author, as far as he is great and at the same time *original* has had the task of *creating* the taste by which he is to be enjoyed."[50] Mill imitates Wordsworth's point with very little alteration. "All . . . thinkers or artists," he writes, "must themselves create the tastes or the habits of thought by means of which they will afterwards be appreciated."[51] Wordsworth admits that, "this remark was long since made to me" by Coleridge,[52] and Coleridge indeed insists even more strongly than Wordsworth on sympathetic criticism. "I know nothing," he writes, "that surpasses the vileness of deciding on the merits of a poet or painter . . . by accidental failures or faulty passages."[53] Or, making the same point in a familiar aphorism, "*until you understand a writer's ignorance, presume yourself ignorant of his understanding.*"[54]

Mill seems to have been entirely convinced by these arguments and everywhere relies not on rules, but on his own feelings for the interpretation of poetry. He suggests that a poem should at first be felt, and only then be analysed. "If everyone approached poetry in the spirit in which it ought to be approached, willing to feel it first and examine it afterwards"[55] all would be well. It is therefore important to read poetry with a "catholic spirit; it we read it captiously we shall never have done finding fault."[56] It is, he realizes, easy to find much "to say against the poem; if we insist upon judging it by a wrong

[49]*Wordsworth's Poetry and Prose*, ed. W.M.Merchant (London, Rupert Hart Davies, 1955), p.233. Subsequently referred to as Wordsworth.

[50]*Ibid.*, p.275.

[51]*Dissertations and Discussions*, I, 321-322.

[52]Wordsworth, p.275.

[53]*Biographia Literaria*, I, 43.

[54]*Ibid.*, 160.

[55]*Early essays*, p.248.

[56]*Ibid.*, p.321.

standard."[57] And Mill is as scathing as Coleridge is about the reviewing of the time, criticising its "strain of dull irony, of which all the point consists in the ill-nature."[58] Interestingly, it is just those "disgraceful articles in the early numbers of the 'Edinburgh Review' on Wordsworth and Coleridge"[59] which Mill selects for particular criticism.

IV

Perhaps the central point of Mill's poetic theories is an echo of Wordsworth's dictum, "all good poetry is the spontaneous overflow of powerful feelings."[60] "Poetry," Mill wrote, is "the expression or uttering forth of feeling."[61] But Mill, characteristically, exaggerates the implications of the idea, in saying that,

> one may write genuine poetry, and not be a poet; for whosoever writes out truly any one human feeling, writes poetry. All persons, even the most unimaginative, in moments of strong emotion, speak poetry . . . poetry is natural to most persons at some period of their lives.[62]

He defines poetry as "feeling expressing itself in the forms of thought."[63] Mill stresses "feeling" more than Wordsworth or Coleridge did, but he does deduce from this a conclusion which Coleridge endorsed, that true poetry can only exist in short, that is lyric, forms. Coleridge suggested that, "a poem of any length neither can be, or ought to be, all poetry."[64] Mill parallels Coleridge's point, arguing that, "it being impossible that a feeling so intense as to require a more rhythmical cadence than that of eloquent prose should sustain itself at its highest elevation for long together . . . a long poem will always be felt . . . to be something unnatural and hollow."[65] In elevating lyric

[57]*Ibid.*, p.245.
[58]*Ibid.*, p.241.
[59]*Ibid.*, pp.214-242.
[60]Wordsworth, p.223.
[61]*Early Essays*, p.208.
[62]*Ibid.*, p.223.
[63]*Works*, XIII, 470.
[64]*Biographia Literaria*, II, 11.
[65]*Dissertations and Discussions*, I, 326-327.

poetry, he deprecates the novel, which he feels like Coleridge to be a kind of epic. Mill draws a "radical distinction between the interest felt in a novel as such, and the interest excited by poetry; for the one is derived from *incident*, the other from the representation of *feeling*,"[66] and he points out that, "an epic poem . . . in so far as it is an epic (i.e. narrative), it is not poetry at all."[67]

The problem which dogged all the Romantic apologists for poetry as pure feeling was the nature of the distinction between poetry and prose. Mill's essay, "What is Poetry," opens with the assertion that the most unsatisfactory definition of poetry is that which "confounds poetry with metrical composition," for poetry "may exist in what is called prose as well as in verse."[68] It is Wordsworth's position that, "between the language of prose and metrical composition . . . there neither is nor can be any essential difference."[69] Coleridge, on the other hand, argued that metre was an organic part of poetry, and Mill is evidently following Wordsworth in preference to Coleridge. But the essay "What is Poetry" was not the last thing which Mill recorded on the subject. In 1841 he wrote to G.C.Lewis,

> I allow that there is a natural, not an arbitrary relation between metre & what *I* call poetry. This is one of the truths I had not arrived at when I wrote those papers in the Repository but what afterwards occurred to me on the matter I put . . . into the . . . article . . . on Alfred de Vigny.[70]

And writing to Lewis again, a week later, he agreed that, "you have just as much right to use the word Poetry . . . as synonymous with 'Art by the instrument of words' . . . Taking Poetry in this sense I admit that metre is of the essence of it or at least necessary to the higher kinds of it."[71]

In the de Vigny article Mill formulated for the first time a real distinction between verse and prose. "Nothing," he wrote, "should be written in verse which is not exquisite. In prose, anything may be said

---

[66]*Early essays*, p.203.

[67]*Ibid.*, p.213.

[68]*Ibid.*, p.201; see also *Works*, XIII, 464.

[69]Wordsworth, p.227.

[70]*Works*, XIII, 464.

[71]*Ibid.*, 466.

which is worth saying at all; in verse, only what is worth saying better than prose can say it. The gems alone of thought and fancy, are worth setting with so finished and elaborate a workmanship." And he goes on to describe the characteristic excellencies of verse as, firstly, "it affords a language more *condensed* than prose" and secondly, "ever since man has been man, all deep and sustained feeling has tended to express itself in rhythmical language."[72]

Mill is here closer to Coleridge than to Wordsworth, especially in the recognition of the condensed and passionate expression which is the mark of poetry, and the result of metre. Wordsworth's discussion of metre is part of his pursuit of a theory of poetic diction. He is faced, in the course of it, with the question, "why have I written in verse?" to which his answer is that metre produces "excitement in coexistence with an overbalance of pleasure." Metre is seen as a sweetener for dour topics, which superadds "the charm which by the consent of all nations is acknowledged to exist in metrical language."[73] It was left to Coleridge to formulate an organic theory of metre.

Coleridge argued, first, that "the elements of metre owe their existence to a state of increased excitement ... every passion has its proper pulse,[74] and secondly that, "metre in itself is simply a stimulant of the attention."[75] Mill's two points were that metre is the language of passion, and secondly that it had unusual penetrating power, that it was, if not a stimulant, a substitute for attention. Allowing for the fact that Mill is not pursuing a theory of poetic diction, but a theory of metre, his arguments are in substance those of Coleridge, and certainly widely divergent from Wordsworth's.

V

Mill did not, in fact, concern himself much with the differences between Wordsworth and Coleridge on the question of the true nature of poetic diction, despite his involvement in the argument about metre.

[72]*Dissertations and Discussions*, I, 325-326.
[73]Wordsworth, p.228.
[74]*Biographia Literaria*, II, 50, 56.
[75]*Ibid.*, 53.

But his only reference to diction[76] suggests that he was more impressed by Coleridge's arguments than by Wordsworth's. Wordsworth had insisted that the language of poetry should be that of natural, uncorrupted speech, and although it is arguable that Wordsworth's formulations were more polemical than definitory, Coleridge makes the obvious case against his cultural primitivism, in the same terms as Mill was to use. "Every passion," Coleridge wrote, "has . . . its characteristic modes of expression . . . an unusual state of excitement . . . of course justifies and demands a corresponding difference of language."[77]

Although Mill looks for the origin of metre in the primitive language of passion, on the whole he acknowledges Coleridge's argument for the development of a sophisticated language appropriate to passion. In true poetry, he writes,

> the ideas or objects . . . are spoken of in words which we spontaneously use only when in a state of excitement . . . This . . . seems to point to the true theory of poetic diction; and to suggest the true answer to as much as is erroneous of Mr. Wordsworth's celebrated doctrine on that subject.[78]

Presumably Mill was influenced in this declaration against Wordsworth by the arguments he had read in *Biographia Literaria*.[79] It is worth noting that Wordsworth's theory, which has been labelled "cultural primitivism" is analogous to Platonic modes of thought, in that it claims that we get nearer to the true idea of language by going back to its origins. Wordsworth typically locates his ideals in his own childhood, as he locates the ideal of language in the childhood of the race. By contrast with this, Coleridge's theory of diction is essentially one based on associational psychology, and probably owes most to the Aristotelian aspects of Hartley.[80] For Coleridge, a special "poetic" diction is a natural development (the concept of natural modes of

---

[76]*Early Essays*, pp.232n-233n.

[77]*Biographia Literaria*, II, 56.

[78]*Early essays*, pp.232 and 232n.

[79]*Biographia Literaria*, II, 29-30.

[80]J.A.Appleyard, *Coleridge's Philosophy of Literature* (Harvard University Press, 1965), p.36; see also Richard Marsh, "The Second Part of Hartley's System," *J.H.I.*, XX (1959), 264-273.

operation of the mind, in this sense, is essential to the associationist position – and the cause of many of its ambiguities),[81] and derives from the associations created by the long continued use of the words in special contexts.

Mill had, of course, his own share of Platonism, and certainly found many of Wordsworth's theories of a return to a more ideal state of nature attractive. But when he was faced with the two sides of the Wordsworth-Coleridge controversy on diction, he immediately saw the relevance to his own philosophical assumptions of Coleridge's associationist argument. Thus Mill agrees that poetic diction,

is derived from one of the natural laws of the human mind, in the utterance of its thoughts impregnated with its feelings. All emotion which has taken possession of the whole being – which flows unrestrictedly, and therefore equably – instinctively seeks a language that flows equably like itself.[82]

But Mill supports this position with an argument which comes from neither Wordsworth, or Coleridge, for, he writes, "the stronger the feeling is, the more naturally and certainly will it prefer the language which is most perfectly appropriated to itself, and keep sacred from the contact of all more vulgar and familiar objects of contemplation."[83] To "keep sacred" from the "vulgar and familiar" (the two are inseparable) is a Victorian demand. It was not withdrawal from life, but true engagement with the proper language of the passions which Wordsworth and Coleridge advocated.

VI

The way in which the Romantic tenets of Coleridge, still containing elements of a demand for the "proper" and decorous in poetry, and based on a criterion of "good sense," turned into the Victorian tenets of Mill's poetics, in which the idea of poetry as fragile and withdrawn from contact with a damaging and harsh world is dominant, can be seen most clearly in the distinction Mill draws

[81]Karl Popper, *The Open Society and its Enemies*, 2 vols. (London, Routledge, 1966), II, 87-93.

[82]*Dissertations and Discussions*, I, 325-326.

[83]*Early essays*, pp.232n-233n.

between poetry and eloquence.

Coleridge had proposed a distinction between real and false poetry, resting on the concept of the creative imagination. This was to replace Wordsworth's disengagement between the artificial and the spontaneous, itself in turn designed to replace distinctions resting ultimately on the distinction between the artful and the crude. The distinctions set up to divide the poetic sheep from the goats in any age are a key to its real standards, and Mill, making the same distinction between good and bad, chooses as his instrument a new, and prophetic division. He distinguishes true poetry, from neither the clumsy, the artificial, nor the Fanciful, but from the eloquent.

Mill works towards this point through a series of contributory distinctions. He first separates poetry from metre, distinguishing it from matter of fact or science, like Coleridge, on the basis that, "the one does its work by convincing or persuading, the other by moving."[84] Next he distinguishes true poetry from other forms of prose by employing Coleridge's distinction between narrative interest and poetic interest. Finally, he writes,

> the distinction between poetry and eloquence appears to us to be equally fundamental with the distinction between poetry and narrative . . . Poetry and eloquence are both alike the expression or uttering forth of feeling. But . . . eloquence is *heard*, poetry is *over*heard. Eloquence supposes an audience . . . All poetry is of the nature of soliloquy.[85]

The link between poet and audience is severed, and any conscious attempt to communicate is seen as staining the purity of poetry. Mill is lead to the conception of poetry as essentially a solitary, individual pursuit, antagonistic to society.

> Poetry, accordingly, is the natural fruit of solitude and meditation; eloquence, of intercourse with the world . . . When the mind is looking within, and not without, its state does not often or rapidly vary; and hence the even, uninterrupted flow, approaching almost to monotony, which a good reader, or a good singer, will give to words or music of a pensive or melancholy cast.[86]

Poetry is written "to exhale, perhaps to relieve, a state of feeling,

---

[84] *Ibid.*, p.202.
[85] *Ibid.*, pp.208-209.
[86] *Ibid.*, pp.209-211.

or of conception of feeling, almost oppressive from its vividness."[87] Mill
cannot say "communicate," so he chooses "exhale" instead. One might
argue that "exhale" and "monotone" are vital words for any
description of Victorian poetry.

There is thus a reaction to the social context of poetry. "In these
days," Mill wrote in 1841, "one composes in verse . . . for oneself
rather than for the public . . . the heresy of the poetical critics of the
present day in France" is that they "hold that poetry is above all &
pre-eminently a *social* thing."[88] Poetry must not be social, "society
. . . is the prominent feature in all the speculations of the French
mind; and thence it is that their poetry is so much shallower than ours,
and their works of fiction so much deeper."[89] This is the initial stage of
the rejection of links between the individual, deeply feeling poet and
his society which was to prove, by the end of the nineteenth century,
to be the primrose path to the ivory tower. Even in the supremely
"social" France, Mallarmé was to follow the same development of late
Romanticism which is here foreshadowed in Mill.[90]

This distinction between poetry and eloquence is characteristic of
Mill, and does not belong to any obvious source. The distaste for
everything French would have found support in Coleridge [but not in
Wordsworth], and the feeling that poetry was solitary exhalation was
in the air, though nowhere else had it received such clear and
uncompromising expression. In making this distinction so clearly, Mill
assumes an important role in the change from Romantic to Victorian
attitudes. Mill adds a new term to the Romantic theory of poetry as
the expression of passion, but now only in private, and therefore not
truly expression at all.

The conception of the sacredness and fragility of poetry over-rides
all else in Mill's poetics in a way which would have been impossible in
Wordsworth or Coleridge. Perhaps Coleridge's belief in the "organic
unity" of the poetic process, or Wordsworth's näive equation between

[87]*Ibid.*, p.229.

[88]*Works*, XIII, 473-474.

[89]*Dissertations and Discussions*, I, 308.

[90]Joseph Chiari, *Symbolism from Poe to Mallarmé, The Growth of a Myth*
(London, Rockliff, 1956), pp.56-58.

the natural and the truly poetic are neither of them adequate. But
Mill's division between poetic experience and any other human
experience or communication is surely invidious.

VII

If Mill ignored the respect for the audience and social context of
poetry which is evident in Coleridge and Wordsworth, he none the less
retained their firm belief that poetry and science, though different, are
in no way contradictory or mutually exclusive. Indeed, Mill was able to
include poetic culture in his mature thought, partly because he could
claim that it did not interfere with more rigorously scientific modes of
explanation. The renewal of the demand for absolute factual sobriety in
all forms of expression which, during the nineteenth century, spread to
a major criticism of religion on similar grounds of scientific dogmatism,
had its roots in the Utilitarians. Bentham was popularly and
mistakenly believed, even by Mill himself, to have held that all poetry
was misrepresentation.[91]

One of the ways in which Mill integrated his increasing love of
poetry with this heritage was to claim that poetry did not in fact
interfere with correct description – it was merely an alternative form of
representation. Poetry, he thought, while being necessary to the
happiness of the individual, in no way affected his empirical
perceptions of reality. In his early advocacy of Wordsworth to the
Utilitarians he urged that,

> the imaginative emotion which an idea, when vividly conceived,
> excites in us, is not an illusion but a fact, as real as any of the other
> qualities of objects; and far from implying anything erroneous and
> delusive in our mental apprehension of the object, is quite consistent
> with the most accurate knowledge and most perfect practical
> recognition of all its physical and intellectual laws and relations.[92]

Wordsworth had also rejected any suggestion of a conflict between
simple reality and the best poetry. He suggested instead that poetry
was the "science of the feelings," and in an important passage he

---

[91]Mary P.Mack, *Jeremy Bentham: An Odyssey of Ideas, 1748-1792* (London,
Heinemann, 1962), p.247.

[92]*Autobiography*, p.151-152.

proclaims the companionship of poetry and science.[93]

As well as insisting that poetic description was in no way misleading, Mill supported poetry as a worthy intellectual activity by showing the necessity of a large element of thought in all poetic expression. Although poetry was spontaneous, this spontaneity needed to be directed by a cultivated mind. Both Wordsworth and Coleridge had emphasized this important point. "Poems," Wordsworth wrote, "to which any value can be attached were never produced . . . but by a man who being possessed of more than usual organic sensibility had also thought long and deeply.[94] But it was Coleridge's formulation, "no man was ever yet a great poet without being at the same time a profound philosopher,"[95] which Mill followed when he, too, claimed that, "every great poet, every poet who has extensively or permanently influenced mankind, has been a great thinker."[96]

Although both Coleridge and Wordsworth sowed this idea in Mill's mind, Coleridge was distinguished by Mill as its only practical exponent. In a carefully constructed comparison between Wordsworth and Shelley, Wordsworth is the poet of thought, with an unpoetical nature; Shelley is the spontaneous, born poet who lacks intellectual culture. But there is a poet who combines the best of both types, and this is represented to Mill by,

> Milton, or to descend to our own times . . . Coleridge, [in whom] a poetic nature has been united with logical and scientific culture . . . it would be absurd to doubt whether two endowments are better than one.[97]

At the time of his crisis Mill had felt that thought was the enemy of emotional culture, "that the habit of analysis had a tendency to wear away the feelings."[98] But Coleridge's arguments and Coleridge's example proved otherwise, and so Mill developed a valuable

---

[93]Wordsworth, p.233.

[94]Wordsworth, p.233.

[95]*Biographia Literaria*, II, 19.

[96]*Early Essays*, p.260.

[97]*Ibid.*, p.235; in *Dissertations and Discussions*, I, 93, the passage is re-written to avoid the reference to Coleridge, which is further evidence of Mill's decreasing enthusiasm for Coleridge between the two versions (1833 and 1867).

[98]*Autobiography*, p.137.

understanding of the need for a cognitive element in poetry.

VIII

The belief that true poetry also involved serious and sustained thought helped poetry to find its place in Mill's Utilitarian system. But as politics began to absorb more and more of Mill's attention in the later eighteen-forties, poetry became increasingly a secondary occupation, in theory as in practice. There is no doubt that Mill was aware of the close relationship between poetry and politics. "Where both politics and poetry, instead of being either a trade or a pastime, are taken completely *au sérieux*, each will be more or less coloured by the other."[99] In 1838 he believed that,

> there is room in the world for poets of both these kinds [radical and conservative]; and the greatest will always partake of the nature of both. A comprehensive and catholic mind and heart will doubtless feel and exhibit all these different sympathies, each in its due proportion and degree; but what that due proportion may happen to be, is part of the larger question.[100]

But in 1842 he was saying to Sterling that, "the highest forms of poetry cannot be built upon obsolete beliefs."[101] He now believes that the intellectual discipline Coleridge saw in poetry, "the so-called training of the intellect – consists chiefly of the mere inculcation of traditional opinions."[102] His admiration of Coleridge's poetry was now being seriously limited by his politics, and he was soon to use the insight into the close relation between thought and poetry, which Coleridge had personified for him, to give practical advice to the young Tennyson, urging him to develop away from Coleridge's example.

At the end of Mill's review of Tennyson's early poems, which is mainly taken up with describing and encouraging the increasing role which intellect is playing in his verse, Mill asks him to,

> guard himself against an error, to which the philosophical speculations of poets are peculiarly liable – that of embracing as

---

[99]*Dissertations and Discussions*, I, 290.
[100]*Ibid.*, 294.
[101]*Works*, XIII, 556.
[102]*Early essays*, p.235.

truth, not the conclusions which are recommended by the strongest evidence, but those which have the most poetical appearance ... That whatever philosophy he adopts will leave ample materials for poetry, he may be well assured. Whatever is comprehensive, whatever is commanding, whatever is on a great scale, is poetical ... .Whoever, in the greatest concerns of human life, pursues truth with unbiased feelings, and an intellect adequate to discern it, will not find that the resources of poetry are lost to him.[103]

Mill is claiming that the evidences of the intellect must guide the feelings, wheras Coleridge's writings insist on the ability of genuine fellings to question the validity of purely speculative conclusions.

Mill was increasingly convinced of the marginal importance of poetry, compared with the great political issues of his age. While he had perhaps never taken the position of what he called "the sentimental weakling, who has no test of the true but the ornamental,"[104] he had, at the time of the crisis, expressed himself strongly on the "need" for poetic culture, and insisted on the value of the arts as "aids in the formation of character."[105] His main praise of Wordsworth is that "he has exercised, and continues to exercise a powerful, and most highly beneficial influence over the formation and growth of not a few of the most cultivated and vigorous of the youthful minds of our time."[106]

Mill had even been able in the early eighteen-thirties to write to Carlyle in terms which made the artist the fully acknowledged legislator.[107] The philosopher, he told Carlyle, was merely the interpreter of the poet; a view which he had completely reversed by the time of the Tennyson article in 1835. Although the comments to Carlyle seem rather isolated in the context of the rest of Mill's thought, it is clear that poetry did have an important place in Mill's life. But in the review of de Vigny's works, written in 1838, Mill returned to a more Benthamite position, and made a different point about art.

The great majority of persons in earnest will ... always ... feel themselves more or less militant in this world - having something to

---

[103]*Ibid.*, pp.266-267.

[104]*Ibid.*, p.267.

[105]*Autobiography*, p.151.

[106]*Early Essays*, p.227.

[107]*Works*, XII, 163.

pursue in it, different from the Beautiful, different from their own mental tranquility and health, and which they will pursue, if they have the gifts of an artist, by all the resources of art, whatever becomes of canons of criticism, and beauty in the abstract.[108]

The rejection of the "canons of criticism" as irrelevant is a telling change after the struggles with them which Mill took so seriously in 1833. In a private letter to Fox in 1841 Mill makes clear what were, in the event, to be his final opinions as to the function of art in society. Re-expressing his conviction that there is more serious business at the present than the pursuit of the beautiful, he describes art as a "safeguard" for an ideal future.

Prose is after all the language of *business*, & therefore is the language to do good by in an age when men's minds are forcibly drawn to external effort . . . True, this is only part of the mission of mankind & the time will come when its due rank will be assigned to Contemplation, & the calm culture of reverence and love. Then poetry will resume her equality with prose, an equality like every healthy equality, resolvable into reciprocal superiority. But that time is not yet.[109]

Even sixteen years later, in 1854, Mill had not altered his feelings about the place of art in the precedence of human endeavour. He wrote in his private journal,

Verse I take to be eternal; but it ought, as well as every other attempt at public Art, to be suspended at the present time. In a militant age, when those who have thoughts and feelings to impress on the world have a great deal of hard work to do, and very little time to do it in . . . it is foppery to waste time in studying beauty of form in the conveyance of a meaning.[110]

A few days later he continues,

that the mind of this age, in spite of its prosaic tendencies, is quite capable of and gifted for Art is proved by its achievements in music . . . [but] greatness in any of them [the arts] absolutely requires intellect, and in this age the people of intellect have other things to do.[111]

These passages belong to a time when art had entirely disappeared

---

[108]*Dissertations and Discussions*, I, 303.

[109]*Works*, XIII, 473-474.

[110]*The Letters of John Stuart Mill*, ed.Hugh S.R.Elliot, 2 vols. (London, Longmans, Green, and Co., 1910), II, 364.

[111]*Ibid.*, 364-365.

from Mill's public writings, and they illustrate very well the reason why. Mill had not ceased to appreciate art, but the return of a sense of purpose and urgency to his life's work left little room for it. It is, indeed, curious that Mill should feel that political concerns ought to displace art when the much more urgent politics of the generation before him had apparently stimulated the creative minds from whom Mill derived most of his ideas about poetry. Mill's final position is perhaps a foretaste of the ultimate result of the belief that art is sacred and withdrawn from life. His vision of a future state when poetry will assume a central position denied to it at the present time of crisis is, of course, catastrophic as a view of the function of art in society.

IX

Mill's writings on art are in no sense a central part of his work. It is almost certainly because Mill himself evidently did not regard these as central, and after a brief active period between 1832 and 1833 left speculations on art to return to politics, that they are so obviously derivative. From what he did write it is clear, though, that it is often Coleridge who is the source of the derivations, and rarely Wordsworth alone. Coleridge's influence is seen especially in Mill's ideas on metre, on diction, and on the relation between thought and poetry. In view of Mill's study of Coleridge at this period this closeness is not really surprising. But it does add another aspect to the picture of Coleridge's early influence over Mill's mind. Coleridge's criticism has always been claimed to have been influential, but many scholars have believed that the influence was not until quite recently general. A study of Mill's criticism shows just how much Coleridge's aesthetic arguments, whatever the vagaries of their formulations, were accepted by at least one active mind of the time.

In the end, two points of interest emerge from the study of Mill's poetics. Firstly, that it illuminates Mill's early contacts with intuitionism, and partial assimilation of what it had to offer to satisfy his own needs at the time. Much was later disgorged, but the experience remained. The vital point for the argument that Coleridge was an influence on Mill is that it was in Coleridge, and in Coleridge's own special domain aesthetics, that Mill found these first contacts with intuitionism. The second point is that Mill represents, uniquely, a stage

in the transition from Coleridge to Matthew Arnold, from Romantic to
Victorian attitudes, at a time when the majority of critics, like Jeffrey
and Wilson,[112] were continuing Augustan criteria only slightly modified
by Romantic notions. The belief that poetry is the solitary exhalation
of feeling, and in no way a form of social eloquence, the arguments for
the sanctity of a specifically "poetic" diction, and the vision of poetry
as a retirement from the struggles of politics, are distinctively
Victorian.

[112]Frances Jeffrey (1773-1850), joint founder of the *Edinburgh Review*; John Wilson
(1785-1854), "Christopher North" of *Blackwoods*.

9 Half-truths

Great minds . . . are never wrong, but in consequence of being in the right, but imperfectly. – S.T.Coleridge[1]

I sometimes think that if there is anything which I am under a special obligation to preach, it is the meaning & necessity of a catholic spirit in philosophy. – John Stuart Mill[2]

The third of Coleridge's major influences on Mill was in guiding him to the formulation of an apologia for eclecticism. This apologia helped Mill in the very process of absorbing ideas both from Coleridge, and from the many other sources that contributed to the colourful patchwork of his mature opinions. This is perhaps the most important of all Coleridge's influences on Mill's mind, though it is probably the most difficult to specify. The ideal of eclecticism was in no way original to Coleridge; it was latent in the intellectual atmosphere of the time. Mill found it, for instance, in Goethe and the French Eclectics, represented by Condorcet. But it seems to have been linked most closely in Mill's mind with Coleridge. Both the verbal formulations of the idea, and the objects of its application centre around Coleridge's influence, and Mill wrote his most eloquent defence of the idea, by design, in his essay on Coleridge. There is every reason to credit Coleridge with an important function in formalizing Mill's

---

[1]S.T.Coleridge, *The Table Talk and Omniana*, ed. T.Ashe (London, G.Bell & Sons, 1923), p.183. Subsequently referred to as *Table Talk*.
[2]*The Collected Works of John Stuart Mill*, ed. F.E.L.Priestley, Vols. XII and XIII, "The Earlier Letters, 1812-1848," ed. F.E.Mineka (University of Toronto Press, 1963), XIII, 411. Subsequently referred to as *Works*, XII and XIII.

eclecticism, although the evidence of Coleridge's role is often only circumstantial.

I

Only at the time of the crisis did Mill become aware of the limitations of sectarianism, and the benefits of a broad-minded eclecticism. He was soon to find words to explain his insight into "truth". In the *Autobiography* he tells us that before the crisis, "what we . . . were sometimes, by a ridiculous exaggeration, called by others, namely a 'school,' some of us for a time really hoped and aspired to be. . . . No one of the set went to so great excesses in this boyish ambition as I did."[3] But, assailed by the irrepressible conviction that his father's theory was not adequate to his needs, Mill found himself less sure about everything; the priggish certainty of the youth became shame at his "sectarian follies."[4] He finally found himself, *"quite sure of scarcely anything respecting Truth, except that she is many-sided."*[5] After the 'crisis' he was left with "no system: only a conviction that the true system was something much more complex and many-sided than I had previously had any idea of."[6] He told Carlyle that,

> My first state had been one of intense philosophic intolerance. . . . Now when I had got out of this state . . . I think it is scarcely surprising that for a time I became catholic and tolerant in an extreme degree, & thought one-sidedness almost the one great evil in human affairs.[7]

On these infirm foundations of doubt Mill was to build rapidly. After some seeking round for a steadier footing his apologia for eclecticism took its familiar shape. Throughout his career Mill is characterized by a readiness to learn from others. His belief in the value of adding together the "half-truths" of opposing sects to make the whole truth is the common justification he gives for the eclecticism

---

[3]J.S.Mill, *Autobiography*, 3rd. ed. (London, Longmans, Green, Reader, and Dyer, 1874), pp.108-109. Subsequently referred to as *Autobiography*.

[4]*Ibid.*, p.114.

[5]*Works*, XII, 181.

[6]*Autobiography*, p.161.

[7]*Works*, XII, 204-205.

which is the root of much that is original, valuable and controversial in his work. Although he later corrected the excesses of his reaction against sectarianism he did not altogether reject the idea of complementary half-truths. It was used to explain the revised opinion of Bentham, and it is the foundation of the "Bentham" and "Coleridge" essays. He used it, for instance, in his criticism of Comte, in 1867, which in summary is that "M. Comte has got hold of half the truth."[8] He even claimed that the *Political Economy* was written to "rescue from the hands of such people the truths they misapply, and by combining these with other truths to which ,they are strangers, to deduce conclusions capable of being of some use to the progress of mankind."[9] The premises of *Liberty* also depend on the belief that truth is the addition of conflicting half-truths.

The *London and Westminster Review* was designed to destroy dogmatism in religion, among other broadening influences; an ambition Coleridge shared for similar, eclectic, reasons.[10] Even "counteracting causes" are only the philosophic expression of eclecticism. They are the many factors which Mill has discovered, disparately, to act together and which he cannot unify but must acknowledge. Bentham and Coleridge are counteracting causes. The *Logic* itself is designed to "embody and systematize, the best ideas ... promulgated on its subject by speculative writers."[11] It is an achievement of eclecticism, by Mill's own admission, not of originality.

This eclecticism is generally agreed to be the cause of many of Mill's difficulties.[12] It is the most characteristic feature of his mind,

---

[8]*Auguste Comte and Positivism*, in *The Collected Works of John Stuart Mill*, ed. F.E.L.Priestley, Vol.X, "Essays on Ethics, Religion and Society," ed. J.M.Robson (University of Toronto Press, 1969), 313. Subsequently referred to as *Works*, X.

[9]*The Letters of J.S.Mill*, ed. H.S.R.Elliot, 2 vols. (London, Longmans, Green and Co., 1910), I, 149.

[10]*Works*, XII, 264-265.

[11]J.S.Mill, *A System of Logic*, 2 vols. (London, Longmans, Green, and Co., 1879), I, v.

[12]Kenneth E.Miller, "John Stuart Mill's Theory of International Relations," *J.H.I.*, XXII (1961), 509; John Bowle, *Politics and Opinion in the Nineteenth Century* (London, Jonathan Cape, 1954), p.196; L.T.Hobhouse, *Liberalism* (London, Williams & Norgate, 1911), p.107; Sir Isiah Berlin, *John Stuart Mill and the Ends of Life* (London, Council of Christians and Jews, 1959), p.21.

and was a central element of his thought from the time of the crisis onward. He used the idea less in later life but it never disappeared, or was replaced, as an explanation of his modifications of the Benthamite tradition.

II

In Coleridge the same eclectic spirit was at work. His thought was, like his political and religious allegiances, marked by a readiness to follow and incorporate truths, no matter how distant. The history of his mind is a history of partly digested systems, whose waste products regurgitated in burning criticisms, and whose choicer elements fed the great visions of Coleridge's dialectic. Hartley, Unitarianism, Platonism, Atheism, Kantianism, Liberalism, Conservatism, all the philosophies of the time fuelled Coleridge's eclectic mind, all their elements combined in the sparks that flew from the conflagration.[13] Coleridge joined the eighteenth and nineteenth centuries; he would never give up what he had once learned. The early systemizations of the mind he retained in a subordinate position in his later philosophy. He added Plato and empiricism to Kant, and the unlikely mixture formed his own mature thought.

These diverse insights were explained more and more towards the end of his life in the phrase, "half-truths." His later conversation is full of comments about the half of the truth possessed by one or other sect, party, or individual. In 1830 Coleridge said that "The Nominalists and Realists . . . were both right, and both wrong. They each maintained opposite poles of the same truth."[14] Again, in 1832 he commented, "the Conservative party see but one-half of the truth,"[15] and a year later, "Mr.Lyell's system of geology is just half the truth, and no more."[16]

[13]Paul Deschamps, *La Formation de la Pensée de Coleridge, 1772-1804* (Paris, Didier, 1964), p.21; see also S.F.Gingerich, "From Necessity to Transcendentalism in Coleridge," *P.M.L.A.*, XXXV (1920), 7.

[14]*Table Talk*, p.62.

[15]*Ibid.*, p.150.

[16]*Ibid.*, p.230.

What were the sources? Eclecticism was hardly Coleridge's invention. Most obviously, the German tradition of the age of Goethe yields a flood of examples of the eclectic spirit,[17] which was to be systematized into a formal dialectic by the Post-Kantians. Less obviously, but probably more importantly for Coleridge, the conciliatory tone of sixteenth and seventeenth century Anglican theology, and its wish to preserve peace in the intervals of sectarian strife must have deeply impressed him with the values of an eclectic tolerance. There was, finally, the more immediate example of the evils of extremism in the French Revolution to convince him of the value of understanding rather than bigotry.[18] In England the Revolution had resulted in the convulsions of political conscience which the first generation of Romantic poets underwent as they were transformed into Jacobins, and back again into Tories. It left a lasting impression of the virtues of tolerance. From this background Coleridge constructed his eclecticism. What was new was not the idea, it had had its place from Plato's dialectic to Locke's *Letter on Toleration*, but the new valuation which seemed to place it above all coherence, and the new formulation, "half-truth."

The words were influential on Coleridge's lips. Many of his disciples express their belief in combining half-truths, and often acknowledge Coleridge as their source. Julius Hare is an example.[19] F.D. Maurice in the introduction to the *Kingdom of Christ* praises Coleridge because,

> he has brought out and applied with singular clearness the fact, that it is in the positive and practical portion of men's creeds, and not in the negations by which they are polemically distinguished, that we are to look for the partial truths which may serve as points of reconciliation.[20]

---

[17]Ronald Gray, *The German Tradition in Literature, 1871-1945* (Cambridge University Press, 1965), p.2; see also S.T.Coleridge, *Aids to Reflection* (London, G.Bell & Sons, 1884), p.67. Subsequently referred to as *Aids to Reflection*.

[18]S.T.Coleridge, *The Friend*, ed. Barbara E.Rooke, 2 vols. (London, Routledge & Kegan Paul, 1969), I, 331. Subsequently referred to as *Friend*.

[19]John Sterling, *Essays and Tales*, ed. J.C.Hare, 2 vols. (London, J.W.Parker, 1848), I, cxxviii.

[20]Anon. review of F.D.Maurice's *Kingdom of Christ* in "The State and the Church," *Foreign Review* (1831), 434.

Thirlwall, too, applies the doctrine in his historical researches. "The right and the truth lies on neither side exclusively," he writes, "there is no fraudulent purpose, no gross imbecility of intellect, on either: but both have plausible claims and specious reasons to allege, though each is too much blinded by prejudice or passion to do justice to the views of his adversary."[21] The idea appealed to many and among them was J.S. Mill.[22]

Mill had heard Coleridge's talk; and a letter of Henry Taylor's records Mill's reaction to Coleridge after one of his visits, a reaction which illustrates both Mill's eclecticism in action and its links with Coleridge.

> As we came home discussing Coleridge, Mill made a remark in which I thought there was justice . . . he said that on such subjects, which are for the most part mere matters of calculation, of plus and minus, a man might be either quite right or quite wrong, and if he was wrong on such subjects what he said was good for nothing, whereas he might be more or less wrong in discussing the moral and political relations of society and yet be very instructive, and if you could not agree with him, still he might lead you to take a survey of society from a new point of view, and impress you with many ideas and sentiments which could never have resulted to you from communication with a person whose conclusions were the same as your own. You might be enriched even by the materials of his erroneous structure.[23]

The distinction between matters of calculation and matters in which, as Mill was to put it in the later essay on *Utilitarianism*, "considerations may be presented capable of determining the intellect to give or withhold its assent,"[24] was part of the basic furniture of Mill's thinking. That he should express this concept after one of his most important contacts with Coleridge suggests that he went to see Coleridge both willing and theoretically prepared to accept from him any "ideas and sentiments" that could "lead" him to a "new point of

[21]Cannop Thirlwall, *Remains, Literary and Theological*, 3 vols. (London, Daldy, Isbister & Co., 1877-1878), III, 8.

[22]Walter E.Houghton, *The Victorian Frame of Mind, 1830-1870* (New Haven, Yale University Press, 1957), p.178.

[23]*Correspondence of Henry Taylor* ed.E.Dowden (London, Longmans, Green, and Co., 1888), pp.39-40.

[24]J.S.Mill, *Utilitarianism, Liberty, Representative Government*, introduction by A.D.Lindsay (London, J.M.Dent & sons, 1962), p.4.

view."

Perhaps, indeed, the idea was reawakened in Mill's mind on that occasion by Coleridge's own declarations of eclecticism. Taylor's letter is dated September 29, 1831, and refers to the visit to Coleridge as "the other day." The only record of a conversation about that time in H.N. Coleridge's *Table Talk* is on September 12th, when Coleridge was talking about his "system" and explaining how it "endeavoured to unite the insulated fragments of truth, and therewith to frame a perfect mirror."[25] H.N.Coleridge does not record another conversation until nearly the end of October, and since Taylor notes that Coleridge, "poor man, he has been for two months past under the influence of cholera and other extra disorders, by which he seems sadly enfeebled and even crippled,"[26] the absence of any record of another conversation around this date might suggest that this was the only evening in the early Autumn of 1831 that Coleridge was able to receive guests. The evidence is tenuous, since only a little of Coleridge's conversation can have found its way fully dated and recorded into H.N.Coleridge's notes. But Coleridge's remarks about eclecticism are more frequent around 1830-31 than at any other time, and these were the years when both Mill and Sterling were visiting him. They were thus likely to have heard his views on "half-truth".

It was the eclecticism which Mill expressed in his remarks to Henry Taylor, on the way down Highgate Hill in 1831, which was to help him to find the other "half" of the truth which Bentham had omitted. What is interesting is to see Mill, at the moment of his early contact with Coleridge, formulating quite explicitly the theory which was to enable him to learn from Coleridge, and to write about him, even in the context of a resolutely Utilitarian career. And it is this eclecticism itself which Mill learnt, at least in part, from Coleridge. For the very openness to the truths of other sects which was the key that unlocked new worlds for Mill at twenty-two was perhaps Coleridge's own greatest message.

Mill seems to regard the idea of combining half-truths as an especially Coleridgean one. But while Coleridge is certainly at pains to

[25]*Table Talk*, pp.138-139.
[26]Taylor, *op.cit.*, p.39.

understand and use opposing ideas, the theory of combining half-truths is not as prominent in reality in Coleridge as Mill's glowing account of it, especially in the 1840 "Coleridge" essay, would make us believe. Mill not only approved of Coleridge's catholicity, but "applied . . . to Coleridge himself, many of Coleridge's sayings about half truths."[27]

The exaggeration is an indication of the preoccupations of the commentator.

III

Coleridge was not, of course, the only example of eclectic and understanding tolerance that Mill knew. His first declaration of dependence for his new anti-sectarian spirit tells us that it was Condorcet's *Life of Turgot* which first "cured me of my sectarian follies . . . [it] sank deeply into my mind . . . .I ceased to *afficher* sectarianism." But Mill qualifies this statement with the observation, "my real inward sectarianism I did not get rid of until much later, and much more gradually."[28] The first seeds of the half-truth theory were sown by the French eclectics, but the idea was to blossom in another context. The anti-sectarianism of the French eclectics was based on a desire for tolerance, Mill's and Coleridge's was based on the needs of the individual mind. Mill's orientation is towards experience, not theories. Theories can be derived from other minds, experience is personal and theories must be made to fit the needs of experience, at whatever cost to their inner consistency. His theory of half-truth is a way of ignoring the consequences of theories in favour of the needs of experience. The conflation of the principles of Bentham and Coleridge is made on the ground that, "as the materials of both were real observations, the genuine product of experience – the results will in the end be found not hostile, but supplementary, to one another."[29] This confidence that whatever the theoretical foundations of a philosophy, if

---

[27] *Autobiography*, p.163.

[28] *Ibid.*, p.114.

[29] *Mill on Bentham and Coleridge*, with an introduction by F.R.Leavis (London, Chatto and Windus, 1962), p.102.   Subsequently referred to as *Bentham and Coleridge*.

it is grounded on "experience" it will be compatible with another similarly grounded theory, emphasizes how strongly Mill was committed to the test of experience. Coleridge's eclecticism is also based on a valuation of personal needs, and personal experience, above the demands of theory. If a theory is "repugnant to the dictates of conscience"[30] the theory can be considered to be proved wrong.

A possible source of the half-truth theory is Goethe, whose "device, 'many-sidedness,' was one which I would most willingly, at this period, have taken for mine."[31] Goethe was the father of much of the eclectic spirit in Germany,[32] but it is not difficult to distinguish Mill's ideas from Goethe's. Goethe's "Vielseitigkeit" is a living ocean of truth,[33]but Mill's half-truth is a simple, practical belief that truth has two sides. The Positivists are another source of Mill's tolerance. Their philosophy of history is constructed on a model in which the oscillating conflict of opinions is the very material from which the coming stability is fused. But the Positivist model is an early form of the historical dialectic which was to be the dominant historiography of the nineteenth century. Mill's ideas are innocent of the sophistication of a belief in the digestive function of conflict in an age of transition. The Positivists taught Mill the relative nature of systems, and showed how historical ideas grow by synthesis into an adequate truth. But Mill sees the historical progress of opinions as an "oscillation between . . . extremes . . . every excess in either direction determines a corresponding reaction."[34] The principal image is that of a pendulum, not a dialectic. He is constructing a model which will enable him to assimilate radically different forms of speculation. But what he proposes to do is to stop the pendulum in the centre of its swing, rather than to absorb the instability into the motive force of a new synthesis. Mill's model of the history of opinions is closest to Coleridge's, when he found it,

> curious to trace the operation of the moral law of polarity in the
> history of politics, religion, &c. When the maximum of one tendency

---

[30]*Aids to Reflection*, p.111.

[31]*Autobiography*, p.163.

[32]Grey, *Op.cit.* p.2.

[33]Shirley R.Letwin, *The Pursuit of Certainty* (Cambridge University Press, 1965), p.237.

[34]*Bentham and Coleridge*, pp.107-108.

has been attained, there is no gradual decrease, but a direct transition to its minimum, till the opposite tendency has attained its maximum; and then you see another corresponding revulsion.[35]

Mill's tolerance, which "meant collecting as many boxes as possible"[36] was as different from the dissenting forbearance of Locke and the English Latitudinarians, as it was from Goethe's mystical sense of the plenitude of truth. Of course, the French Eclectics played their part, as did Goethe, in eradicating Mill's sectarianism, but it is Coleridge's words, "half-truth", and not Goethe's "many-sidedness", or Condorcet's "sectarianism", that Mill uses. The Continental writers speak of many sides of truth, or of many sects. Both Mill and Coleridge, on the other hand, habitually think of only two opposing points of view; they always speak of halves, even when there are three or more. They both, that is, had their roots in the English two-party system.

Coleridge did sometimes talk of fusing a multitude of truths into a unity, drawing on the German tradition, but he tended, especially in conversation, to express himself in terms of half-truths.[37] But Mill thinks almost exclusively in terms of two halves. He never questioned whether the simple addition of two opposite halves of truth might be an impossible operation, or whether it might not produce, not the whole truth, but something wholly false. He always assumed that the addition of truths was, per se, a beneficial action. And he saw himself as the adept carpenter of truths, and not the speculative formulator of increasingly flawless theories. He seems to have thought that, "in the competition among opinions truth survives as an accumulating residue."[38] His belief in the tolerance of half-truths is a curiously ill-formulated and scantily analysed conception. It is based on an optimism about the nature of truth which is singularly näive in its prognostication of the success of transplant operation of any kind. And Mill is thinking of transplanting, and not of infusion. The image is

[35]*Table Talk*, pp.155-156.

[36]Letwin, *op.cit.*, p.239.

[37]E.g. *Table Talk*, pp.138, 230, 415.

[38]William Irvine, "Carlyle and T.H.Huxley," *Booker Memorial Studies: Eight Essays in Victorian Literature*, in memory of John Manning Booker, 1881-1948, ed. Hill Shine (Chapel Hill, University of North Carolina Press, 1950), p.119.

perhaps an apt model of the difference between Mill and Continental eclecticism.

IV

The closeness of Mill's and Coleridge's ideas of half-truth is illustrated most forcibly by the continuous parallels in their exposition and use of the idea. Their theories of half-truths were constructed in similar words on similar grounds; and their applications are also parallel. Mill criticised Bentham, for instance, in terms strikingly similar to Coleridge's criticisms of Locke. Coleridge writes, "the position . . . on which Mr. Locke's Essay is grounded, is irrefragable; Locke erred only in taking half the Truth for a whole Truth."[39] And Mill writes, "there is hardly anything positive in Bentham's philosophy which is not true. . . . To reject his half of the truth because he overlooked the other half, would be to fall into his error."[40]

What they both insist must be avoided are the mistakes of that, "Order of intellects, who, like the *pleuronectae* (or flat fish) in ichthyology which have both eyes on the same side, never see but half of a subject at one time, and forgetting the one before they get to the other are sure not to detect any inconsistency between them."[41] Or, as Mill puts it,

> what led them wrong at first, was generally nothing else but the incapacity of seeing more than one thing at a time; and that incapacity is apt to stick to them when they have turned their eyes in an altered direction . . . they have in general an invincible propensity to split the truth, and take half, or less than half of it.[42]

Coleridge's remedy for these men was to show them the whole truth. "For myself," he wrote, "I act and will continue to act under the belief that the whole truth is the best antidote to falsehoods which are

---

[39]*Aids to Reflection*, p.44.
[40]*Bentham and Coleridge*, p.64.
[41]*Aids to Reflection*, p.270.
[42]"The Spirit of the Age," *Examiner*, January 9th, 1831, p.21.

dangerous chiefly because they are half-truths."[43] Mill applied the same antidote to Bentham's ideas; his critique of Bentham and his modifications of Utilitarianism conspicuously follow this idea of adding new truth, not subtracting old error.

Both Mill and Coleridge agree in seeing the early nineteenth century as an age specially endowed with the sectarian spirit. "There never was an age," Coleridge writes, "since the days of the apostles, in which the catholic spirit of religion was so dead, and put aside for love of sects and parties, as at present."[44] and he insists that, "the spirit of sectarianism has been hitherto our fault, and the cause of our failures."[45] Mill, too, felt that "the spirit of philosophy in England, like that of religion, is still rootedly sectarian."[46]

The tolerant mind shared by Coleridge and Mill was, they were both aware, liable to place them in an unpopular position. Mill recognized that one of the reasons for his failure to achieve re-election to Parliament was that,

> all persons of Tory feeling were . . . embittered against me . . . As I had shown in my political writings that I was aware of the weak points in democratic opinions, some Conservatives, it seems, had not been without hopes of finding me an opponent of democracy: as I was able to see the Conservative side of the question, they presumed that, like them, I could not see any other side.[47]

He frequently found similar difficulties in explaining his independence of party dogmas to his allies. But it is Coleridge, talking about himself, who most clearly expressed Mill's position.

> Party men always hate a slightly differing friend more than a downright enemy. I quite calculate on my being one day or other holden in worse repute by many Christians than the Unitarians and open infidels. It must be undergone by everyone who loves the truth

[43]*Friend*, I, 189. The first edition read, "The Friend . . . acts," which was later changed to, "For myself . . . I act." I have preferred to follow the 4th ed. (London, William Pickering, 1850), I, 250.

[44]*Table Talk*, p.148.

[45]S.T.Coleridge, *Biographia Literaria*, ed. J.Shawcross, 2 vols. (Oxford, Clarendon, 1907), I, 170.

[46]*Bentham and Coleridge*, p.104.

[47]*Autobiography*, p.309.

for its own sake beyond all other things.[48]

Eclectic sympathies could be unpopular, as both men knew. But truth was their first concern, and truth was, again for both men, more important even than tolerance. Mill saw tolerance as both a source, and a result, of the belief in the need to add separate half-truths to form a whole truth. Since truth could only be reached by adding together all opinions, there was a need for "antagonistic modes of thought" in a society. And this need Mill felt to be the only "rational or enduring basis of philosophical tolerance; the only condition in which liberality in matters of opinion can be anything better than a polite synonym for indifference."[49] The equation of that tolerance which is not built upon a sound love of truth with indifference parallels Coleridge. He discussed tolerance at length in *the Friend*, and came to the conclusion that,

> either the intolerant person is not master of the grounds on which his own faith is built . . . In this case he is angry, not at the opposition to Truth, but at the interruption of his own indolence and intellectual slumber . . . Or, secondly, he has no love of the Truth for its own sake.[50]

He is here castigating the intolerance of free-speech: he has a different attitude to tolerance of ideas.

> The only true spirit of Tolerance consists in our conscientious toleration of each other's intolerance. Whatever pretends to be more than this, is either the unthinking cant of fashion, or the soul-palsying narcotic of moral and religious indifference. As much as I love my fellow-men, so much and no more will I be *intolerant* of their Heresies and Unbelief.[51]

"We are," Coleridge reminded his hearers at Highgate, "none of us tolerant in what concerns us deeply and entirely."[52]

Coleridge is not contradicting himself in these passages; he is making a distinction between tolerance of men, and of ideas. "As far as opinions, and not motives, principles and not men are concerned," he

---

[48] *Table Talk*, p.95; see also Crane Brinton, *The Political Ideas of the English Romanticists* (London, Oxford University Press, 1926), pp.83-84.

[49] *Bentham and Coleridge*, p.104.

[50] *Friend*, I, 279.

[51] *Ibid.*, 96-98.

[52] *Table Talk*, p.329.

insisted, "I neither am *tolerant*, nor wish to be regarded as such."[53]

Mill has evidently taken over this distinction in his praise of "tolerance (not in the sense which Coleridge justly disavows, but in the good sense.)"[54] Like Coleridge, he is proud of his intolerance of what he conceives to be false ideas, while also insisting on his tolerance of men." I have," he writes, "opinions to which I attach importance, and which I earnestly desire to diffuse, but I am not desirous of aiding the diffusion of opinions contrary to my own."[55] But he would not want to limit free-speech either. He is following Coleridge in his distinction between tolerance which is founded on understanding, and that founded on indifference which nourishes "the worst intellectual habit of all, that of not finding, and not looking for, certainty in anything."[56]

From this perception of what is valuable in the spirit of toleration springs a parallel insistence on the need to understand the point of view of an opponent as an essential priority in any attempt to criticise him. Coleridge writes,

> Let it be remembered that no Assailant of an Error can reasonably hope to be listened to by its Advocates, who has not proved to them that he has seen the disputed subject in the same point of view, and is capable of contemplating it with the same feelings as themselves.[57]

Mill, similarly, insists that "to be just to any opinion, it ought to be considered, not exclusively from an opponent's point of view, but from that of the mind which propounds it."[58]

It hardly needs comment that Mill follows Coleridge's account of toleration both closely and explicitly. Their attitude goes beyond the shallow indifference they both deplore and is guided by a rational desire for the truth which does not neglect the responsibility of fighting for what is genuinely believed to be that truth. It is possible to multiply these parallels. Mill and Coleridge undoubtedly thought and expressed themselves on the subject of eclecticism and tolerance in

---

[53] *Friend*, I, 96.

[54] *Works*, XII, 85.

[55] Elliot, *op.cit.*, I, 180-181.

[56] J.S.Mill, *Dissertations and Discussions*, 4 vols. (London, Longmans, Green, Reader, and Dyer, 1867-1875), I, 201-202.

[57] *Friend*, I, 227.

[58] *Works*, X, 332.

closely similar ways.

This is not to disguise the fact that they had many common sources – not only Goethe and the French Eclectics, but Locke, Hume and many other writers of the Enlightenment insist on a broader approach to the problems of "truth". The crucial factor, however, is that Mill was reading Coleridge at a time when he was open to such ideas. Much of the liberality and reasonableness of Mill's polemical manner may come from this seed.

V

Mill's "Coleridge" essay is one of the main tributes to Coleridge's greatness in the first half of the nineteenth century. It is, at the same time, the fullest verbal formulation of Mill's belief in eclecticism, and its most telling application. By design, Mill wrote his most eloquent defence of eclecticism in an essay exemplifying it in action. He told Sterling,

> I have set to work upon an article on Coleridge . . . I shall be glad to have this among [my essays] . . . because some of the others, without this, would give a false view of my general mode of thinking – & besides I sometimes think that if there is anything which I am under a special obligation to preach, it is the meaning & necessity of a catholic spirit in philosophy, & I have a better opportunity of shewing what this is, in writing about Coleridge, than I have ever had before.[59]

Coleridge was paired with Bentham as the other half of the truth, and Mill's understanding of Coleridge provided the clearest example of a thinker's ability to surmount the barriers of sect and party.

The essay is intended to demonstrate Mill's own catholic spirit by showing the extent to which he was prepared to sympathize with Coleridge. But the obligation Mill feels, while it may refer predominantly to an obligation to his audience, an obligation of honesty, also refers to an obligation of debt. He wishes not only to make a full avowal of his own catholicism but also to pass on some of what he had learnt of Coleridge's. Mill felt that it was Coleridge, more than any other figure, who should be the subject of an essay devoted

---

[59]*Works*, XIII, 411.

specifically to his clearest public statement of his half-truth theory.

The essay itself satisfied both obligations. Mill begins by insisting that both Bentham and Coleridge are essential for a complete philosophy and that an eclectic use of their ideas is therefore necessary. At the end of the essay he records Coleridge's own catholicism.

> Few men have ever combined so much earnestness with so catholic and unsectarian a spirit . . . .That almost all sects, both in philosophy and religion, are right in the positive part of their tenets, though commonly wrong in the negative, is a doctrine which he professes as strongly as the eclectic school in France. Almost all errors he holds to be 'truths misunderstood', 'half-truths taken on the whole' . . . Both the theory and practice of enlightened tolerance in matters of opinion, might be exhibited in extracts from his writings more copiously than in those of any other writer we know.[60]

It is difficult to believe that Coleridge's catholicism so strongly praised here in 1840, did not deeply affect the formulation of Mill's own half-truth theory at the time of his 'crisis', when for the first time he was reading Coleridge with the experience to understand his ideas.

VI

The half-truth theory was obviously at its most useful to Mill at the time of his change of opinions. The theory and its application grew together at his crisis out of his new needs. As his opinions became more established at the end of the eighteen thirties, his theory ceased to be so important, or so frequently used. By 1840 the major influences on Mill's mind – Carlyle, Coleridge, Sterling, Comte, Tocqueville – had had their main effects, and Mill was settling down to a period of steady productivity with his newly marshalled ideas. But in his later rejection of Comte the theory of half-truths was to remain useful.

Mill's relation to Positivism had two main stages, the initial absorption of its ideas, and the ultimate rejection of Comte in *Comte and Positivism*. Mill's first contact in 1828 with Gustave D'Eichthal, the Saint-Simonist envoy in England, was followed by a remarkably rapid absorption of Saint-Simonist ideas. For D'Eichthal, the missionary, the experience must have been frustrating. Mill, a rising

---

[60]*Bentham and Coleridge*, pp.160-161.

and potentially important young intellectual, already the leader of a small group, showed every signs of becoming a convert. He understood and agreed with the main doctrines of Saint-Simonism the moment they were explained to him. Yet he continued to hang back. For all his complimentary and encouraging letters, which had hardly a critical word to say against the doctrines, Mill remained independent. Only when pressed hard did he declare that he found Saint-Simonism useful, but he could not become a follower.[61]

The explanation of both the rapid acceptance, and the deceptive stance, lies in Mill's previous teachers. Especially, it was Coleridge who prepared him for Saint-Simonism.[62] The Saint-Simonists and Coleridge drew sustenance from similar sources in the *philosophes* of eighteenth century France, and in the new German school, and for Mill Saint-Simon was thus an interesting extension of ideas of already familiar attraction. But more than the new historiography, the theory of half-truths, derived in part from Coleridge, assisted Mill in his approach to Positivism, and in his definition of the limits of his admiration for them. At the beginning of his correspondence with D'Eichthal, he tried to avoid antagonism, he sought rather to learn than to criticise. He told his correspondent that, "I have a great dislike of controversy . . . I am adverse to any mode of eradicating error, but by establishing and inculcating . . . the opposite truth."[63] This attempt to minimize the difference between them, and to get at the other half of the truth, is typical of Mill's attitude to other sects at this time. He is approaching the Positivists through his theory of half-truths.

The *Spirit of the Age* essays, written at this time (1831), show that Mill was already deeply influenced by Positivist ideas, but there are important divergences from their doctrines which point to the influence of Coleridge. Mill adopts the Positivist distinction between organic and critical periods of history,[64] but explains the difficulties inherent in an age of transition by a different, and familiar theory. "Ancient doctrines . . . are thrown aside," he explains, "but men

---

[61]*Works*, XII, 109.

[62]Iris Mueller, *John Stuart Mill and French Thought* (Urbana, University of Illinois Press, 1956), p.57.

[63]*Works*, XII, 45.

[64]"Spirit of the Age," *Examiner*, January 9th, 1831, p.21.

usually resolve that the new light . . . shall be the sole light."[65] He seems to have in mind the idea of half-truths, and not the Positivist idea of organic and critical historical periods. These two modes of thought are not antagonistic, but they are distinct. Coleridge's concept of half-truths, which Mill adopts, is not fundamentally a relativistic one. It pre-supposes rather an inaccessible, but enduring ideal of truth to which valid, if partial, approaches can be made irrespective of the historical context. It is essentially Platonic. The Positivists, however, valued systems only in the context of their time. Mill's attitude by contrast is a mixture of liberalism and Platonism.

The mixture is sometimes a strange one. The Positivists' attitude on the other hand is clear and consistent in its own terms, but, as Mill finally realized, at times damagingly dogmatic. It is here that Coleridge's example of tolerance played its most important role. When Mill first read Comte, the Positivist with whom he had the closest contacts, he felt that he had found a complete and satisfactory system. By the time that their correspondence ceased, however, he felt that Comte was too dogmatic, and that truth was more complex than Comte realized. This he explained directly to Comte, pointing out that because of this Positivism, "ne me paraît pas encore bien en état de se produire avec advantage comme école."[66] Comte's system, Mill wrote in his final summary, "is the most warning example we know, into what frightful aberrations a powerful and comprehensive mind may be led by the exclusive following out of a single idea."[67] His rejection is summarized in the simple explanation,

> M.Comte has got hold of half the truth, and the so-called liberal or revolutionary school possesses the other half; each sees what the other does not see, and seeing it exclusively, draws consequences from it which to the other appear mischievously absurd.[68]

Thus, although Mill learnt a great deal from Comte, the dominant and finally triumphant mode of Mill's thought was the belief in the complexity of truth and the need to "unite" its separate fragments.

Mill's analysis of the dangers of Positivist thought is only one of

[65]*Ibid.*
[66]*Works*, XIII, 656.
[67]*Works*, X, 351.
[68]*Ibid.*, 313.

the ways in which he used his concept of half-truths, but it points to the significance of Coleridge's contribution to Mill's thought in directing and encouraging this liberal conception of the importance of tolerance in the cross-pollination of systems. Although the idea could have many sources, the formulation which Mill applies in all his thinking, the idea of half-truths, is specifically Coleridge's.

VII

The parallels between Coleridge's and Mill's expressions are more striking on half-truths than on any subject, and there are some distinctions between Mill's idea, and other sources of the same idea. Yet the fact remains that eclecticism was in the air. The intellectual and historical conflicts of the eighteenth century all pointed to the need for tolerance. The throwing off of the dogmatism of religion had wide effects. In Germany, and subsequently in England, a new liberalism was appearing in individual interpretation of dogma and the Bible. Even more than the philosophy, the history of the late eighteenth century made tolerance a necessary ideal. Tolerance, openness, flexibility, and the value of change are all, paradoxically, key notes of the Victorian mind. Paradoxically, because rigidity and dogma are also characteristically Victorian. But Walter Houghton argues, the open and flexible mind was,

> in one sense ... more Victorian because, unlike the rigid dogmatic mind with its long history, it was largely indigenous to the nineteenth century. Though by no means new, in fact or theory, it was perhaps more common in the fifties and sixties and more emphatically extolled as a supreme virtue than had ever been the case in the past.[69]

Against this background it would hardly be wise to claim that Coleridge was the sole or original source of Mill's half-truth theory. Yet his role in shaping the spirit of eclecticism Mill inherited with his date of birth would seem to be appreciable. There is in Coleridge's insistence on the need to "unite the insulated fragment of truth, and therewith to frame a perfect mirror,"[70] in his belief in the ultimate

---

[69]Houghton, *op.cit.*, p.176.
[70]*Table Talk*, pp.138-139.

validity of experience for judging systems of thought, and in his attitude to toleration, much that must have provided food for thought for Mill at that time.

Coleridge's influence was probably effective, not only in single ideas, but in the formulation of a whole method of approach to the problem of truth. The importance of this can only be measured by the limits of the importance of this method in Mill's development, as an example of openness of mind, and comprehensiveness of understanding and insight. This was something beyond party politics – and beyond the fact that Coleridge was politically, religiously, and in many other ways at the opposite pole to Mill.

10 A teacher on teachers: Mill on Bentham and Coleridge

Now that his fame is recognized by the second generation, the true umpires, it must be permanent. – J.S.Mill[1]

What then was Coleridge's real effect on Mill? Divergencies in epistemology, parallels in theology, poetics, politics and eclecticism provide the evidence; it must now be weighed. Mill himself had attempted this task, for in addition to the brief comments in the *Autobiography*, and the explicit summary in the letter to Nichol, he wrote a major essay on Coleridge. Coleridge is thus accorded a detailed and extended assessment in a carefully considered and important essay. Only Tocqueville, Comte, Hamilton, Bentham and James Mill had equal attention paid to the accurate valuation of their achievements. Coleridge is therefore among the privileged.

Mill's essays on Bentham and Coleridge have become an important part of nineteenth century cultural history.[2] They are keys to the influence of men at the centre of the two major streams of thought in the period as seen by a third, representative mind. They are also intended to be a public exposition of Mill's catholicity of mind, and a demonstration of his ability to accept what was useful in Coleridge.

[1]*Memories of Old Friends, Being extracts from the Journals and Letters of Caroline Fox, from 1835 to 1870*, ed.H.N.Pym, 2 vols. (London, Smith, Elder & Co., 1882), I, 147.

[2]F.R.Leavis, "Introduction," to *Mill on Bentham and Coleridge* (London, Chatto and Windus, 1962), p.12. Subsequently referred to as *Bentham and Coleridge*.

They are also a statement of debt to two opposing masters. Their success in providing honest and compatible attitudes to the two teachers determines whether Mill stands or falls between two stools.

His aim in the Bentham essay was to systematize and stabilize his long established critique of Bentham with a sustained analysis of his value. It was to establish a status quo in his shifting relations with Benthamism. It would seem that this was an occupation of an entirely different stature from an appraisal of Coleridge. Yet Mill found, for historical and probably for personal reasons, that he had to turn to Coleridge to balance his debate with Benthamism.[3] Historical reasons indicated Coleridge as the only opposing thinker to Bentham with whom Bentham's virtues and defects could be compared. To Bentham's contemporaries, Burke might have been a more ready choice, but in Mill's age and circle Coleridge had more disciples and more influence than Burke. Personal reasons were as strong. Coleridge and the Coleridgeans had played their part as teachers as Mill came to maturity. To locate Bentham's influence he needed to refer to Coleridge; to clear the way, he needed to write about Coleridge as well as Bentham.

It is perhaps the most persuasive evidence of Coleridge's importance for Mill, beyond the mere fact that he is the subject of a major essay, that Coleridge should be so necessary a part of Mill's assessment of Bentham. It is also evidence of Coleridge's importance as an educator that the two essays from a watershed between Mill's early and late work. The essays, with their poised assessment, are a testimony of maturity. Before 1838, Mill made widely varying estimates of Bentham and Coleridge as he went through the intellectual pilgrimage which was the aftermath of the crisis. After 1838, he no longer hesitates in his assessment of his teachers. The essays stand as an apologia, both to the public, and to his private fascination with the history of his own mind.

---

[3]N.N.Feltes, "'Bentham' and 'Coleridge,' Mill's 'Completing Counterparts'," *The Mill News Letter*, II, (1968), 3.

I

Mill's clearest summary of his attitude to Bentham is the analogy, "The field of Bentham's labour was like the space between two parallel lines; narrow to excess in one direction, in another it reached to infinity."[4] His value, which was incalculable, lay in his proposals for the reform of the machinery of justice, in the introduction of the method of detail, and in his constructive criticism of existing institutions. These are the clear achievements which Mill acknowledges. But his assessment of Bentham's originality is limited. His "arguments and his examples together,"[5] are the terms on which Mill's admiration rests, but in practice the examples receive more attention than the arguments. He claims that "Bentham broke the spell,"[6] and draws particular attention to his role, not as an originator, but as a disseminator of much needed criticisms. "But were these discoveries of his?" Mill then asks, and the answer is "No."[7]

Mill sees more extensive inadequacies in Bentham's thought than lack of originality. He finds Bentham's method "is a security for accuracy, but not for comprehensiveness."[8] He has two faults which prevent him from taking full account of the "unanalysed experience of the human race."[9] Firstly, he "failed in deriving light from other minds,"[10] and, secondly, his own experience was inadequate. The result of this is that "man, that most complex being, is a very simple one in his eyes." He "is never recognized by him as being capable of pursuing spiritual perfection as an end."[11] Bentham's ethical thought is undermined by his limited insight into human nature. From his perception of these limitations in Bentham, Mill develops his criticisms of Benthamism along the familiar lines which were to emerge in *Utilitarianism* and the *Autobiography*.

[4]*Bentham and Coleridge*, p.75.
[5]*Ibid.*, p.41.
[6]*Ibid.*, p.42.
[7]*Ibid.*, p.45.
[8]*Ibid.*, p.56.
[9]*Ibid.*, p.59.
[10]*Ibid.*, p.58.
[11]*Ibid.*, pp.66-68.

In order to explain his ability to criticise Bentham's achievement in this way without abandoning a favourable estimate of it, Mill uses the idea of complimetary half-truths. He writes, not of Bentham's error, but rather of his "one-sidedness,"[12] and insists "that there is hardly anything positive in Bentham's philosophy which is not true."[13] He explains,

> For our own part we have a large tolerance for one-eyed men, provided their one eye is a penetrating one . . . Almost all rich veins of original and striking speculation have been opened by systematic half-thinkers. . . . no whole truth is possible but by combining the points of view of all the fractional truths, nor, therefore, until it has been fully seen what each fractional truth can do by itself.[14]

When this has been seen, "it is a comparatively easy task . . . to harmonize those truths with his."[15] The air of confidence with which Mill approaches the combination of half-truths is conspicuous. He is evidently satisfied with it as an explanation of his ambiguous attitude, and he is evidently sure that to be half-right is so qualitatively different from being half-wrong that it excuses all inadequacies and explains all praise. The half-truth theory is, then, the fundamental apologia of his treatment of Bentham. It emerges in the Coleridge essay as the framework for both essays.

If the Bentham essay describes one half of the truth, the Coleridge essay is clearly designed to represent the other half. Mill saw three problems in writing the Coleridge essay. Firstly, it would be difficult to explain the importance he felt Coleridge to have, for,

> as there is so much of Coleridge which is not to be found except by implication in his published works, which are only one of the channels through which his influences have reached the age, I am fearful of understanding both his merit & his importance – or rather of not producing sufficient detailed evidence to bear out my general estimate.

Mill is therefore anxious to avoid,

> overlooking any of the great thoughts . . . which he has contributed to the philosophy either explicit or implicit of the age, or which he

[12]*Ibid.*, p.93.
[13]*Ibid.*, p.64.
[14]*Ibid.*, p.65.
[15]*Ibid.*, p.64.

had powerfully aided in deepening or diffusing.[16]

Secondly, Mill is intending to make a difficult public declaration. He wrote,

> It will not be a popular article, & perhaps no one person who reads it will like it; probably few will derive much benefit from it; but if I do what I have thought of doing, viz. to collect the few things I have printed which are worth preserving & republish them in a volume, I shall be glad to have this among them because some others, without this, would give a false view of my general mode of thinking.[17]

Thirdly, the programme of re-reading Coleridge in preparation for this essay reaffirmed Mill's belief that Coleridge "stands almost alone" in seeing the foundation of political philosophy in the study of the balancing interests in a state, "& I think with him that these great interests are two, *Permanence & Progression*," and it is therefore *Church and State* which must take the most prominent part in the essay.[18]

Mill had, then, these three major aims in his essay on Coleridge: to insist, at the danger of being disbelieved, on Coleridge's seminal importance; to express in particular his approval of the ideas in *Church and State*; and, most important, to show the full extent of both Coleridge's and his own catholic spirit in philosophy. The essay is designed not merely as an evaluation of Coleridge, but as the central exposition of Mill's philosophy of half-truths.

In the Bentham essay the half-truth theory had assumed a relatively marginal importance. The major attention of the essay is given to a discussion of Bentham's limitations. But in the Coleridge essay there is a shift of balance. At the beginning of the essay the theory of complementary half-truths is greatly expanded. "In every respect," Mill writes, "the two men are each other's 'completing counterpart'."[19] Following this plan of presenting Coleridge and Bentham as complementary, Mill makes the exposition of the half-truth theory the fullest to be found in his writings.

---

[16]*The Collected Works of John Stuart Mill*, ed. F.E.L.Priestley, Vols. XII and XIII, "The Earlier Letters, 1812-1848," ed. F.E.Mineka (University of Toronto Press, 1963), XIII, 406. Subsequently referred to as *Works*, XII or XIII.

[17]*Ibid.*, 411.

[18]*Ibid.*, 408-409.

[19]*Bentham and Coleridge*, p.102.

> It might be plausibly maintained that in almost every one of the
> leading controversies . . . both sides were in the right in what they
> affirmed, though wrong in what they denied.[20]

It is as one half of this diagram of truth that Coleridge fits. Mill
sees Coleridge's thought as part of the reaction against the eighteenth
century. "In every respect it flies off in the contrary direction to its
predecessor."[21] The characterisation of the eighteenth century as a
period of purely destructive criticism, is carried to much greater
lengths than in the Bentham essay, for it is central to Mill's purpose to
exhibit every deficiency in the thought of the Enlightenment in order
to define Coleridge's position as the other half of the truth. Only in
this context can Coleridge's value be understood.

However, the simple complementary pair proves to be more
difficult and more elusive than Mill's initial remarks suggest. Although
he sets up a framework founded on an apologia for eclecticism, he finds
himself led to make further points which prevent Coleridge from
becoming the complementary to Bentham which the structure of the
essays seems to invite. The difficulty is a vital symptom of Mill's
changing attitudes to Coleridge.

The first sign is Mill's remark that Coleridge's share in this
interaction, "from his posteriority in date, was necessarily a
subordinate one."[22] He compares Coleridge unfavourably with
Bentham as regards his originality.

> In one respect, indeed, the parallel fails. Bentham so improved and
> added to the system of philosophy he adopted, that for his successors
> he may almost be accounted its founder; while Coleridge . . . was
> anticipated in all the essentials of his doctrine by the great
> Germans.[23]

The passage contrasts with Mill's emphasis in the previous essay
on Bentham's limited originality. Coleridge's relative importance is
reduced and this is the first indication that he is not the equal
complement to Bentham that Mill's introductory comments envisaged.
Mill declares that he is "entirely at one with Coleridge"[24] on his

[20]*Ibid.*, p.108.
[21]*Ibid.*, p.108.
[22]*Ibid.*, p.133.
[23]*Ibid.*, p.103.
[24]*Ibid.*, p.148.

doctrine of the clerisy, but remarks that "by setting in a clear light what a national church establishment ought to be ... he has pronounced the severest satire upon what in fact it is."[25] And he states quite succinctly, in opposition to Coleridge, that "when society requires to be rebuilt, there is no use in attempting to rebuild it on the old plan."[26]

It is at this point that Mill finds his attempt to make Coleridge the simple counterpart to Bentham becoming difficult. In the Bentham essay he had written, "it is a comparatively easy task that is reserved for us, to harmonize those truths with his."[27] In the Coleridge essay, however, he sees that "to combine the different parts of a doctrine with one another, and with all admitted truths, is not indeed a small trouble."[28] This change in tone is the key to the shift in emphasis between the two essays. The structure of the essays prepares a place for Coleridge which Mill ultimately cannot allow him to occupy. There is a tension between Mill's perception of Coleridge's value and the assessment to which he is forced when he tries to analyse it in detail. The essays were intended to bring out the areas of Coleridge's thought which complemented Bentham's. But the aspects of Coleridge which received that judicious portion of praise which Mill accords, in equal amounts, to both his subjects, are those of his political speculations which are essentially Liberal and not Conservative. Mill concludes,

> We may have done something to show that a Tory philosopher cannot be wholly a Tory, but must often be a better liberal than Liberals themselves. . . . And even if a Conservative philosophy were an absurdity, it is well calculated to drive out a hundred absurdities worse than itself . . . Not from him shall we have to apprehend the owl-like dread of light, the drudge-like aversion to change. . . . 'Lord, enlighten thou our enemies,' should be the prayer of every true Reformer: sharpen their wits, give acuteness to their perceptions, and consecutiveness and clearness to their reasoning powers: we are in danger from their folly, not from their wisdom; their weakness is what fills us with apprehension, not their strength. . . . The first step . . . is to inspire them with the desire to systematize and rationalize their own actual creed: and the feeblest attempt to do this has an

---

[25] *Ibid.*, p.147.

[26] *Ibid.*, p.128.

[27] *Ibid.*, p.64.

[28] *Ibid.*, p.113.

intrinsic value; far more, then, one which has so much in it, both of moral goodness and true insight, as the philosophy of Coleridge.[29]

Nothing could be more sectarian in spirit than this. Mill has passed from claiming for Coleridge that he saw just those truths to which Bentham was blind, to claiming that Coleridge's value lies in his presence as a clandestine Liberal in the ranks of the Tories. It is a startling reversal and raises uncomfortable questions. Mill's essay reveals an ambiguous attitude to Coleridge's value and influence. He is both a valuable corrective to the errors of Bentham and the eighteenth century, and an intellectual fifth columnist in the Tory ranks, working more for than against those very values for which he was earlier claimed to be the anti-dote. Coleridge, as the subject of an extended essay, is credited as a major balancing force, a powerful mind of considerable individuality. Yet this estimate hardly fits with the picture of him as a Tory, unconsciously damning his own party.

The reason for these differing estimates is historical and personal. Historical, because Mill's attitude to Coleridge has changed rapidly in the final stages of the maturing process; the inflated estimate belongs to the time of the crisis when Coleridge was a vital force, the later estimate to the time of the *Logic* when Mill had returned to a deliberate and coherent philosophy of his own. Personal, because the balancing effect of Coleridge's speculations was one on Mill's own mind. By 1840, however, the supra-personal claims of the radical cause resulted in the personal gratitude being overlaid by an inconsistently sectarian conclusion.

What estimate of Coleridge's influence emerges, on the whole, from the "Coleridge" essay? The answer is a deeply personal respect for Coleridge as a thinker, a realization of a very solid worth as a teacher, coupled with a distaste for most of his political affiliations. By the time the essay was written, in 1839, the distaste had grown stronger than the sense of personal debt. Hence Mill felt that it was almost too late for the essay to be written. Without Sterling's encouragement it might never have been completed.[30] Even with it, it remains an ambiguous testimony to Coleridge. And this explains Mill's sense of difficulty in

[29]*Ibid.*, pp. 167-168.
[30]*Works*, XIII, 411.

writing the essay. He knows it will not please his associates, nor will its tempered praise please the very ardent Coleridgeans. Equally, he wishes to claim an importance for Coleridge as a balancing force which his conclusions cannot support.

Thus Mill's essay on Coleridge, superficially a graceful and generous appreciation of an often maligned opponent, is under the surface a difficult and ambiguous attempt to reconcile the major irreconcilables in Mill's mind, the strong influence of idealism, and the re-established Utilitarianism. In this sense the essay is an excellent summary of Mill's relations to Coleridge.[31] It demonstrates visibly the conflicts that this relation caused, it stands historically at the end of the period of real debt to Coleridge, and illustrates well why Coleridge is little mentioned after 1840.

But even the structure of the essay is more influenced by Coleridge than its explicit declarations would suggest. The reader feels that all but Coleridge's *Church and State* was of passing interest to Mill. Yet the very structure of the essay itself, the arrangement and the reasons, are themselves curiously Coleridgean. The essays were designed to show in operation the half-truth theory which Coleridge himself had played a major part in creating. But further than this, Mill sees the English enlightenment through Coleridge's eyes. The points Mill criticises are these. Firstly, the Church had become a mockery, being "required to be, practically, as much a nullity as possible."[32] Secondly, "government altogether was regarded as a necessary evil,"[33] or, as Coleridge puts it, a mere committee for public safety. Thirdly, in religion,

> belief ... was left to stand upon miracles ... it is melancholy to see on what frail reeds able defenders of Christianity preferred to rest, rather than upon that better evidence which alone gave to their so-called evidences any value as a collateral confirmation. In the interpretation of Christianity the palpablest *bibliolatry* prevailed ... the reason for doing good is declared to be, that God is stronger than we are, and is able to damn us if we do not. This is no exaggeration of the sentiments of Paley, and hardly even the crudity

[31]See also J.S.Mill, *A System of Logic*, 2 vols. (London, Longmans, Green, and Co., 1879), II, 233-238.

[32]*Bentham and Coleridge*, p.135.

[33]*Ibid.*, p.137.

of his language.[34]

Mill is using Coleridge's criticisms to value Coleridge's remedies. Mill even uses Coleridge's own valuation of the working of his influence to describe that influence. Coleridge felt that,

> the Public, indeed, have given no heed: but if only ten minds have been awakened by my writings, the intensity of the Benefit may well compensate for the narrowness of its extension.[35]

And Mill argues that, in the case of both Bentham and Coleridge, "their readers have been few: but they have been the teachers of the teachers."[36] Thus the concepts on which the whole essay and some of the individual judgements are based owe a great deal to Coleridge.

Although Mill derived from Coleridge several ideas which were of the first importance in his thought, he is still essentially alien. Mill is contemptuous of Coleridge's intuitionism; he can only value his religious thought in a way which has little relevance to its real intentions; his economic thought is "drivel"; and his cultural thinking, whatever its value, is essentially derivative. On the other hand Mill does accept Coleridge's idea of the clerisy, his theory of the constitution as a balance of two great class interests, as opposed to Bentham's idea of the summation of innumerable individual interests, and his insistence on the need for a catholic spirit in philosophy.

II

> But mercy on us! is there no such thing as two men's having similar Thoughts on similar Occasions? – S.T.Coleridge[37]

In order to incorporate the evidence of the essay on Coleridge into an informed judgement of Coleridge's place in Mill's thought the parallels and opposites discussed throughout this study must be

---

[34]*Ibid.*, pp.138-139.

[35]B.M.Add. Ms. 47544, Notebook 49, f.14. Numbered by Coleridge as Notebook 17, p.28. Entry dated 21st November, 1830.

[36]*Bentham and Coleridge*, p.39.

[37]*Collected Letters of Samuel Taylor Coleridge*, ed. E.L.Griggs, 4 vols. (Oxford, Clarendon, 1956-1959), III, 429. Subsequently referred to as *Letters*.

summarized.

J.S. Mill's mental crisis is an event as complex in its recorded history as in its substance. Mill's own accounts are curiously inconsistent; his commentators often biased. What still emerges, however, is the feeling that the experience was neither as violent, as unusual, nor as unnatural as has been supposed. But the most interesting conclusion is that the cause and effect relationships that surround the crisis suggest that what Mill saw as the result of the crisis – a new interest in art, and an understanding of Romantic theories of art – may have played a part in the instigation of the crisis.

After the crisis, Mill went through a period of intellectual expansion when he read widely outside the Benthamite tradition of his education. One of these new influences was Coleridge. The evidence for attributing a special place to him among the bewildering variety of sources of the new Idealistic elements in Mill's thought lies in an early, personal and enthusiastic testimony of debt to Coleridge in a letter to Nichol. Whatever the exaggerations of his account there – and it is almost mysterious in some of its enthusiasms, such as that for Coleridge's system – the evidence is clear. Mill had read virtually all of Coleridge's published works, some of his unpublished work, had visited Coleridge himself and had close acquaintances with several Coleridgeans, especially Sterling, who was his closest friend.

The basic ideas of Mill and Coleridge show the intense opposition of their epistemologies. They are Platonist and Aristotelian. But they also follow similar paths in passing through an early phase of attraction to the opposite system, and in preserving elements of this other system in their mature ideologies. The result is a certain overlap in their ideas and certain inconsistencies and uncompleted trains of thought in both writers. The motives and the results which cause this overlap are similar. Both Coleridge's and Mill's motives are personal. Coleridge wants to reconcile his ideals with the world, to create security in a personal relation with God; Mill wishes to reform philosophy, and through philosophy the economic and social institutions of the world. Both motives are pressingly human; both motives spring from a valuation which places the experienced needs of humanity above the consistencies of logic.

Coleridge's philosophy is based as much in the English Platonic tradition, as in Continental Idealism, though he evidently owed much

to Kant and Post-Kantianism. He is concerned with Ideas, whereas
Mill's philosophy starts with an attack on the concept of universals.
Yet both thinkers have a similar attitude to the syllogism as a useful
generalizing device, a preserver if not a discoverer of truth.

Coleridge's epistemology is based on a conviction of the mind's
activity in perception, Mill's on its passive dependence on laws of
association. Here there is an almost total opposition, though Mill's
uncertainties about his father's *Analysis of the Phenomena of the
Human Mind*, and the fragments of Hartley remaining in Coleridge,
temper this opposition. Yet, again, both insist on free-will, though Mill
has difficulty reconciling it with his overall logical standpoint. They
also exhibit a philosophical relativism, which in both thinkers allows
the inexplicable and the unexplored to lie undisturbed in close
contradiction to their established ideas.

Mill's and Coleridge's criticisms of the opposing systems are telling.
They are both the criticisms of men with personal experience of the
other system, though both are informed by a tolerant relativism. This
alone would make them interesting. They are parallel in their insistence
that it is in the misuse of language that most of the errors of the
opposing doctrine lie; in the claim that it is only the superficial clarity
which allows the other system to survive, and in the belief that the
consequences of the opposed ideology is some form of vicious and
infinitely regressive circularity of argument. Thus although their
critiques are pungent, they both start from a common belief in the
nature of truth as a complex and continuous process founded in deep
assumptions, and not in simple formulations; and they both direct their
critiques at the less modest manifestations of the alternative system.

It is noticeable that Mill does not choose Coleridge as a target for
his critique of intuitionism. Once the philosophical basis of Mill's and
Coleridge's thought is firmly established it becomes clear that their
opposition is real, but not total. Room is left for some communities of
ideas, and subsequent evidence shows that there is a considerable area
where Mill and Coleridge hold common beliefs.

Thus they both see philosophy as a means, rather than an end.
Coleridge's responsiveness to human needs reaches the level where he
has been plausibly charged with irrationalism. Mill prefers the
experienced need to the inferred conclusion, and some of the difficulties
of his later essays are the inevitable, and openly faced, result of this

philosophical eclecticism. The parallel is an important one, for it is in this way of assessing the values of truth that Mill's closeness to Coleridge, and Coleridge's impact on Mill as a teacher seems to lie. It is the eclecticism which Mill found in Coleridge which was the great solvent of Mill's rigid Benthamism. Through eclecticism utilitarianism turned into the pliant liberalism of the nineteenth century. Eclecticism might be defined as distinguishing between competing systems by other means than by establishing their total logical coherence. These means, the distinctive and distinguishing factor in Coleridge's and Mill's minds, were experienced human needs. This is the most striking parallel between them.

In the methodology of politics Mill seems to have owed a lot to Coleridge in the process of arriving at his established ideas, if not in the final result. He has a similar dissatisfaction with eighteenth century political theories, a similar balance between first principle and practical modification, a similar political gradualism, and a similar quasi-historicist outlook. Evidence of the impact of idealism on Mill is derived from analysing Mill's most durable and influential works, the essays on *Utilitarianism* and *Liberty*. It would seem that it is impossible to defend Mill purely as an Utilitarian, and Idealism must be allowed to have played a considerable part in both essays. Mill's liberalism is specifically Romantic in tone. His position, like Coleridge's, is a philosophically hybrid blend of argument, and assumed valuations based on experienced human needs.

Surprisingly it is in religious ideas that the parallels between Mill and Coleridge seem strongest. Mill's later religious essays confirm the tendency of mind explained to Carlyle in an earlier declaration of lack of faith. Mill, the only Benthamite to take religion seriously, had read and been impressed by Coleridge's religious works, and Coleridge's ideas appeared in his speculations. The fact has little historical importance, for Mill's *Three Essays on Religion*, apart from a flutter of surprise and consternation at their apparent concessions to religion, had little permanent effect. But they are vital evidence of Coleridge's overall effect on Mill's mind. It is Coleridge's liberal interpretation of the Christian myth, and his humanist insistence on the priority of human needs as factors determining the valuation of religious ideals, that Mill's essays echo. The criteria, for both men, are human ethical ideals, not divinely imposed duties.

Mill's theology, though interesting, is a minor aspect of his work. His belief in the clerisy is not. Mill's clearest debt to Coleridge lies in his acceptance of Coleridge's doctrine of an endowed class for the cultivation of the nation. He changed Coleridge's intentions significantly in using his arguments to militate against the preservation of the established Church which Coleridge so loved. But he retained the essence of Coleridge's idea, and it became a defence against the extremes of Comte and Tocqueville.

Mill's poetics is heavily indebted to the Romantics, especially Coleridge. The ideas of Imagination and genius, the sympathetic and interpretative approach to criticism, the attitude to poetic diction in particular, come from Coleridge and not from Wordsworth. But Mill's conclusions were neither Coleridgean, nor Wordsworthian, but prophetically Victorian.

The example of Coleridge's eclecticism seems to have stimulated the development of Mill's own important theory of half-truths. Although Mill had many sources for this idea, some quite close parallels with Coleridge's attitudes to eclecticism and tolerance point to Coleridge as a major factor in the formation of a belief which was to distinctively colour and direct Mill's later thought.

III

These parallels might, coupled with Mill's early letter to Nichol, suggest a very serious debt. But this would contradict the relative coolness of Mill's later assessment in the *Autobiography*, and the conclusion of the "Coleridge" essay, and would ignore the large areas of Mill's thought which are radically divergent from anything in Coleridge. Mill's support of the feminist cause, his wish for radical reforms of parliamentary government, tenure of property and inheritance, his economics and scientific sociology, not to mention his work as a teacher of logic; all this is in direct opposition to Coleridge and Coleridge's influence.

The truth is perhaps that here is an ambiguous situation. Idealism had a deep, but suppressed, influence on Mill. It altered Benthamism from something eccentric, parochial and impractical to a liberalism which was widely acceptable to the nineteenth century. Mill's honesty led him to make an unusually full account of his debts to Coleridge –

yet his position as one of the fathers of nineteenth century liberalism led him to reject Coleridge. Hence the ambiguity, and the difficulty, in formulating Coleridge's importance to Mill.

Coleridge was only one of many Idealist influences on Mill. There were also Carlyle, Macaulay, Burke, Wordsworth, and Shelley. Yet Coleridge stands out in two ways. He is the subject of unusual declarations of debt, and the only one to receive extended consideration in a major essay. Secondly, he is the most radical in philosophy as in politics, and therefore the nearest to Mill. The various parallels spring from this radicalism. Coleridge had a philosophy of human needs, a revolutionary religious liberalism, a belief in hortatory rather than supervisory education. He offered new theories of art, of the role of the imagination, and of genius; he expounded an ideal of the "clerisy," and above all of eclecticism. These ideas differentiate him from other Romantics. Shelley was too idealistic to have much to offer Mill; Burke, Wordsworth, Carlyle and Macaulay were too conservative, and too little the speculators. Thus Coleridge stands as the only English Idealist who was close enough to Mill to have exerted any considerable influence.

There were, of course, other influences besides the English ones. Plato, Goethe, Tocqueville, and Comte all played their part. Coleridge was not the only influence on Mill, nor was he first or last. In common with other idealist influences, his effect was not fully acknowledged. Yet Coleridge should stand as an important example of idealist influences on Mill, and through Mill on nineteenth century liberalism. It has been held that Coleridge might have saved Mill, had Mill paid more attention to him,[38] and that Mill failed to understand either Coleridge's originality, or his deeply English roots.[39] The influence of Idealism on Mill has never been in doubt, despite his own failure to correctly estimate its effect on him.[40] But the importance of the "Coleridge" essay as a public declaration of his differences in sympathy

[38]D.G.James, "The Thought of Coleridge," in *The Major English Romantic Poets; A Symposium in Reappraisal*, ed.Clarence D.Thorpe; Carlos Baker and Bennet Weaver (Carbondale, Southern Illinois University Press, 1957), p.112.

[39]R.J.White, "John Stuart Mill," *Cambridge Journal*, V (1951-52), 94.

[40]Shirley R.Letwin, *The Pursuit of Certainty* (Cambridge University Press, 1965), p.233.

from the majority of the Utilitarians has always been clear.[41]
Coleridge's influence as a radical has also been admitted. Mill gladly
accepted Coleridge's radical ideas as tools for his own purpose – the
clerisy is the prime example. But Coleridge had three roles as one of
Mill's teachers: as a radical, as an idealist, and as an eclectic. The
first and last have not been properly appreciated. The evidence
collected here will, it is hoped, correct this.

IV

The routes by which the fragments of Coleridge's ideas have
retained their vital life in other minds, and so survived as living forces,
must defy any catalogue. The seeds of his ideas have stimulated
educators, theologians, and critics. In some ways they have crystallized
as institutions, as Churches and schools with liberal ideas, as university
English schools, established on rationales which owe much to
Coleridge's pioneering of literature's vital importance. In the same way
Mill's ideas survive as contemporary forces. They are probably more
institutionalized even than Coleridge's. Who can estimate the influence
of utilitarianism on legislators, or the vast effect of *Liberty* on public
conscience? And through *Utilitarianism* and *Liberty* Coleridge's ideas,
too, remain vital.

Both Coleridge and Mill believed that their ideas would be
influential, but their concept of usefulness was vague. Coleridge hoped
that the "Light shall stream to a far distance from the taper in my
cottage window."[42] He believed that if the seed of his ideas stimulated
only a few minds he would not have lived and worked in vain. One
almost senses self-pity in the humility of such justifications, pity for his
ostrich eggs,[43] his emblem of his wasted talents blamed on an
indifferent world. Mill's intellectual pieties are equally vague. He
himself did solid work, yet men like Austin and Sterling, who did little
through ill health, he believed to be sources of "great elevation of

---

[41]J.H.Burns, "J.S.Mill and Democracy, 1829-61," *Political Studies*, V (1957), 170.
[42]*Letters*, I, 277.
[43]S.T.Coleridge, *Biographia Literaria*, ed. J.Shawcross, 2 vols. (Oxford, Clarendon,
1907), I, 32.

character" through their examples and conversations. Coleridge, too, he thought "might plead" this "set off."[44]

Mill's argument that Coleridge was a teacher of teachers, a seminal and ignored mind, and thereby mysteriously almost more important, the seed growing most strongly in the dark, comes directly from Coleridge. Mill has thus been responsible for propagating Coleridge's justification with Coleridge's ideas, and paradoxically the weak argument of the taper in the cottage window became in part a reality. The exact measure of this reality is another subject. This study is designed to show merely that Coleridge's Idealism was more active, even in an opposed tradition, than has often been supposed. Coleridge's liberal and eclectic love of truth, and its foundation on human needs and experiences, found permanent admiration and emulation throughout Mill's writings. It is not therefore what was, to some extent, derivative in Coleridge's thought, but what was essentially his own, his "moral goodness and true insight,"[45] which was most influential.

Something of this spirit was transmitted by Coleridge's writings and by his disciples to the minds who were capable of assimilating it. Coleridge's distinctive and lasting value as a prose writer probably lies in his approach to truth. He has a largeness and flexibility of mind which is more than tolerance, and a depth of insight which supercedes paradox in its spirit if not in its expression. Matthew Arnold makes what is still a fair assessment of Coleridge (and Arnold had far less sympathy with Coleridge than Mill had).[46]

> How little . . . of his philosophy can we expect permanently to stand!
> But that which will stand of Coleridge is this: the stimulus of his
> continual effort . . . to get at and lay bare the real truth of his
> matter in hand. . . . Coleridge's great usefulness lay in his supplying
> in England . . . a stimulus to all minds capable of profiting by it.[47]

Mill acknowledges just this stimulus from Coleridge as his "moral

[44]J.S.Mill, *Autobiography*, 3rd ed. (London, Longmans, Green, Reader, and Dyer, 1873), p.75.

[45]*Bentham and Coleridge*, p.168.

[46]Leon Gottfried, *Matthew Arnold and the Romantics* (London, Routledge & Kegan Paul, 1963), p.191.

[47]Matthew Arnold, *Lectures and Essays in Criticism*, ed. R.H.Super, The Complete Prose Works of Matthew Arnold, III (Ann Arbor, University of Michigan Press, 1962), pp.189-190.

goodness and true insight." It was surely this that made him claim that Coleridge was a seminal mind, one of the teachers of the teachers. And it is Mill more than anyone else who has propagated the belief in the seminal value of Coleridge's fragmentary work.

Bibliography

Abrahams, Meyer H., *The Mirror and the Lamp; Romantic Theory and the Critical Tradition* (New York, Oxford University Press, 1953).

Adair, Patricia M., *The Waking Dream; A Study of Coleridge's Poetry* (London, Edward Arnold, 1967).

Allsop, T. (ed.), *Letters, Conversations and Recollections of S.T.Coleridge*, 2 vols. (London, Edward Moxon, 1836).

Annan, Noel, *Leslie Stephen* (London, MacGibbon & Kee, 1951).

Anon., 'On Tendencies Towards the Subversion of Faith', *The English Review*, X (1848), pp. 399-444.

Anon., Review of F.D.Maurice's *Kingdom of Christ* in 'The State and the Church', *Foreign Review* (1831), p. 434.

Anschutz, R.P., 'J.S.Mill: Philopsopher of Victorianism', in *1840 and After*, ed. Arthur Sewell (Auckland, N.Z., 1939).

Appleyard, J.A., *Coleridge's Philopsophy of Literature* (Harvard University Press, 1965).

Armour, Richard W., and Raymond F.Howes (*eds*), *Coleridge the Talker, A Series of Contemporary Descriptions and Comments* (New York, Cornell University Press, 1940).

Arnold, Matthew, *Lectures and Essays in Criticism*, ed. R.H.Super, *The Complete Prose Works of Matthew Arnold*, Vol.III (Ann Arbor, University of Michigan Press, 1962).

— *The Letters of Matthew Arnold to Arthur Hugh Clough*, ed. H.F.Lowry (London, Oxford University Press, 1932).

August, Eugene, *John Stuart Mill* (New York, Scribner, 1975).

— *John Stuart Mill: A Mind at Large* (London, Vision Press, 1976).

Babbit, Irving, 'Coleridge and the Moderns', *The Bookman*, LXX (October, 1929).

Bain, Alexander, *John Stuart Mill, a Criticism* (London, Longmans, Green and Co., 1882).

Baker, Herschel, *William Hazlitt* (London, Oxford University Press, 1962).

Baker, J.V., *The Sacred River; Coleridge's Theory of the Imagination* (Louisiana State University Press, 1957).

Balfour, Arthur James, *Theism and Humanism* (London, Hodder and Stoughton, 1915).

Ball, Patricia, *The Science of Aspects: The Canging Role of Fact in the Work of Coleridge, Ruskin and Hopkins* (London, Athlone Press, 1971).

Barfield, Owen, *What Coleridge Thought* (Wesleyan University Press, 1971).

Barth, J. Robert, *Coleridge and Christian Doctrine* (Harvard University Press, 1969).
— *The Symbolic Imagination: Coleridge and the Romantic Tradition* (Princeton University Press, 1977).
Bate, Walter J., *Coleridge* (London, Weidenfeld & Nicolson, 1969).
Baumgardt, David, 'Bentham's "Censorial" Method', *Journal of the History of Ideas*, VI (1945).
Bayley, John, *The Romantic Survival: A Study in the Poetic Evolution* (London, Constable and Co., 1957).
Beer, John, (*ed.*), *Coleridge's Variety: Bicentenary Studies* (University of Pittsburgh Press, 1975).
— *Coleridge's Poetic Intelligence* (London, Macmillan, 1977).
Benn, A.W., *The History of English Rationalism in the Nineteenth Century*, 2 Vols (London, Longmans, Green and Co., 1906).
Benzinger, James, 'Organic Unity: Leibnitz to Coleridge', *P.M.L.A.*, LXVI (1951).
Berkoben, L., *Coleridge's Decline as a Poet* (The Hague, Mouton, 1975).
Berlin, Sir Isiah, *John Stuart Mill and the Ends of Life* (London, Council of Christians and Jews, 1959).
Binyon, C.G., *The Christian Socialist Movement in England* (London, S.P.C.K., 1931).
Blake, William, *Poetry and Prose of William Blake, ed.* Geoffrey Keynes (London, Nonesuch Press, 1943).
Blegvad, Morgens, 'Mill, Moore, and the Naturalist Fallacy', in *Philosophical Essays Dedicated to Gunnar Aspelin* (Lund, 1963).
Boulger, J.D., *Coleridge as Religious Thinker* (New Haven, Yale University Press, 1961).
Bouton, Clark W., 'John Stuart Mill: On Liberty and History', *Western Political Quarterly*, XVIII (1965), pp. 573-574.
Bowle, John, *Politics and Opinion in the Nineteenth Century* (London, Johnathan Cape, 1954).
Bradley, A.C., *English Poetry and German Philosophy in the Age of Wordsworth* (Manchester University Press, 1909).
Brett, R.L., *Reason and Imagination* (London, Oxford University Press, 1960).
— (*ed.*), *Coleridge* (London, G.Bell, 1971).
Brinkley, R.F., 'Coleridge on Locke', *Studies in Philology*, XLVI (1949).
Brinton, Crane, *The Political Ideas of the English Romanticists* (London, Oxford University Press, 1926).
Britton, Karl, 'J.S.Mill: A Debating Speech on Wordsworth, 1829', *Cambridge Review*, LXXIX (1958).
Broad, C.D., *Five Types of Ethical Theory* (London, Kegan Paul, Trench, Trubner & Co., 1934).

Bunsen, Christian Carl Josias von, *Die Verfassung der Kirche der Zukunft* (Hamburg, 1845), translated by the author as *The Constitution of the Church of the Future* (London, Longmans and Co., 1847).

Burns, J.H., 'J.S.Mill and Democracy, 1829-61', *Political Studies*, V (1957).

Byatt, Antonia, *Wordsworth and Coleridge in their Time* (London, Nelson, 1970).

Caine, T.Hall, *Recollections of Rosetti* (London, Elliot Stock, 1882).

– *Life of Samuel Taylor Coleridge* (London, Walter Scott, 1887).

Carlyle, Thomas, *New Letters of Thomas Carlyle, ed.* Alexander Carlyle, 2 vols (London, John Lane, 1904).

– *The Life of John Sterling*, World's Classics, CXLIV (London, Oxford University Press, 1933).

Carlyon, Clement, *Early Years and Late Reflections*, 4 vols (London, Whittacker and Co., 1836-1858).

Carpenter, Maurice, *The Indifferent Horseman; The Divine Comedy of Samuel Taylor Coleridge* (London, Elek Books, 1954).

Carr, Robert, 'The Religious Thought of J.S. Mill', *Journal of the History of Ideas*, XXIII (1962).

Caskey, Jefferson, *Samuel Taylor Coleridge: A Selective Bibliography of Criticism, 1935-1977* (Greenwood Press, 1978).

Cassirer, Ernst, *The Problem of Knowledge: Philosophy, Science, and History since Hegel*, translated by W.H.Woglom and C.W.Hendel (New Haven, Yale University Press, 1950).

Castle, W.R., 'Newman and Coleridge', *Sewanee Review*, XVII (1909), pp. 39-152.

Chambers, E.K., *Samuel Taylor Coleridge, A Biographical Study* (Oxford, Clarendon, 1938).

Chiari, Joseph, *Symbolism from Poe to Mallarmé, The Growth of a Myth* (London, Rockliff, 1956).

Christensen, Jerome, *Coleridge: Blessed Machine of Language* (Cornell University Press, 1982).

Coburn, Kathleen (*ed.*), *Inquiring Spirit: A New Presentation of Coleridge from his Publications and Unpublished Prose Writings* (Toronto, University of Toronto Press, 1979).

– *Experience into Thought: Perspectives in the Coleridge Notebooks* (University of Toronto Press, 1982).

Cockshut, A.O.J., *The Unbelievers, English Agnostic Thought, 1840-1890* (London, Collins, 1964).

Coleridge, S.T., *Aids to Reflection, in the Formation of a Manly Character* (London, William Pickering, 1825).

– *Aids to Reflection* (London, G.Bell and Sons, 1884).

– *Anima Poetae*, (*ed.*) E.H.Coleridge (London, W.Heinemann, 1895).

– *Biographia Literaria, or Biographical Sketches of my Literary Life and Opinions*, 2 vols (London, Rest Fenner, 1817).

254

- *Biographia Literaria*, (*ed.*) J.Shawcross, 2 vols (Oxford, Clarendon Press, 1907).
- *Coleridge's Miscellaneous Criticism*, (*ed.*) T.M.Raysor (London, Constable and Co., 1936).
- *Coleridge's Shakespearean Criticism*, (*ed.*) T.M.Raysor, 2 vols (London, Constable and Co., 1930).
- *Collected Letters of Samuel Taylor Coleridge*, (*ed.*) E.L.Griggs, 4 vols (Oxford, Clarendon Press, 1912).
- *Confessions of an Inquiring Spirit*, edited from the author's manuscript by Henry Nelson, esq., M.A. (London, William Pickering, 1840).
- *Confessions of an Inquiring Spirit*, (*ed.*) H.StJ.Hart (London, A & C Black, 1956).
- *On the Constitution of Church and State, with Reference to the Idea of Each, with Aids Towards a Right Judgement on the Late Catholic Bill* (London, Hurst, Chance & Co., 1830).
- *The Friend*, (*ed.*) Barbara E. Rooke, 2 vols (London, Routledge & Kegan Paul, 1969).
- *Lay Sermons*, in White, R.J. (*ed.*), *Political Tracts of Wordsworth, Coleridge and Shelley* (Cambridge University Press, 1953).
- *The Notebooks of Samuel Taylor Coleridge, 1794-1808*, (*ed.*) Kathleen Coburn, 4 vols (London, Routledge & Kegan Paul, 1957).
- *The Philosophical Lectures*, (*ed.*) Kathleen Coburn (London, Pilot Press, 1949).
- *Table Talk and Omniana*, (*ed.*) T.Ashe (London, G.Bell and Sons, 1923).
- *Two Addresses on Sir Robert Peel's Bill, April 1818*, (*ed.*) Edmund Gosse (London, Printed for Private Circulation, 1913).

Colmer, John, *Coleridge, Critic of Society* (Oxford, Clarendon Press, 1959).
Cooke, Katharine, *Coleridge* (London, Boston, Routledge & Kegan Paul, 1979).
Cooper, Wesley (*ed.*), *New Essays on John Stuart Mill and Utilitarianism* (Neilsen & Patten, Canadian Association for Publishing in Philosophy, 1979).
Cornwell, John, *Coleridge Poet and Revolutionary, A Critical Bibliography* (London, Allen Lane, 1973).
Corrgian, Tim, *Coleridge, Language and Criticism* (University of Georgia Press, 1982).
Courtney, William Leonard, *Life of John Stuart Mill* (London, Walter Scott, 1889).
- *The Metaphysics of John Stuart Mill* (London, Kegan Paul and Co., 1879).
Cowling, Maurice, *Mill and Liberalism* (Cambridge University Press, 1963).
Cox, Catherine M., *The Early Mental Traits of Three Hundred Geniuses* (London, Harrup & Co., 1926).

Cumming, Robert D., 'Mill's History of his Ideas', *Journal of the History of Ideas*, XXV (1964), pp. 235-256.

Davis, H.F., 'Was Newman a Disciple of Coleridge?', *Dublin Review*, CCXVII (October, 1945), pp. 165-173.

De Quincey, Thomas, 'Samuel Taylor Coleridge', *Tait's Edinburgh Magazine*, I (1834). Reprinted in *Recollections of the Lakes and Lake Poets*, in *Works* (Edinburgh, Adam and Charles Black, 1862).

Deschamps, Paul, *La Formation de la Pensée de Coleridge, 1772-1804* (Paris, Didier, 1964).

Dewey, J., 'James Marsh and American Philosophy', *Journal of the History of Ideas*, II (1941), p.32.

Dicey, A.V., *Lecture on the Relation Between Law and Public Opinion in England during the Nineteenth Century* (London, Macmillan and Co., 1914).

Doughty, Oswald, *'Perturbed Spirit': The Life and Personality of Samuel Taylor Coleridge* (Associated University Presses, 1981).

Douglas, Charles Mackinnon, *The Ethics of John Stuart Mill*, edited with an introduction by C.M.Douglas (Edinburgh, W.Blackwood & Sons, 1897).

— *John Stuart Mill, A Study of his Philosophy* (Edinburgh, W.Blackwood & Sons, 1895).

Downie, R.S., 'Mill on Pleasure and Self-Development', *Philosophical Quarterly*, XVI (1966).

Duncan, Graeme, *Marx and Mill: Two Views of Social Conflict and Social Harmony* (Cambridge University Press, 1973).

Eisenach, Eldon, *Two Worlds of Liberalism: Religion and Politics in Hobbes, Locke and Mill* (Chicago University Press, 1981).

English Institute, *New Perspectives on Coleridge and Wordsworth. Selected Papers Presented in 1970 and 1971* (Columbia University Press, 1972).

Escott, T.H.S., 'Coleridge as a Twentieth Century Force', *London Quarterly Review*, CXXI (1914).

Fairchild, H.N., *Religious Trends in English Poetry*, 5 vols (New York, Columbia University Press, 1949).

Feltes, N.N., '"Bentham" and "Coleridge," Mill's "Completing Counterparts"', *The Mill News Letter*, II (1968).

Friedman, Richard B., 'A New Exploration of Mill's Essay "On Liberty"', *Political Science*, XIV (1966).

Feuer, Lewis S., 'John Stuart Mill and Marxian Socialism', *Journal of the History of Ideas*, X (1949), pp. 297-304.

Fogle, R.H., *The Idea of Coleridge's Criticism, Perspectives in Criticism*, 9 (Berkeley and Los Angeles, California University Press, 1962).

Fox, Caroline, *Memories of Old Friends, Being Extracts from the Journals and Letters of Caroline Fox, 1835-1871*, (ed.) H.N.Pym, 2 vols (London, Smith, Elder and Co., 1882).

Froude, James Anthony, *Thomas Carlyle, A History of the First Forty Years of Life, 1795-1835*, 2 vols (London, Longmans, Green and Co., 1891).

Fruman, Norman, *Coleridge the Damaged Archangel* (New York, George Braziller, 1971).

Garforth, Francis, *John Stuart Mill's Theory of Education* (New York, Barnes & Noble, 1979).

— *Educative Democracy: John Stuart Mill on Education in Society* (Published for the University of Hull by Oxford University Press, 1980).

Gilpin, George, *The Strategy of Joy: An Essay on the Poetry of Samuel Taylor Coleridge* (University of Salzburg, 1972).

Gingerich, S.F., 'From Necessity to Transcendentialism in Coleridge', *P.M.L.A.*, XXXV (1920).

Goehlert, Robert, *John Stuart Mill: A Bibliography* (London, 1982).

Gottfried, Leon, *Matthew Arnold and the Romantics* (London, Routledge & Kegan Paul, 1963).

Grant, Allan, *A Preface to Coleridge* (New York, Scribner, 1972).

Gray, John, *Mill on Liberty: A Defence* (London, Routedge and Kegan Paul, 1983).

Grey, Ronald, *The German Tradition in Literature, 1871-1945* (Cambridge University Press, 1965).

Grow, Lynn, *The Consistency of Biographia Literaria* (Wichita, Kansas, 1973).

Hainds, John R., 'Mill's Examiner Articles on Art', *Journal of the History of Ideas*, XI (1959), pp. 215-234.

Hainds, John R., Ney MacMinn and James McCrimmon, *Bibliography of John Stuart Mill*, Northwestern University Studies, 12 (Northwestern University Press, 1945).

Hall, Everett Wesley, 'The "Proof" of Utility in Bentham and Mill', in *Categorical Analysis* (Chapel Hill, University of North Carolina Press, 1964).

Halliday, Richard, *John Stuart Mill* (London, Allen & Unwin, 1976).

Hamburgher, Joseph, 'James Mill on Universal Suffrage and the Middle Class', *Journal of Politics*, XXIV (1962).

— *Intellectuals in Politics: John Stuart Mill and the Philosophic Radicals* (New Haven, Yale University Press, 1966).

Hammond, Albert L., 'Euthyphro, Mill and Mr. Lewis', *The Journal of Philosophy*, XLIX (1952).

Haney, John Louis, 'Coleridge the Commentator', in *Coleridge: Studies by Several Hands*, (eds) Edmund Blunden and E.L.Griggs (London, Constable and Co., 1934).

— 'The Marginalia of Samuel Taylor Coleridge', in *Schelling Anniversary Papers by his Former Students* (New York, The Century Co., 1923).

Hare, Julius Charles and Augustus William, *Guesses at Truth, by Two Brothers*, 2 vols (London, John Taylor, 1827).

Hare, Julius Charles, 'Samuel Taylor Coleridge and the English Opium Eater', *British Magazine*, VII (January, 1835).
— 'Introduction', to John Sterling, *Essays and Tales*, (*ed.*) J.C.Hare, 2 vols (London, J.W.Parker, 1848).
Harris, Abram L., 'John Stuart Mill: Servant of the East India Company', *Canadian Journal of Economics and Political Science*, XXX (1964).
— 'John Stuart Mill's Theory of Progress', *Ethics*, LXVI (1955-1956).
Harrison, John S., *The Teachers of Emerson* (New York, Sturgis and Walton Co., 1910).
Harrold, Charles Frederick, *Carlyle and German Thought, 1819-1834* (New Haven, Yale University Press, 1934).
Hartley, David, *Observations on Man, his Frame, his Duty, and his Expectations*, 2 vols (London, S. Richardson, 1949).
Haven, Richard, *Patterns of Consciousness: An Essay on Coleridge* (University of Massachusetts Press, 1969).
— *Samuel Taylor Coleridge: An Annotated Bibliography of Criticism and Scholars* (Boston, G.K.Hall, 1975).
Havens, Michael, *Coleridge on Language and Imagination* (Syracuse University Press, 1980).
Hayter, Alethea, *A Voyage in Vain: Coleridge's Journey to Malta in 1804* (London, Faber & Faber, 1973).
Hazlitt, William, *The Complete Works of William Hazlitt*, (*ed.*) P.Howe, 21 vols (London, J.M.Dent & Sons, 1930-1934).
Heath, William, *Wordsworth and Coleridge: A Study of their Literary Realations in 1801-1802* (Oxford University Press, 1970).
Helmholz, Anna, *The Indebtedness of Coleridge to A.W. von Schlegel*, Bulletin of the University of Wisconsin, CLXII (Madison, University of Wisconsin Press, 1907).
Himmelfarb, Gertrude, *On Liberty and Liberalism: The Case of John Stuart Mill* (New York, Knopf, 1974).
Hobhouse, L.T., *Liberalism* (London, Williams & Norgate, 1911).
Holthoon, F.L. van, *The Road to Utopia — John Stuart Mill's Social Thought* (London, 1971).
Honderich, Ted, 'Mill on Liberty', *Inquiry*, X (1967).
Hort, F.J.A., 'Coleridge', in *Cambridge Essays* (London, J.W.Parker, 1856).
Hough, Graham, 'Coleridge and the Victorians', in *The English Mind, Studies in the English Moralists, Presented to Basil Willey*, (*ed.*) Hugh Sykes Davies and George Watson (Cambridge University Press, 1964).
— *The Last Romantics* (London, Gerald Duckworth and Co., 1949).
Houghton, Walter E., *The Victorian Frame of Mind, 1830-1870* (New Haven, Yale University Press, 1957).
Howard, Claud, *Coleridge's Idealism, A Study of its Relationship to Kant and to the Cambridge Platonists* (Boston, R.G.Badger, 1924).

Howe, Susanne, *Wilhelm Meister and his Kinsmen: Apprentices to Life* (New York, Columbia University Press, 1930).

Hyman, S.E., *The Armed Vision* (New York, Alfred A. Knopf, 1952).

Ince, R.B., *Calverley and Some Cambridge Wits of the Nineteenth Century* (London, Cayne Press, 1929).

Irvine, William, 'Carlyle and T.H.Huxley', *Booker Memorial Studies: Eight Essays in Victorian Literature*, in memory of John Manning Booker, 1881-1948, (*ed.*) Hill Shine (Chapel Hill, University of North Carolina Press, 1950).

Irving, Edward, *For Missionaries after the Apostolical School: A Series of Orations in Four Parts* (London, Hamilton, Adams and Co., 1825).

Jackson, J.R. de J., *Method and Imagination in Coleridge's Criticism* (London, Routledge & Kegan Paul, 1969).

Jackson, James, *Coleridge: The Critical Heritage* (London, Routledge & Kegan Paul, 1970).

Jackson, Reginald, *An Examination of the Deductive Logic of John Stuart Mill* (London, Oxford University Press, 1941).

James, D.G., 'The Thought of Coleridge', in *The Major English Romantic Poets: A Symposium in Reappraisal*, (*ed.*) Clarence D.Thorpe, Carlos Baker and Bennet Weaver (Carbondale, Southern Illinois University Press, 1957).

Jevons, W.S., 'John Stuart Mill's Philosophy Tested', in *Pure Logic and Other Minor Works* (London, Macmillan & Co., 1890).

Kamm, J., *John Stuart Mill in Love* (London, 1977).

Keats, John, *The Letters of John Keats, 1814-1821*, (*ed.*) Hyder Rollins, 2 vols (Cambridge University Press, 1958).

Korner, S., *Kant* (London, Penguin Books, 1966).

Kort, Fred, 'The Issue of a Science of Politics in Utilitarian Thought', *American Political Science Review*, XLVI (1952).

Kubitz, A.O., 'The Development of John Stuart Mill's *System of Logic*', *University of Illinois Studies in the Social Sciences*, XVIII (1932).

Laine, Michael, *Bibliography of Works on John Stuart Mill* (University of Toronto Press, 1976).

Lawrence, Berta, *Coleridge and Wordsworth in Somerset* (London, 1970).

Leavis, F.R., 'Coleridge in Criticism', *Scrutiny*, IX (1940-1941).

— *New Bearings in English Poetry* (London, Chatto and Windus, 1932).

Lefebure, Molly, *Samuel Taylor Coleridge: A Bondage of Opium* (London, Victor Gollancz, 1974).

Letwin, Shirley, *The Pursuit of Certainty* (Cambridge University Press, 1965).

Levere, Trevor, *Poetry Realized in Nature: Samuel Taylor Coleridge and Early 19th Century Science* (Cambridge University Press, 1981).

Levi, Albert William, 'The Value of Freedom: Mill's Liberty (1859-1959)', *Ethics*, LXX (1959-1960).

— 'The Writing of Mill's Autobiography', *Ethics*, LXI (1950-1951), pp. 284-296.

Lewis, George Cornwall, *Letters*, *(ed.)* G.F.Lewis (London, Longmans, Green and Co., 1870).

Lichtman, Richard, 'The Surface and Substance of Mill's Defence of Freedom', *Social Research*, XXX (1963).

Litchfield, L., *The Conservative Response to the Problem of Authority in 19th Century Britain: Coleridge, Carlyle, Bagehot* (University of New York, Buffalo, 1973).

Lloyd, Charles, *Edmund Oliver*, 3 vols (Bristol, 1798).

Locke, John, *An Essay Concerning Human Understanding*, *(ed.)* A.S.Pringle-Pattison (Oxford, Clarendon Press, 1924).

Lockridge, Laurence, *Coleridge the Moralist* (Cornell University Press, 1977).

Lovejoy, A.O., 'Kant and the English Platonists', in *Essays Philosophical and Psychological in Honour of William James*, by his colleagues at Columbia University (New York, Longmans, Green and Co., 1908).

Lowes, John Livingstone, *The Road to Xanadu: A Study in the Ways of the Imagination* (London, Constable and Co., 1933).

Lucas, Edward, 'Mr. Mill upon Liberty of the Press', *Essays on Religion and Literature*, third series, *(ed.)* Henry Edward Manning, Archbishop of Westminster (London, S.King & Co., 1874).

Lucas, F.L., *The Decline and Fall of the Romantic Ideal* (Cambridge University Press, 1937).

Macaulay, T.B., 'Mill's Essay on Government', *Edinburgh Review*, XCVII (March, 1829), pp. 159-189; reprinted in *Critical and Miscellaneous Essays*, 5 vols (Philadelphia, Carey and Hart, 1841-1844), V, pp. 328-367.

McCloskey, H.J., 'Mill's Liberalism', *Philosophical Quarterley*, XIII (1963).

— *John Stuart Mill: A Critical Study* (London, Macmillan, 1971).

M'Cosh, James, *An Examination of John Stuart Mill's Philosophy* (London, Macmillan and Co., 1866).

MacCunn, J., *Six Radical Thinkers* (London, Edward Arnold, 1910).

McFarland, G.F., 'J.C.Hare: Coleridge, DeQuincey, and German Literature', *Bulletin of the John Reynolds Library*, XLVII (1964-1965).

McFarlane, Tom, *Coleridge and the Pantheist Tradition* (Oxford University Press, 1969).

McRae, Robert, 'Phenomenalism and John Stuart Mill's Theory of Causation', *Philosophy and Phenomenological Research*, IX (1948-1949).

Marcel, Gabriel, *Coleridge and Schelling* (Paris, Aubier- Montaigne, 1971).

Marcoux, H., 'The Philosophy of Coleridge', *Revue de l'Université d'Ottawa*, XVIII (1959).

Marks, Emerson R., 'Means and Ends in Coleridge's Critical Method', *E.L.H.*, XXVI (1959).

— *Coleridge on the Language of Verse* (Princeton University Press, 1981).

Marsh, James, *Coleridge's American Disciples: The Selected Correspondence of James Marsh* (University of Massachussetts Press, 1973).

Marsh, Robert, 'The Second Part of Hartley's System', *Journal of the History of Ideas*, XX (1959).

Martineau, James, 'Joseph Priestley: Life and Works', *Monthly Repository*, VII (1833), pp. 19-30; reprinted in his *Essays, Reviews, and Addresses*, 4 vols (London, Longmans, Green and Co., 1890-1891).

Maurice, F.D., *The Kingdom of Christ*, (*ed.*) A.R.Vidler, 2 vols (London, S.C.M. Press, 1958).

Maurice, F.D., *The Life of Frederick Denison Maurice*, 2 vols (London, Macmillan and Co., 1884).

Mazlish, Bruce, *James and John Stuart Mill: Father and Son in the 19th Century* (New York, Basic Books, 1975).

Medawar, P.B., *Induction and Intuition in Scientific Thought* (London, Methuen and Co., 1969).

Mileur, J.P., *Vision and Revision: Coleridge's Art of Immanence* (University of Cambridge Press, 1982).

Mill, Anna Jean, 'John Stuart Mill's Visit to Wordsworth, 1831', *Modern Languages Review*, XLIV (1949).

— *John Stuart Mill's Boyhood Visit to France, 1820-1821* (University of Toronto Press, 1960).

Mill, James, *Analysis of the Phenomena of the Human Mind*, 2 vols (London, Baldwin and Cradock, 1829).

Mill, John Stuart, *Auguste Comte and Positivism*, in *The Collected Works of John Stuart Mill*, (*ed.*) F.E.L.Priestley, X, 'Essays on Ethics, Religion, and Society', (*ed.*) J.M.Robson (University of Toronto Press, 1969).

— *Autobiography* (London, Longmans, Green, Reader and Dyer, 1874).

— 'The Earlier Letters, 1812-1848', (*ed.*) F.E.Mineka, Vols XII and XIII of *The Collected Works of John Stuart Mill*, (*ed.*) F.E.L.Priestley (University of Toronto Press, 1963).

— 'Essays on Ethics, Religion and Society', (*ed.*) J.M.Robson, Vol. X of *The Collected Works of John Stuart Mill*, (*ed.*) F.E.L.Priestley (University of Toronto Press, 1969).

— *Early Essays by John Stuart Mill*, (*ed.*) J.W.N.Gibbs (London, G.Bell and Sons, 1897).

— *Dissertations and Discussions*, 4 vols (London, Longmans, Green, Reader and Dyer, 1867-1875).

— *An Examination of Sir William Hamilton's Philosophy* (London, Longmans, Green, Reader and Dyer, 1878).

— *The Letters of John Stuart Mill*, (*ed.*) H.S.Elliot, 2 vols (London, Longmans, Green and Co., 1910).

— *Mill on Bentham and Coleridge*, with an introduction by F.R.Leavis (London, Chatto and Windus, 1962, reprinted 1980).

— *Principles of Political Economy* (London, Longmans, Green and Co., 1900).
— 'The Spirit of the Age', *Examiner*, January 23rd., 1831.
— *A System of Logic*, 2 vols (London, Longmans, Green and Co., 1879).
— *A System of Logic, Ratiocinative and Inductive: Being a Connected View of the Principles of Evidence and the Methods of Scientific Investigation*, Vols VI and VII in *The Collected Works of John Stuart Mill* (University of Toronto Press, 1974).
— *Three Essays on Religion* (London, Longmans, Green and Co., 1885).
— *Utilitarianism with Critical Essays*, edited by Samuel Gorowitz (London, 1971).
— *Utilitarianism: On Liberty, Essay on Bentham with Selected Writings of Jeremy Bentham and John Austin*, edited with an introduction by Mary Warnock (New American Library, 1974).
— *Utilitarianism*, edited with an introduction by George Sher (Hackett Publications, 1979).
— 'Whatley's *Elements of Logic*', *Westminster Review*, IX (1828).
Miller, Kenneth E., 'John Stuart Mill's Theory of International Relations', *Journal of the History of Ideas*, XXII (1961).
Mineka, F.E., *The Dissidence of Dissent: The Monthly Repository, 1806-1838* (Chapel Hill, University of North Carolina Press, 1944).
Moran, Michael, 'Coleridge', in *The Encyclopedia of Philosophy.*, (*ed.*) Paul Edwards, 8 vols (New York, Macmillan & Co., 1967).
Morley, John, *19th Century Essays* (University of Chicago Press, 1970).
Mueller, Iris, *John Stuart Mill and French Thought* (Urbana, University of Illinois Press, 1956).
Muirhead, J.H., *Coleridge as Philosopher* (London, Allen & Unwin, 1954).
— 'Metaphysician or Mystic?', in *Coleridge: Studies by Several Hands*, (*ed.*) E.Blunden and E.L.Griggs (London, Constable and Co., 1934).
Murphey, Howard R., 'The Ethical Revolt Against Christian Orthodoxy in Early Victorian England', *American Historical Review*, LX (1955).
Nesbitt, George L., *Benthamite Reviewing: The FIrst Twelve Years of the Westminster Review, 1824-1836* (New York, Columbia University Press, 1934).
Orsini, G.N.G., *Coleridge and German Idealism: A Study in the History of Philosophy with Unpublished Materials in Coleridge's Manusripts* (Southern Illinois University Press, 1969).
Overton, John H., *The English Church in the Nineteenth Century, 1800-1833* (London, Longmans, Green and Co., 1894).
Pappé, H.O., *John Stuart Mill and the Harriet Taylor Myth* (Melbourne University Press, 1960).
Parker, Reeve, *Coleridge's Meditative Art* (Cornell University Press, 1975).
Parrish, Stephen, *The Art of the Lyrical Ballads* (Harvard University Press, 1973).

Pattison, Mark, 'Tendencies of Religious Thought in England, 1688-1750', in his *Essays*, *(ed.)* H.Nettleship, 2 vols (Oxford, Clarendon Press, 1889).

Poe, Edgar Allen, 'The Poetic Principle', in *The Complete Poetical Works with Three Essays on Poetry*, *(ed.)* R.Brimley Johnson (London, Oxford University Press, 1909).

Popper, Karl, *The Logic of Scientific Discovery* (London, Hutchinson, 1959).

— *The Open Society and its Enemies*, 2 vols (London, Routledge, 1966).

Preyer, R., *Bentham, Coleridge and the Science of History*, Leipziger Beiträge zur Englischen Philogie, 41 Heft (Bochum-Langendeer, Verlag Poppinghaus, 1958).

Prickett, Stephen, *Coleridge and Wordsworth: The Poetry of Growth* (Cambridge University Press, 1970).

— *Wordsworth and Coleridge: 'The Lyrical Ballads'* (London, Edward Arnold, 1975).

— *Romanticism and Religion: The Tradition of Coleridge and Wordsworth in the Victorian Church* (Cambridge University Press, 1976).

Pucelle, Jean, *L'Idéalism en Angleterre, de Coleridge à Bradley* (Neuchâtel, La Baconnière, 1955).

— *La Nature et L'Esprit dans le Philosophie de T.H.Green* (Paris, Louvain, 1960).

Pym, David, *The Religious Thought of Samuel Taylor Coleridge* (London, 1978).

Raphael, D.Daiches, 'Fallacies in and about Mill's *Utilitarianism*', *Philosophy*, XXX (1955).

Reading, C., *Approaches and Applications, ed.* Walter Crawford (Cornell University Press, 1979).

Rees, J.C., 'A Phase in the Development of Mill's Ideas on Liberty', *Political Studies*, VI (1958).

— 'A Re-reading of Mill on Liberty', *Political Studies*, VIII (1960), p.116, from *London Review*, XIII (1859).

Richards, I.A., *Coleridge on Imagination* (London, Routledge & Kegan Paul, 1934).

Richter, Melvin, *The Politics of Conscience: T.H.Green and his Age* (London, Weidenfeld and Nicolson, 1964).

Rickaby, Joseph, *Free Will and the Four English Philosophers: Locke, Hobbes, Hume and Mill* (New York, Books for Libraries Press, 1969).

Ritchie, David, *The Principles of State Interference: Four Essays on the Political Philosophy of Herbet Spencer, John Stuart Mill and T.H. Green* (New York, Books for Libraries Press, 1969).

Robberds, J.W., *A Memoir of the Life and Writing of the Late William Taylor of Norwich*, 2 vols (London, John Murray, 1843).

Robinson, Daniel, *Toward a Science of Human Nature: Essays on the Psychologies of Mill, Hegel, Wundt, and James* (Columbia University Press, 1982).

Robson, John, *The Improvement of Mankind: The Social and Political Thought of John Stuart Mill* (University of Toronto Press, 1968).

Russell, Bertrand, *Autobiography, 1922-1969*, 3 vols (London, Allen & Unwin, 1967-1969).

— 'Lecture on a Master Mind: John Stuart Mill', *Proceedings of the British Academy*, XLI (1955).

Ryan, Alan, *The Philosophy of John Stuart Mill* (London, Macmillan, 1970).

— *John Stuart Mill* (London, Boston, Routledge and Kegan Paul, 1974).

Sampson, R.V., 'J.S.Mill: An Interpretation', *Cambridge Journal*, III (1950).

Saunders, C.R., *Coleridge and the Broad Church Movement* (Durham, North Carolina, Duke University Press, 1942).

Schneewind, Jerome B., 'Mill', in *Encyclopedia of Philosophy*, (*ed.*) Paul Edwards, 8 vols (New York, Macmillan and Co., 1967).

— *Mill: A Collection of Critical Essays* (University of Notre Dame Press, 1982).

Schwartz, Pedro, *The New Political Economy of John Stuart Mill* (London, Weidenfeld & Nicolson, 1972).

Seth, James, 'The Alleged Fallacies in Mill's Utilitarianism', *Philosophical Review*, XVII (1908), pp. 469-472; reprinted in his *Essays in Ethics and Religion*, (*ed.*) A.Seth Pringle-Pattison (Edinburgh, W.Blackwood & Sons, 1926), pp. 22-25.

— *English Philosophers and Schools of Philosophy* (London, J.M.Dent, 1912).

Shairp, J.C., *Studies in Poetry and Philosophy* (Edinburgh, Edmonston and Douglas, 1868).

Shapiro, J.Selwyn, 'John Stuart Mill, Pioneer of Democratic Liberalism in England', *Journal of the History of Ideas*, IV (1943).

Shepherd, Richard, *The Bibliography of Coleridge: A Bibliographical Listing of Publications and Prose Writings Including his Contributions to Annuals, Magazines and Periodical Publications, Posthumous Works, Memoirs, Editions etc.* (Folcroft Press, 1970).

Shelley, P.B., *Shelley's Prose*, (*ed.*) David Lee Clarke (Albuquerque, University of New Mexico Press, 1954).

Sidgewick, Henry, *The Methods of Ethics* (London, Macmillan and Co., 1893).

Smith, Alexander, 'The Philosophy of Poetry', *Blackwoods*, XXXVIII (December, 1835).

Smith, Norman Kemp, *Polegomena to an Idealist Theory of Knowledge* (London, Macmillan and Co., 1924).

Snyder, A.D., *Coleridge on Logic and Learning* (New Haven, Yale University Press, 1929).
— *The Critical Principle of the Reconciliation of Opposites as Employed by Coleridge*, Contributions to Rhetoric, No.9 (Ann Arbor, University of Michigan Press, 1918, reprinted Folcroft Press, 1970).
Somervell, D.C., *English Thought in the Nineteenth Century* (London, Methuen and Co., 1929).
Spencer, Herbert, *Social Statistics* (London, Williams and Norgate, 1868).
Stanley, Arthur Penrhyn, *The Life and Correspondence of Thomas Arnold, D.D.* (London, B.Fellowes, 1852).
Stephen, Leslie, *An Agnostic's Apology and other Essays* (London, Duckworth and Co., 1937).
— 'Coleridge', in *Hours in a Library*, 3 vols (London, Stevens-Cox, James, *Samuel Taylor Coleridge and Mary Lamb: Two Recent Discoveries* (Toucan Press, 1971).
Smith, Elder & Co., 1899).
— 'The Importance of German', in *Studies of a Biographer*, 4 vols (London, Duckworth and Co., 1898-1902).
Sterling, John, *Arthur Conningsby*, 3 vols (London, Effingham Wilson, 1833).
— *Essays and Tales*, (ed.) J.C.Hare, 2 vols (London, John W.Parker, 1848).
Stillinger, Jack, (ed.), *The Early Draft of Mill's Autobiography* (Urbana, University of Illinois Press, 1961).
Stokoe, F.W., *German Influence in the English Romantic Period, 1788-1818* (Cambridge University Press, 1926).
Storr, Vernon F., *The Development of English Theology in the Nineteenth Century, 1800-1860* (London, Longmans, Green and Co., 1913).
Street, Charles Larabee, *Individualism and Individuality in the Philosophy of John Stuart Mill* (Milwaukee, Morehouse Publishing Co., 1926).
Strong, E.W., 'William Whewell and John Stuart Mill: Their Controversy about Scientific Knowledge', *Journal of the History of Ideas*, XVI (1955), pp. 209-231.
Swiatecka, M.J., *The idea of the Symbol: Some 19th Century Comparisons with Coleridge* (New York, Cambridge University Press, 1980).
Taylor, Henry, *Autobiography, 1800-1875*, 2 vols (London, Longmans, Green and Co., 1885).
— *Correspondence of Henry Taylor*, (ed.) E.Dowden (London, Longmans, Green and Co., 1888).
Ten, C.L., *Mill on Liberty* (Oxford, Clarendon Press, 1980).
Thirlwall, Cannop, *Remains, Literary and Theological*, 3 vols (London, Daldy, Isbister & Co., 1877-1878).
Thompson, Dennis, *John Stuart Mill and Representative Government* (Princeton University Press, 1976).

Trail, H.D., *Coleridge*, English Men of Letters (London, Macmillan and Co., 1884).

Triiling, Lionel, *Matthew Arnold* (London, Allen & Unwin, 1939).

Tulloch, John, *The Movement of Religious Thought in Britain During the Nineteenth Century* (London, Longmans, Green and Co., 1885).

Ulam, Adam B., *Philosophical Foundations of English Socialism* (Cambridge, Harvard University Press, 1951).

Vidler, Alec R., *F.D.Maurice and Company* (London, S.C.M. Press, 1966).

Vlasoplos, Anca, *The Symbolic Method of Coleridge* (Wayne State University, 1983).

Walsh, William, *The Use of Imagination: Educational Thought and the Literary Mind* (London, Chatto and Windus, 1959).

Ward, Wilfred, 'John Stuart Mill', *Quarterly Review*, CCXIII (1910).

— *The Life of Cardinal Newman*, 2 vols (London, Longmans, 1912).

Watson, George, (*ed.*) *The New Cambridge Bibliography of English Language and Literature*, 5 vols (Cambridge University Press, 1969).

Watson, John, *Comte, Mill and Spencer* (Glasgow, James Maclehose & Sons, 1895).

Watson, Lucy E., *Coleridge at Highgate* (London, Longmans, Green and Co., 1925).

Wellek, René, *Kant in England* (Princeton University Press, 1931).

Wellman, Carl, 'A Reinterpretation of Mill's Proof', *Ethics*, LXIX (1958-1959).

West, E.G., 'Liberty and Education: John Stuart Mill's Dilemma', *Philosophy*, XL (1965).

Wheeler, Kathleen, *Sources, Processes and Methods in Coleridge's Biographia Literaria* (Cambridge University Press, 1980).

— *The Creative Mind in Coleridge's Poetry* (London, Heinnmann, 1981).

White, R.J., 'John Stuart Mill', *Cambridge Journal*, V (1951-1952).

— (*ed.*) *Political Tracts of Wordsworth, Coleridge and Shelley* (Cambridge University Press, 1953).

Winkelman, Elizabeth, *Coleridge und die Kantische Philosophie*, Palaestra, 184 Heft (Leipzig, Mayer & Müller, 1933).

Williams, Raymond, *Culture and Society, 1780-1950* (London, Chatto and Windus, 1958).

Willey, Basil, *Samuel Taylor Coleridge* (New York, Norton, 1972).

Wood, Herbert G., *Frederick Denison Maurice* (Cambridge University Press, 1950).

Woodring, Carl R., *Politics in the Poetry of Coleridge* (Madison, University of Wisconsin Press, 1961).

Wylie, Laure J., *Studies in the Evolution of English Criticism* (Boston, Ginn & Co., 1903).

Zinkernagel, Peter, 'Revaluation of John Stuart Mill's Ethical Proof', *Theoria*, XVIII (1952).

Index